TO OUR DEAR FRIEND, MICHAEL

THIS IS TO WISH YOU A VERY HAPPY
BIRTHDAY AND ALL THE BEST FOR
THE NEXT STEP IN YOUR LIFE'S JOURNEY.

WE HOPE THAT PAGING THROUGH THIS
BOOK, YOU WILL BE REMINDED OF
MANY HAPPY TIMES IN ARIZONA AND
ALL THE HEARTS YOU HAVE TOUCHED
DURING YOUR YEARS HERE.

WE WILL MISS YOU AND MARY BUT
ARE EXCITED FOR WHAT LIES AHEAD
FOR YOU.

PLEASE KEEP IN TOUCH AND VISIT OFTEN!

LOVE AND GOD BLESS, ALWAYS

THE FORRESTER FAMILY.

GREATER

PHOENIX

THE

DESERT

IN

BLOOM

CONVERSATION PIECE BOLA

GREATER

PHOENIX

THE

DESERT

IN

BLOOM

INTRODUCTION BY

HUGH DOWNS

ART DIRECTION BY

BRIAN GROPPE

URBAN
TAPESTRY
SERIES

TOWERY
PUBLISHING, INC.

CONTENTS

BY HUGH DOWNS

Whenever I'm away from home—that is, away from the Phoenix area—I find myself fielding the same simple and unanimous question over and over again: "Why on earth?" Or, in even shorter form, "Phoenix?" This question always seems to be accompanied by wrinkled brows, pursed lips, and suspicious looks. ❧ The answer to these questions is also simple and unanimous. Simple in that I have made this part of Arizona my home because I like it. Several aspects of my personality never run out of reasons to expand on this notion of actually enjoying the place I call home. The list is not only endless, but endlessly changing. There is so much more to this desert city than outsiders can imagine that when I try to start detailing the various charms and quirks and hot spots and trends that make Phoenix unique, I inevitably end up surprising whoever it was who asked "Why on earth?" in the first place. ❧ And, over the years, I have learned to be patient. Outsiders think that Phoenix is a dusty and hot backwater, a cowboy town that clings to its Wild West heritage. Saguaros. Rattlesnakes. Gun racks in every truck (and *every-body* drives a truck). A quaint place to vacation, perhaps, but not a place for civilized people to live. I'm happy to say that not all of these images are phony. You can, after all, wear a gun in public, and pointy, lizard-skin boots do qualify as dress shoes (I have worn these with a tux). But such images are becoming the stuff of

Dorothy Bigg, director of the International Trade and Investment Division of the Arizona Department of Commerce

myth, a faded memory held by only a few of the die-hard Phoenix old-timers.

The truth is closer to this: Phoenix is now the sixth-largest city in the nation, a thriving metropolis of 2.6 million people with a $50 billion marketplace, an educated and youthful population, and a diverse and interesting culture. The community still makes a big deal of its numerous rodeos, but they don't outdraw a Rolling Stones concert or even *Phantom of the Opera*. Trucks abound, but so do imported sports cars and limos, none of which are adorned with rear-window gun racks. Instead, these vehicles prominently display bike racks and baby carriers.

Both geographically and socially, Phoenix is situated somewhere between Texas and California. We're not as Western as Texas or as laid-back as California, but we enjoy a bit of both. Phoenix–aka The Valley of the Sun, or, to locals, simply The Valley–balances hard work with a healthy desire to play. It's a good place to visit, and it's a good place to work. It's no wonder that some 50,000 people every year tell their family and friends they're moving to Phoenix. They endure the questions–"Why on earth?"–and come anyway, just as we did. And they come in record numbers: Phoenix has enjoyed a growth rate higher than any other community in the nation during the 1990s, with the arrival of nearly 600,000 new residents.

▶ © MARK R. ZEMNICK

At least one reason for this migration is no mystery: jobs. Phoenix is a working town, with plenty of opportunity in just about every business sector. Once dependent only on real estate development and tourism, Phoenix's economy is now a balanced mix of service, distribution, agriculture, construction, high-tech manufacturing, aerospace, health care, and telecommunications. The booming industries in the Phoenix area are creating 50,000 new jobs every year. Unemployment in Phoenix is 2.5 percent, the lowest it has ever been and a full two percentage points below the national average.

Another reason has to do with Phoenix's being one of the most affordable places to live. The cost for everything from Arizona Cardinals tickets to milk to

housing is, on average, less than other communities. To give you an idea, the median price for a single-family home is $105,300, compared to a national average of $118,000.

While these are certainly compelling reasons, there's another that I think is often overlooked: Phoenix is pleasantly located within striking distance of a host of exciting places and recreation areas. An hour's drive outside the city and you can be waterskiing at Roosevelt Lake. Two hours' drive and you're in Flagstaff, where you can snow ski at Snowbowl, one of the state ski resorts. (At the right time of the year, either late winter or late fall, it's possible to participate in both types of skiing, snow and water, on the same weekend. Those of us who live here have come to love the contrast.)

Two hours to the south and you're just outside Tucson, with its many old Spanish attractions, not to mention all that's going on at the University of Arizona. Four hours' drive and you can make the Mexican border and the coastal city of San Carlos, where the jumbo shrimp and tequila are cheap. Five hours and you can be standing on the edge of one of the natural wonders of the world, the Grand Canyon. Six hours' drive takes you either to San Diego or Las Vegas (provided the traffic is kind to you).

But it's not as if we have to travel all that far to find intriguing vistas or engaging activities. There's plenty on hand locally to keep most people busy throughout the year. For instance, a popular early morning exercise is a hike to the top of Camelback Mountain, so named because its profile follows that of a prone camel. Rush hour is 5 a.m. on the 1,000-foot-high, rock-spined mountain, which is covered rock wall to rock wall with The Valley's go-getters. It's a more popular place to be seen than even the most fashionable restaurant. It says you're serious (up early), not afraid of hard work (the climb is tough), and can work well in groups (there can be hundreds up there at any one time). What's more, the mountain is the centerpiece of metropolitan Phoenix's most tony zip code, the aptly named Paradise Valley, where the typical home goes for better than $1 mil-

lion. On any given morning, you might find the CEO of a billion-dollar company making his way to the top, or a sweat-covered socialite or a glad-handing politician enjoying the trek.

Another popular hiking spot is South Mountain Park, which lies along the southern border of Phoenix and comprises the largest municipal park in the world. The 16,500-acre park encompasses a series of desert mountains and has a patchwork of 50 miles of trails that are shared (sometimes with considerable competition) by hikers, runners, mountain bikers, and horseback riders. Desert wildflowers and the full range of cacti found in Arizona dot the park's landscape. With some exploration, you can even discover ancient Indian pottery shards or find rocks decorated with petroglyphs.

© CHRISTINE KEITH

✳

P hoenix is a sports town—both spectator sports and the kind where you wake up sore the next day. With the addition of Major League Baseball's Arizona Diamondbacks, which began their inaugural season in 1998, Phoenix is now one of just 10 communities in the nation to have a team in each of the four major professional sports leagues—baseball, football, hockey, and basketball. After years of hosting spring training for about half the big league's baseball teams, Phoenix was ready for one of its own. Season tickets for the 42,000-seat Bank One Ballpark sold out before construction was completed on the retractable-roof stadium. So far, wins have been hard to come by, but the fans don't seem to mind. At big moments in the game, they wave replicas of rattlesnake tails.

This may seem like the last place where ice hockey would be popular, but in just two seasons here the Phoenix Coyotes have found a huge pack of fans. Getting tickets to one of the games, even for seats with obstructed views, can be a

Dwight Patterson, the man responsible for bringing Cactus League baseball to Arizona.

challenge. Fans show their solidarity by howling at full volume and dressing from head to paw in white.

Although it's been more than a decade since the Arizona Cardinals relocated to The Valley from St. Louis, the team—much like its namesake—has been uncomfortable in the desert environment. For a number of reasons, residents haven't seemed to embrace it like they have the other major teams. Some home games seem to draw more fans of the opposing team, such as the Cowboys and Vikings, than they do Cardinals fans, although this is probably more a reflection of the origins of most of Phoenix's residents. But the team's popularity is on the upswing, thanks in part to the 1997 debut of former Arizona State University standout Jake Plummer as the Cardinals' starting quarterback, as well as the signing of some

© J. PETER MORTIMER

quality free agents and the drafting of quite a few promising college players. The future, indeed, looks bright.

Still, it is the NBA's Phoenix Suns that hold the hearts of Phoenicians. The Suns, which first arose 30 years ago, have sold out games spanning more than eight seasons. During the 1993 NBA play-offs, the Suns brought the city to a virtual standstill as hundreds of thousands of residents focused on nothing but their team. Only in Phoenix can an outfit that's a combination of purple and orange, the team's colors, be considered fashionable.

For the person who is more of a participant of sports than a spectator, Phoenix is an ideal location. Nearly year-round warm weather (more than 300 days a year of sunshine), little rain (on average, about eight inches a year), and an endless supply of sporting amenities make the city a natural haven for those who like to be active.

In fact, there doesn't seem to be a sport that isn't practiced here. Some of the most popular are golf, tennis, running, in-line skating, mountain biking, hiking,

street hockey, basketball, softball, and volleyball, but that's not saying that you can't find virtually any outdoor activity with plenty of devotees in the Phoenix area.

n ot surprisingly, water is coveted here. Pools. Lakes. Fountains. Puddles. Anything. Backyard pools, of which we have more per capita than any other city in the nation, dot the landscape. There's even a pool at Bank One Ballpark, just over the right-center-field wall. The pool area can be rented on a per-game basis for up to 35 people for around $4,000.

Several neighborhood communities are designed around shallow, man-made lakes. Homes adjacent to the water sell for a significant premium.

Water has become the central design element for two Valley cities. Tempe has started construction on a man-made lake just north of its downtown in the usually dry bed of the Salt River. The two-mile-long lake will be built using inflatable dams. The long-awaited lake is expected to draw more than $1 billion worth of development, and should become a focal point of culture and recreation in this city that's best known as the home of Arizona State University. Meanwhile, Scottsdale is transforming a portion of a canal at the city's core into a San Antonio-like waterway. Like Tempe's water project, it is expected to become the centerpoint of the city and spur millions of dollars' worth of development.

One of the most popular summer activities involves floating down the upper Salt River in an inflated truck tube, an activity that practically requires a pair of cutoff jeans and, usually, a couple of six packs of beer. On any given weekend, from May through August, thousands flock to the river to float for miles down the slow-flowing river.

On a less languid note, we've even transported a portion of the ocean here. Big Surf is an accurate imitation of about an eighth of a mile of ocean and beach, complete with white sand and a surf-worthy wave every few minutes. ☞

Despite Phoenix's reputation as an arid, desert city, newcomers are shocked to learn it has seven lakes and large rivers located just a short drive outside town. Boating, skiing, and fishing are welcome and wildly popular summer diversions. Often, it seems that there are more boats per capita in Phoenix than anywhere else in the country. You see nothing but boats just an hour's drive from downtown Phoenix when you visit Lake Pleasant, which attracts so many watercraft during weekends that park rangers have to turn away late arrivals. On just about any warm and sunny day—which pretty much describes the entire climatological calendar for Phoenix—Jet Skis, ski boats, houseboats, small fishing boats, and sailboats fill the waterways.

Not unlike inner cities throughout the country, downtown Phoenix began to experience an exodus in the 1950s. Tired of fighting traffic as well as parking and crime problems, businesses and residents found solace in the up-and-coming suburbs. By the mid-1970s, there was no major shopping, few restaurants, and virtually no residents in the area. Office buildings sat empty. On weekends, downtown was more like a ghost town.

All that began to change in the early 1990s, when the Rouse Company built a retail and office complex called Arizona Center in the heart of downtown. It begat restaurants and shops, and began to bring people back to the area. The Phoenix Suns later built America West Arena just a few blocks south of Arizona Center, which in turn attracted tens of thousands of residents at night and on weekends.

Since then, the rebirth of Phoenix has continued—a $30 million expansion of the Phoenix Civic Center; construction of a new, $80 million city hall; renovation of the Orpheum Theatre; construction of the $75 million Arizona Science Center;

a 24-screen megaplex at Arizona Center; and a slew of small shops, restaurants, and bars. The surest sign of a full revival: the opening of the downtown area's first McDonald's restaurant.

This revitalization reached its peak in 1998 with the addition of Bank One Ballpark and the Arizona Diamondbacks. The $375 million stadium means 82 home games a year and hundreds of thousands of new visitors for downtown. Perhaps more important, it means visitors during the baseball season, a time when the summer heat has traditionally driven people away from downtown.

In 1996, an extensive, $14 million restoration of the Orpheum Theatre in downtown Phoenix was completed. Once regarded as the most luxurious playhouse west of the Mississippi River, the Orpheum was the venue for such stars as

Mae West and W.C. Fields. All the original features of the Spanish baroque-style Orpheum, built in 1929, have been meticulously revived, including gargoyles, silver and gold peacocks, a retooled Wurlitzer, and an interior mural festooned with balconies and minarets.

Summer in Phoenix is a survivor sport. I should point out what I have learned about heat and humidity: All the clichés are true. But I'd rather be in Phoenix at 110 degrees than New Jersey at 90. Sure, it's a dry heat, but it can become a dry heat from a blow-torch. There are times during the summer when it feels like the city is fulfilling the mythological calling of its name. The temperature has been recorded as high as 122 degrees, which closed down Sky Harbor International Airport. (Aviation officials weren't sure planes could take off in that kind of heat.)

Phoenix residents warily await the first day when the temperature pops over 100 degrees. By that point, there's no more deluding ourselves: Summer has arrived. ☛

When temperatures begin to hit well into the triple digits, somewhere around 108 degrees, Phoenix residents run for cover—covered parking, covered heads, and skin covered with lots of sunscreen.

Summer means as many as 100 consecutive days when the temperature never drops below 100 degrees. Never. Morning, noon, and night, it can stay hot. Newcomers open their doors at dawn, expecting to catch a refreshing waft of cool air, and are greeted with a blast furnace that leaves many of them reeling. Locals are used to this early morning inferno, even though we remain somewhat in awe of the heat's relentless authority.

When that first triple-digit mark is eclipsed, it sets off a flurry of activity. The last of the snowbirds begin their slow migration east. Air-conditioner repair

companies work around the clock, as do travel agents. Outdoor cafés close up their patio tables and umbrellas and herd their customers inside to the cooler, air-conditioned interiors. Walks around the block give way to laps on the air-conditioned track at the local health spa or club. And in many of even the most staid offices, jackets are not worn, ties disappear, and bare legs and sandals become the standard dress code.

A simple cooling system can be found at many restaurants, along some walkways, on some golf carts, and in countless backyards. It involves spraying a fine mist of water into the air above. It evaporates almost immediately, but brings the temperature down at least 10 degrees.

The heat does some strange things to Phoenicians. We put insulated pads on our dogs' feet to keep them from burning. We begin exercising at 4 a.m. We fry eggs in the street. We ship in tons of what snow may remain from northern Arizona for one last gasp of cool. But most of all, we take vacations. So many Phoenicians head to San Diego for at least a week or two during the summer that we've earned the nickname there of "Zonies." Residents of San Diego like to think that their city becomes Phoenix West from June through August. ☛

Yet, winter is why Phoenicians put up with the triple-digit summers. Temperatures are moderate and rarely reach the frost level. Snow has been known to fall, but it's so rare that it usually leads the evening news. Winter in Phoenix means you can still play outdoor sports, and it's possible to get a tan during Christmas break. Locals gleefully watch the national weather news. If we want snow, we drive about two hours to the north, where we have an abundance of it at the state's major skiing areas.

Winter here is so pleasant that we experience a taste of what we inflict on San Diego each summer: snowbirds. After the holidays, the migration begins, when some 400,000 winter residents descend on The Valley, filling every apartment, hotel, mobile home park, or rental house they can find. Although they

pump about $1 billion into the economy annually, most full-time locals confess to mixed emotions about our fair-weather residents. The trouble, you see, is that their arrival signals an increase in prices for everything from golf to groceries to rent. The snowbirds pack the already overcrowded freeways with slow-moving Winnebagos and giant Buicks. Many have had their left-hand turn signals on since Indiana. Restaurant waiting times go from minutes to hours.

Somehow, though, we remember the reception those of us with Arizona license plates get each summer when we arrive in San Diego, and we all manage to get along just fine.

There is as much food variety available in Phoenix restaurants as in New York. The sunsets are unrivaled. The friendliness of the inhabitants is world-class. The cultural spectrum, from highbrow to lowbrow, is wide enough to be at least cosmopolitan. And the feeling of being at home doesn't require being born here. Any time you sink a taproot in Phoenix, you know that in time you will become a native. These are just a few of the reasons why I don't even flinch when I see those wrinkled brows and pursed lips and hear the inevitable question: "Why on earth . . . Phoenix?" The answer, as I mentioned, is really very simple indeed. ✒

28

he summer sky explodes with Fourth of July fireworks and Mother Nature's always-stunning light shows. Independence Day usually coincides with the start of Greater Phoenix's monsoon season, which brings massive cloud formations, lightning, showers, and dust storms through mid-September.

rizona's unique weather enhances its spectacular scenery, with double rainbows making rare appearances over the massive expanse of South Mountain Park. At 16,500 acres, South Mountain is the nation's largest municipal park, its desert environment complete with hiking trails, petroglyphs, native plants, and panoramic views of Greater Phoenix.

Day or night, saguaro cacti—most of which live as long as 100 years and weigh in at six to seven tons—dot the Arizona landscape. Saguaros can take 30 years to reach a height of two feet, and 60 years before sprouting their distinctive arms.

Today, as always, the sun figures prominently in Phoenix-area art, from ancient petroglyphs to the blazing sphere that shines over the entrance to City Hall.

Heading north on Interstate 17, the bustling metropolis of Phoenix gives way to high desert and high country. Sunset Point, overlooking the ghost town of Bumble Bee and the Bradshaw Mountains, is a popular rest stop between Phoenix and the Verde Valley.

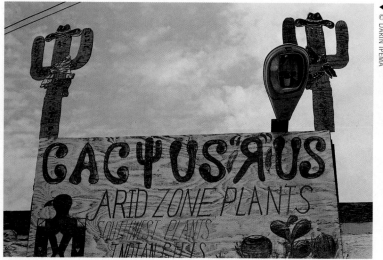

Behind the blossoming smiles on the faces of Arizona's saguaro cacti lies an inherently prickly nature. A mainstay on the Arizona desert, saguaros bloom toward the end of May.

s an aloe a cactus or a succulent? How much should you water a cactus? You'll find the answers to these questions at the Desert Botanical Garden. Located in Papago Park, the garden displays one of the world's largest collections of desert plants in a tranquil setting, as well as demonstrations and classes about desert landscaping.

 he fragile beauty of the thistle (TOP), night-blooming cereus (BOTTOM LEFT), and yellow flowers of the prickly pear (BOTTOM RIGHT) provides a deceptive contrast to their ability to survive in a harsh environment. Rita Jo Anthony, owner of the Wild Seed, has spent 16 years harvesting and selling native Arizona seeds—with landowners' permission—and observing the damage caused by civilization encroaching on the Sonoran Desert.

Beautiful Picacho Peak State Park, located between Phoenix and Tucson along Interstate 10, produces some of Arizona's most profuse poppy fields. Oddly enough, it is also the site of Arizona's only Civil War battle, which is reenacted every March.

The rainy fall weather in Phoenix guarantees exceptionally beautiful wild-flowers come spring. Since 1937, the Desert Botanical Garden has been cultivating and displaying these and other desert plants (THIS PAGE). Its collection is among the most extensive in the world.

Phoenix's desert fauna spans the botanical gamut, from towering palm trees to the crimson blooms of the barrel cactus. The city's always-dramatic sunsets add an inferno of color to the natural beauty of plant life.

The Desert in Bloom

amelback Mountain has long been one of Phoenix's most popular landmarks thanks to its rigorous hiking, the breathtaking views, and the striking Praying Monk rock formation (OPPOSITE).

outhwest painter and Phoenix native Ed Mell is known worldwide for his dramatic, angular landscapes and striking cloud formations. His view of Echo Canyon depicts the scene as he remembers it from childhood—before upscale homes sprang up along the landscape surrounding Camelback Mountain.

Whether on canvas or film, the evening light illustrates the grandeur of the Arizona skies. Landscape artist Ed Mell captures the beauty of northern Arizona in his painting *Skies over* *Ward Terrace* (OPPOSITE), which bears a striking resemblance to the west slopes of the Estrella Mountains, just southwest of Phoenix (ABOVE).

ocated east of Phoenix near Apache Junction, the aptly named Superstition Mountains are known as much for the legend of the Lost Dutchman goldmine as for their distinct, rugged beauty. According to local lore, Dutch prospector Jacob Waltz claimed to have discovered gold in the Superstitions. Though his find was never confirmed, many have died or disappeared in the mountains while searching for the precious metal.

The Desert in Bloom

our Peaks, in the Tonto National Forest, often emerges with a blanket of snow after a winter rain in the Valley. Viewed from Phoenix, Scottsdale, and the East Valley, these distinctive peaks serve as a reminder of Arizona's climatic extremes.

oosevelt Lake is one of four man-made lakes on the Salt River that provide water to the metro Phoenix area. With 88 miles of shoreline, it is the largest reservoir managed by the Salt River Project. Its location 80 miles east of Phoenix also makes it a secluded oasis for boating, fishing, and camping.

63

THE DESERT IN BLOOM

lthough it's the smallest of the Phoenix area's Salt River reservoirs, Canyon Lake is a popular spot for swimming and boating (OPPOSITE). Another watery attraction is Fountain Hills, a master-planned community east of Scottsdale that is home to one of the world's tallest fountains, which shoots water about 560 feet upward from a lagoon (ABOVE).

Once the world's tallest masonry dam, Roosevelt Dam was begun in 1905 and dedicated by President Theodore Roosevelt upon completion in 1911 (OPPOSITE). The dam became even taller in 1996 after a major project was undertaken to increase the lake's capacity. Roosevelt Bridge, another recent addition, was built near the dam to allow Highway 188 to cross the lake (ABOVE).

When you live in the desert, any respite from the Greater Phoenix heat is welcome, whether it's lounging at Tonto Creek (OPPOSITE LEFT), rock climbing among the waterfalls of the Grand Canyon (OPPOSITE RIGHT), or taking in the splendor of Oak Creek near Sedona (ABOVE).

The confluence of the Salt and Verde rivers offers a gorgeous place for hikers in need of a refreshing pause. Dams on the two rivers create a total of six lakes, with water diverted into a series of canals that traverse the Phoenix metro area.

Canal construction figures prominently in Greater Phoenix's past as far back as 550 years, when the Hohokam tribe developed an extensive, 500-mile canal system. The canals in use today were built by Phoenix work crews some 100 years ago (OPPOSITE). A virtual computer tour of a proposed riverwalk entertainment district on a canal near Scottsdale and Camelback roads shows how far along engineering has come since the backbreaking era of the early 1900s (ABOVE).

arming has come a long way since the soil at Camelback Mountain had to be tilled with horse-drawn plows (TOP). Today, herb gardens and pecan orchards dot the rural landscape of Greater Phoenix, as do commercial flower gardens along Baseline Road in South Phoenix (OPPOSITE).

Organically grown fruits and vegetables head the menu at the Farm, a critically acclaimed restaurant nestled in the idyllic serenity of South Mountain. And though you'll have to look elsewhere for chicken, the Farm *does* offer two different turkey sandwiches—made from organically raised birds, of course—for hungry carnivores.

from haze over the farmlands to dust storms in the posh neighborhood of Paradise Valley (ABOVE), the weather in Greater Phoenix is seldom less than visually arresting.

AZ. DEPT. OF LIBRARY, ARCHIVES AND PUBLIC RECORDS, HISTORY AND ARCHIVES DIV., PHOENIX, #97-0955

Although prohibition is a thing of the past, Arizona is indeed dry. And while the scorching Phoenix heat can be enough to drive people out of town—sometimes for good—the ones who stick it out will admit that, while it's hot, at least it's a *dry* heat—dry enough for the 100-degree-plus temperatures to crack the earth and peel paint.

80

GREATER PHOENIX

ining—whether for gold, silver, or copper—has long played a major role in Arizona's economy. Just ask Dean Stevens (TOP RIGHT), the area's self-proclaimed Last of the Old-Time Prospectors. Meanwhile, the gold-mining town of Humbug—abandoned since the late 1880s—has been recently restored to give an idea of how the miners used to live (OPPOSITE). Old silver mines can still be found near Sedona, around Turkey Creek (BOTTOM).

reater Phoenix has definitely earned its Valley of the Sun nickname as the yellow hues of sunset engulf such downtown high-rises as the contemporary, 20-story City Hall (OPPOSITE) and its neighbor, the Wells Fargo Building (BOTTOM). Further north, the Viad Tower's distinctive shape is a cornerstone of the uptown skyline (TOP).

On Valentine's Day, 1912, Arizona became the 48th state to enter the union. Built in 1900, the domed, neoclassic State Capitol Building previously served as the area's territorial capitol (TOP AND OPPOSITE). Today, lawmakers work in the nearby Capitol Annex, while the original building is a museum with exhibits, such as the historical secretary of state's office (BOTTOM).

Old and new collide with the side-by-side positioning of the Spanish baroque Orpheum Theatre and the ultramodern Phoenix City Hall. The former was built in 1929, and reopened in 1997 as a performing arts center after an $11.4 million restoration helped preserve its historic beauty.

The arts community in Phoenix has thrived, thanks in part to the philanthropic efforts of locals, such as Delbert and Jewell Lewis (OPPOSITE BOTTOM), who spearheaded the renovation of the Orpheum Theatre. At Symphony Hall (TOP LEFT), the city's acclaimed Phoenix Symphony performs under the artistic direction of Maestro Hermann Michael (OPPOSITE TOP) and the business leadership of President and CEO Joan H. Squires (BOTTOM).

The Valley's cultural and literary scenes are amply represented by David Speers (OPPOSITE), general director of the Arizona Opera Company, and author Clive Cussler (LEFT). Speers joined the opera in 1998 and is working to expand the company's artistic repertoire, while streamlining its business operations. Paradise Valley resident Cussler is known worldwide as the Grandmaster of Adventure, with sales of nearly 100 million copies of his Dirk Pitt adventure novels.

Beyond the distinctive architecture of Tempe's Arizona State University (ASU), the school has been nationally recognized for educational excellence. Jewell Parker Rhodes, author of such novels as *Voodoo Dreams* and *Magic City*, is director of ASU's Creative Writing Program, which placed among *U.S. News and World Report*'s top 20.

rom the sparkling skies over the Superstition Mountains (TOP) to performances at the Herberger Theater Center (BOTTOM AND OPPOSITE BOTTOM), there are plenty of places to catch a glimpse of the Greater Phoenix stars. At the Arizona Science Center, films on molecular structure take center stage on the big screen (OPPOSITE TOP).

Arizona's night skies attract both amateur stargazers and professional astronomers. Marc Buie, who earned a Ph.D. from the University of Arizona, is one of the staff astronomers at the Lowell Observatory near Flagstaff (OPPOSITE). The observatory has a long and distinguished history, dating to its founding in 1894 by Dr. Percival Lowell. In 1930, a Lowell astronomer discovered the planet Pluto.

he natural wonders of the Phoenix area, abundant in the nearby Superstition Mountains (OPPOSITE TOP), surround a wealth of folklore, much of it part of a rich Native American heritage. As an intermediary between the gods and man, a kachina—or katsina as the Hopi Indians pronounce it—is a benevolent spirit believed to bring rain, fertility, and good health. The internationally acclaimed Heard Museum (OPPOSITE BOTTOM) features the 420-piece Goldwater Katsina doll collection among its numerous art and artifact pieces focusing on the Native American Southwest.

FOLLOWING THE SUN AND MOON
Hopi Katsina Dolls

hether illuminating the Praying Hands formation of the Superstition Mountains (OPPOSITE) or casting an eerie orange glow over Red Mountain (ABOVE), the moon adds a touch of the surreal to the lush Phoenix sky.

Anasazi pot fragments are among the few tangible reminders of Arizona's original residents, yet their traditions are kept alive through the costumes and dances of the White Mountain Apache Crown Dancers and other tribes (OPPOSITE AND TOP LEFT). Another reminder of the past, the Heard Museum's annual World Championship Hoop Dance Contest is a colorful, fast-paced exhibition that draws the best hoop dancers in North America (TOP RIGHT).

The Phoenix-based Ballet Arizona has gained international fame and success through its top-ranked performances of such classics as *The Nutcracker* and *Romeo and Juliet*, not to mention the group's original world premieres.

culpture plays a big part in the art scene of the Phoenix area. Among the greats, Scottsdale's Paolo Soleri is best known for his sculptures and bronze wind-bells (OPPOSITE TOP AND OPPOSITE, BOTTOM LEFT). Soleri is also a ground-breaking urban planner and visionary architect who studied with Frank Lloyd Wright in the 1940s. Other statues and figures—including a bevy of John Waddell's bronze nudes located outside the Herberger Theater—strike artful, dramatic poses throughout Greater Phoenix.

他Far East meets the West every year during Phoenix's Matsuri Festival. Held during Japan Week, the event is a showcase for Japanese arts, traditions, and clothing (OPPOSITE). Chinese architecture is integrated into the landscape at the COFCO Chinese Cultural Center, a huge office and shopping complex built by the Chinese government to exhibit its country's rich culture and to help serve as an economic bridge between Asia and the United States.

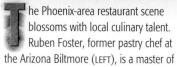

The Phoenix-area restaurant scene blossoms with local culinary talent. Ruben Foster, former pastry chef at the Arizona Biltmore (LEFT), is a master of innovative desserts, while Michael DeMaria, owner of Michael's in Scottsdale, puts a unique spin on classic American cuisine (RIGHT).

ou may have seen chocolate maven Donna Nordin on PBS's *Great Chefs of the West*, or read her critically praised cookbook *Contemporary Southwest*. Her eatery, Café Terra Cotta, is a Scottsdale favorite. Phoenix restaurateur Mark Tarbell—owner of Tarbell's—is a respected wine authority who makes regular appearances on local television.

Dining at home can be quite elegant when the menu includes tasty Arizona quail (OPPOSITE). Farther along the food chain, Basha's supermarkets have been a fixture in Arizona since the family started selling groceries in 1932. CEO Eddie Basha (ABOVE) has become a Phoenix-area icon for his support of education and his political clout: He nearly defeated an incumbent governor in 1994.

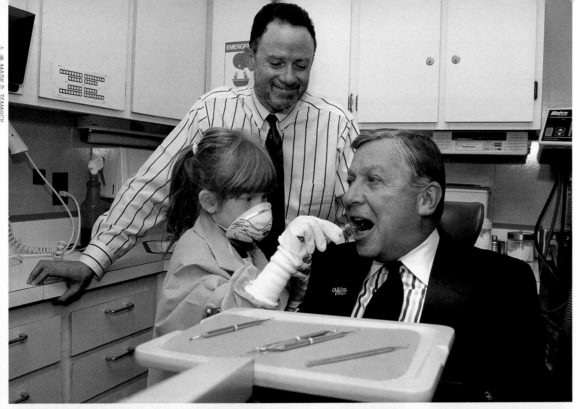

ood dental hygiene isn't a hare-brained idea. Just ask Greg McFarland, executive director of the Arizona Dental Association (OPPOSITE TOP), or the good folks at Finova Group, whose dental mobile provides quality care to low-income students (TOP). Even Finova CEO Sam Eichenfield stops by for an occasional checkup. A great smile is just one class requirement for Professor of Communications Sandra Petronio (OPPOSITE BOTTOM), whose academic speciality at Arizona State University is the study of behavior that causes embarrassment in humans.

ike most college towns, there's plenty to do in Tempe, located east of Phoenix and home of the color-splashed Arizona State University campus (OPPOSITE BOTTOM). Downtown diversions abound, including restaurants, shops, theaters, and coffee houses.

DOWNTOWN
Tempe

from the taps of a Tempe brew pub to the concert stage at the annual Old Town Tempe Spring Festival of the Arts, there's usually some reason to smile in this bustling college town.

n Phoenix, concerts in the shade are just one of the attractions at downtown Patriots Park (LEFT). People line the streets of Central Avenue for the annual Fiesta Bowl Parade (RIGHT), a New Year's tradition and a fine place to clown around.

Phoenix musicians span the gamut of genres. Keith Secola and the Wild Band of Indians incorporate Native American influences into their socially conscious roots rock (OPPOSITE TOP), while Big Pete Pearson earned the title of King of Arizona Blues through a career that stretches back to the 1940s (LEFT).

The heritage of Arizona's cowboy tradition is reflected in the area's obvious affinity for country and bluegrass music. J. David Sloan (OPPOSITE) is an ace fiddler as well as proprietor of Mr. Lucky's in west Phoenix. Pinetop's annual White Mountain Bluegrass Festival (TOP) gives musicians a chance to pick and swap songs in a cozy, down-home atmosphere.

Live

owboy fever can strike at any age, and the legacy of the Old West is still very much alive throughout Arizona cities such as Tombstone, where the legendary shoot-out at the OK Corral is reenacted daily for tourists (BOTTOM).

urely you joust: Dueling knights and fire-breathers are among the attractions at the Arizona Renaissance Festival, held each February and March in the desert just east of Apache Junction (LEFT AND OPPOSITE TOP). The old ways of the Japanese warriors are maintained during Phoenix's Matsuri Festival, a celebration of history and culture (OPPOSITE BOTTOM).

© DAN COOGAN

When the giant saguaros die, all that remains are the brittle ribs (RIGHT AND OPPOSITE, TOP RIGHT). Yet some entities do have an afterlife, such as the character at the Heard Museum's Day of the Dead celebration (OPPOSITE, BOTTOM RIGHT), which is based on the Mexican belief that ancestors' spirits visit on the first of November. At the Renaissance Festival (OPPOSITE, BOTTOM LEFT), a tree not only lives, but appears to walk as well. The by-product of several lives, the dancing Indian sculpture was once part of a housing development, but later moved to Mesa's Hohokam Park.

THE DESERT IN BLOOM

The motorcycle gang in Greater Phoenix includes multitalented Valley celebrity Mary McCann (OPPOSITE). Known to her KZON radio listeners as the Bone Mama, she is a popular disc jockey and a poetry slammer of some note. Keeping the criminals at bay in Maricopa County is the responsibility of the Sheriff's Department and its 3,200-member volunteer posse.

Arizona's Attorney General Janet Napolitano (TOP) helped make history in 1999 when she was sworn in along with the state's four other top-ranking females—Governor Jane Dee Hull, Secretary of State Betsey Bayless, Treasurer Carol Springer, and Superintendent of Public Instruction Lisa Graham Keegan—by another famous Arizona woman, U.S. Supreme Court Justice Sandra Day O'Connor. Less famous perhaps, but no less valuable, are the backbone members of Arizona's legal profession, including Phoenix attorney Paul Weiser (OPPOSITE) and paralegal Wendy Wise (CENTER).

The sound of the chain gang is music to the ears of Maricopa County Sheriff Joe Arpaio (ABOVE), whose "get tough" policies on crime are always sure to generate controversy. Because of overcrowding at the main jail, for instance, Arpaio created a tent city jail, using army surplus tents and countless miles of barbed wire.

The old ball and chain weighs down even the sculpture in the Phoenix area, where jailbirds of all stripes would probably welcome a chance to flee.

murals have become vehicles for communicating in the hands of local artist Rose Johnson (ABOVE). Using downtown buildings as her colorful canvas (OPPOSITE, LEFT AND BOTTOM RIGHT), she works to create positive images that address inner-city woes. Other colorful murals also adorn the city's exteriors with messages of their own (OPPOSITE, TOP RIGHT).

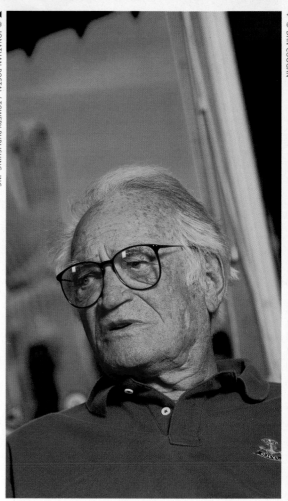

Among the politicians who have served beneath the beaming Arizona state flag are former Governor Rose Mofford (OPPOSITE, BOTTOM LEFT) and the late U.S. Senator Barry Goldwater (OPPOSITE, BOTTOM RIGHT). Mofford was the state's first female governor, while Goldwater began his career with the Phoenix City Council, going on to spend 30 years in the Senate. Phoenix Mayor Skip Rimsza (BOTTOM) shows his love for the city on the customized license plate of his vintage Ford truck: "RCITY1."

Patriotism brings out the red, white, and blue among Greater Phoenix residents, including David Hanna, former CEO of Bank of America's Arizona operations (OPPOSITE). Maintaining its link to the past, Mesa has immortalized pioneer Charles L. Robson in a bronze statue located in Pioneer Park (BOTTOM LEFT).

The grounds of the State Capitol serve as a moving public memorial. Named for the secretary of state who died shortly after assuming Arizona's governorship, the Wesley Bolin Memorial Plaza commemorates the achievements of Bolin and other prominent Arizonans (ABOVE AND OPPOSITE RIGHT). Nearby, the anchor of the USS *Arizona* provides a reminder of the death and destruction caused during the 1941 raid on Pearl Harbor when the ship was sunk (OPPOSITE LEFT).

All things high-tech can be found around Phoenix, from the Boeing plant in Mesa (OPPOSITE) to the latest in archery gear (TOP). The Wilderness, an outdoor and tactical shop owned by Ralph Holzhaus II, is a veritable North Pole of gun accessories and outdoor gear (BOTTOM).

viation combat history is celebrated at the Champlin Fighter Aircraft Museum in Mesa, with a bevy of flying war machines, including P-40 Tomahawks and Rumpler Taubes (TOP AND CENTER). Area war veteran Warren Ledbetter (BOTTOM) has stockpiled mementos from his days in World War II when he flew over Nagasaki dropping leaflets warning Japan to surrender before the atomic bomb attack. And the late Ed Horkey (OPPOSITE) was the developer of the P-51 Mustang fighter plane, a favorite among World War II pilots and today's model builders alike.

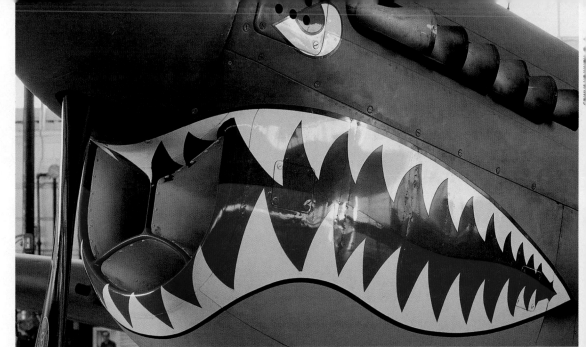

W hatever your wingspan, a bird's-eye view of the beautiful Arizona landscape is sure to include a flyover of the snow-capped Superstition Mountains.

The near-flawless Arizona weather can be perfect for all manner of "sky" jinks—from bungee jumping to parachuting.

The skys of Greater Phoenix provide the canvas for a stunning array of visual sights, from the eerie trail left after a missile launch (OPPOSITE TOP) to a crystal-clear view of 1997's Hale-Bopp comet (TOP). Preserving the combat aircraft that combed the skies during World War II are members of the Arizona chapter of the Confederate Air Force Ghost Squadron (OPPOSITE BOTTOM). Closer to earth, the open-pit copper mine has yielded treasures both profitable and historical (BOTTOM).

ome claim to have seen mysterious objects soaring the Phoenix skies—and a few of those craft may have even landed. Alien sightings are strictly unconfirmed, though, unless you count the metallic faces in the window of Jackson LaBaer's The Clotherie (OPPOSITE BOTTOM). For celebrity sightings, or at least a glimpse of some star-touched memorabilia, your best bet might be a visit to Planet Hollywood.

ootball is a mainstay at Arizona State University's Sun Devil Stadium, which—in addition to the collegiate Devils—hosts the annual Fiesta Bowl and the NFL's Arizona Cardinals. A presence in Phoenix since 1988, the Cardinals are led by former ASU quarterback Jake Plummer (BOTTOM).

hen Major League Baseball debuted in Phoenix with the 1998 Arizona Diamondbacks expansion team, it did so in style. Bank One Ballpark—known affectionately among locals as the BOB—is an engineering marvel, complete with a retractable roof, air-conditioning, and natural turf. Center fielder and free agent Devon White was one of the Diamondbacks' first players to leave the fledgling expansion team (BOTTOM).

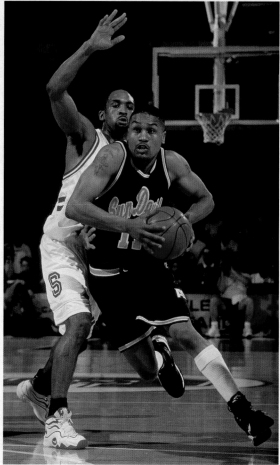

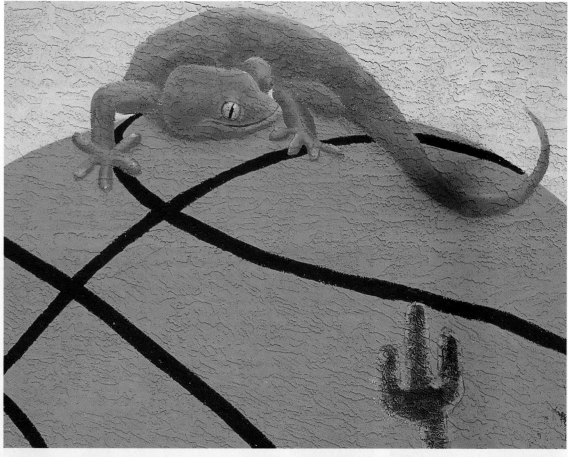

The sporting menu is deep at the America West Arena (OPPOSITE TOP), where the National Hockey League's Phoenix Coyotes set up shop in 1996 (OPPOSITE, BOTTOM LEFT). The team shares its home venue with the NBA's massively popular Phoenix Suns (BOTTOM LEFT), and the WNBA's Phoenix Mercury, one of the league's most successful teams (BOTTOM RIGHT). On the college level, the ASU Sun Devils (OPPOSITE, BOTTOM RIGHT) call Wells Fargo Arena home.

ike the season itself, the boys of summer arrive early in Arizona to participate in the Cactus League. Spring training begins in March at Scottsdale Stadium, the preseason home of the San Francisco Giants (TOP), while the Phoenix-based Arizona Diamondbacks, including pitcher Brian Anderson (BOTTOM LEFT) and former 'backs slugger Brent Brede (BOTTOM RIGHT), prep for the real season in Tucson Electric Park. Diamondbacks President Rich Dozer, one-time bat boy for the Chicago Cubs and White Sox, strikes a pose on his field of dreams (OPPOSITE).

s befits a place nicknamed the Valley of the Sun, the Phoenix area is ideal for outdoor sports pretty much year-round. Golf is a mainstay here, with nearly 200 courses to keep everyone busy, from pros such as Tiger Woods (OPPOSITE BOTTOM) to area duffers like Barbara Gordon (TOP).

ater sports are yet another forum for exercise and achievement in Greater Phoenix, where swimmers of all ages stay in shape at pools throughout the area. Gary Hall Sr. and Gary Hall Jr. (OPPOSITE, TOP LEFT) share more than a name. Gary Sr., a Phoenix ophthalmologist, is a three-time Olympian, winning silver medals in 1968 and 1972, and a bronze in 1976. Gary Jr. bested his old man by winning four medals—two golds and a pair of silvers—in the 1996 Olympic Games. And All-American Jonelle G. Schmidt (OPPOSITE, BOTTOM RIGHT), a resident of Scottsdale, competes for the Arizona Masters.

PAYSON FEED & PET SUPPLY

"We Deliver"

474-4165

172

The rodeo remains one of the West's most enduring institutions. Today's fans can catch the action across Arizona, most notably north of Phoenix in Payson, site of what is purported to be the world's oldest continuous rodeo, as well as the place where they name a Miss Rodeo Arizona.

cottsdale may be a cosmopolitan resort destination, but it still clings to its touted reputation as the West's most Western town, with images of cowboys and their steeds never far from the eye.

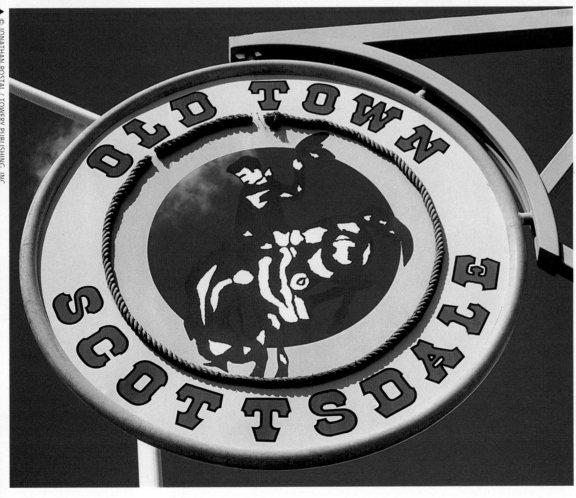

orse and cattle ranches are still a way of life in the state. And if you weren't born into it, you can learn it at Lloyd Bridwell's Arizona Cowboy College in Scottsdale (TOP).

The name itself means "enchanted" in Spanish, so it's no surprise that Encanto Park (ABOVE) is a lush oasis surrounded by charming homes dating from the 1930s. Two golf courses, a lagoon, and plenty of rides at Enchanted Island amusement park (OPPOSITE, TOP LEFT) have made the site a Phoenix favorite for generations.

ith 1,300 animals, including native and imported birds, the Phoenix Zoo (TOP RIGHT AND BOTTOM) always has something to keep the kids entertained. Visitors can experience environments ranging from the rainforest to the desert, not to mention camel rides for the whole family.

rizona trails cater to just about any mode of transportation, from the llama to the Hummer. But a strong set of legs and some sturdy hiking boots tend to be the most common vehicle for taking in the area's stunning vistas.

One of the Phoenix area's unique natural resources is its mountain preserves—set aside to assure that future generations will enjoy the unspoiled beauty of the land. The city's parks department maintains some 32,000 acres within the city limits, which include more than 100 miles of trails for hiking, mountain biking, and horseback riding.

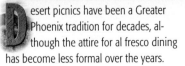esert picnics have been a Greater Phoenix tradition for decades, although the attire for al fresco dining has become less formal over the years.

Remote spots for camping include the lush greenery of Oak Creek Canyon (BOTTOM RIGHT) and Pyramid Peak (OPPOSITE), where the view is as tasty as the picnic menu.

ome sweet home Phoenix style can exist within a gated community on Scottsdale's McDowell Mountain Ranch (OPPOSITE TOP), in front of a roaring fire, or surrounded by the cozy confines of a sunny ranch house.

ar from its reputation as a mere haven for retirees and snowbirds, Greater Phoenix boasts a resident median age of under 35, with young families concentrated in flourishing suburbs such as Gilbert. And given the scorching heat that blankets the region, backyard swimming pools are pretty much necessities.

The cave dwellings of Arizona's early residents tell a rich history of the state's pre-European past. Located east of Phoenix on the Apache Trail, Tonto National Monument features pueblos built by the Salado people between 1100 and 1400 (OPPOSITE). At Montezuma Castle National Monument in the Verde Valley, two stone pueblos begun by the Sinagua people in the 12th century are among the best-preserved in the state (LEFT).

n the northeastern section of the state—the Four Corners region where Arizona, New Mexico, Colorado, and Utah converge—Canyon de Chelly National Monument, part of the Navajo Reservation, extends for some 100 miles, and is home to the prehistoric dwelling sites of the Anasazi (TOP LEFT). Around 100 miles to the northwest, Monument Valley straddles the Arizona-Utah border, and continues to serve as a homeland for generations of Navajo (BOTTOM). Closer to home, Besh-Ba-Gowah Archaeological Park east of Phoenix is a partially reconstructed Salado pueblo site (TOP RIGHT).

Phoenix's Pueblo Grande Museum & Cultural Park is the village site of a Hohokam tribe dating back to A.D. 300. Located not far from the Sky Harbor Airport in the midst of the city, the partially excavated ruins are open to the public for tours, and the museum displays artifacts of the Hohokam, who mysteriously disappeared around 1450.

There may be no royalty in Phoenix, but the city boasts at least two castles. Nestled in the foothills of South Mountain, the 8,000-square-foot Mystery Castle (OPPOSITE TOP) was built by eccentric recluse Boyce Luther Gulley out of used construction materials and found objects. From October to June, his daughter Mary Lou runs tours of the 18-room fantasy home. Situated atop a saguaro-studded hill near 50th and Van Buren streets, the Tovrea Castle (RIGHT) was built in the 1920s as a resort hotel. The grand estate—named for its second owner, prominent cattleman E.H. Tovrea—is slated to undergo a $1.3 million restoration that will result in its opening to the public. Arizona Mills Mall, meanwhile, brings a touch of splendor to the retail world in the form of a decorative tile mosaic (OPPOSITE BOTTOM).

eritage Square's Victorian homes remain as the sole remnants of the city's original townsite. The Rosson House (OPPOSITE) was the home of erstwhile Phoenix Mayor Dr. Roland Lee Rosson. The Evans House, located downtown across from the Carnegie Library, (TOP AND BOTTOM) was built in 1893 and has been nicknamed the Onion House for its prominent dome. The city's history has been a longtime fascination of artist Muriel Freund (CENTER), whose mural in the Madison School District boardroom illustrates about a century's worth of the past.

rank Lloyd Wright's Taliesin West is an embodiment of the groundbreaking architect's singular vision. Opened in 1937 near the deserts of Scottsdale as his winter camp and school, Taliesin is home to the Frank Lloyd Wright Foundation and School of Architecture. Public tours offer a glimpse of Wright's innovative use of open space, visible particularly in the Garden Room (OPPOSITE).

Designed by Frank Lloyd Wright disciple Albert Chase McArthur, the Arizona Biltmore reveals the master's influence on his students. The 1929 resort is regarded as one of the world's finest bastions of rest and relaxation, from its distinctive edifice and five-star gourmet food to the lush gardens and grounds of its 39 acres.

From the ruins of an ancient Native American Indian civilization, Phoenix—true to its mythic name—has risen. The city's downtown core today is being reinvigorated, anchored in part by the recently expanded Phoenix Art Museum (CENTER). Adapting to the changing needs of the city, the historic Westward Ho Hotel (OPPOSITE) opened in 1928 and was transformed into low-income housing for the elderly in the 1980s. Decades of growth in the Valley of the Sun have been fueled by a strong economy, which continues to drive new developments such as the Kierland Office Park (BOTTOM).

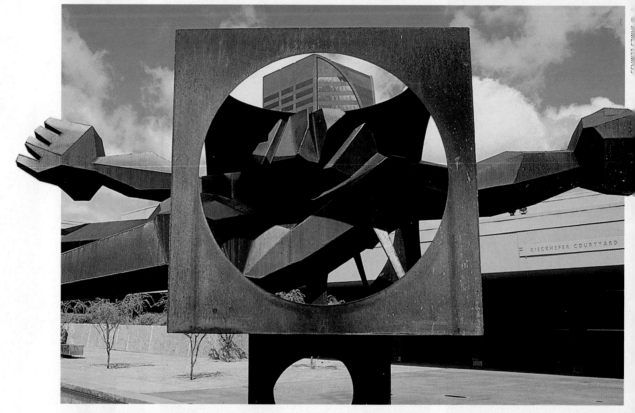

oung families and senior citizens alike are calling Greater Phoenix "home" these days. Since the mid-1990s, more than 30,000 new houses have been built annually, the growth spilling over into nearby cities such as Scottsdale (OPPOSITE), where residential developments compete for space with gorgeous mountain scenery.

espite election pleas to slow down the rapidly expanding Phoenix-area population, the signs of the times reflect a growth rate that shows little indication of reversing.

The Voladores, members of a Totonac tribe from Papantla, Mexico, bring their ritual pole dances to Phoenix as a reminder of the area's Native American heritage. Performing at the Heard Museum, the "flying men" take to the skies and then slowly spiral downward, becoming symbolic intermediaries between the sun and the earth in an effort to bring fertility to the community.

Getting into the swing of commercial and residential growth is Chuck Wahlheim, president of WCB Development.

hile City of Phoenix archaeologist Todd Bostwick digs for the old (OPPOSITE TOP), Opus West commercial real estate developer David Krumweide (BOTTOM) is erecting the new—in this case, the fourth expansion of the Camelback Esplanade. Like the sculptured ram that stands proudly at its entrance, the looming, 11-story office center—as well as the proliferation of downtown public art—is a symbol of Phoenix's booming economy.

The Phoenix of ancient Greek and Egyptian mythology symbolizes immortality, resurrection, and life after death. Its likeness appears in locations throughout the city, including its prominent imprint on the helmets of firefighters—inspiration in the midst of often chaotic darkness.

The sands of time yield a variety of objects, depending on your era. In prehistoric days, Arizona was home to the Salado people, whose cultural artifacts lie buried near Roosevelt Lake. Archaeological digs of the future will no doubt reflect a high-tech bent.

The many faces of Phoenix range from tourists at the Heard Museum to local financial wizard Steve Wunsch, president of the Arizona Stock Exchange, an electronic version of a stock auction.

ithin the desert communities
of Arizona, ancient traditions are
maintained even as technological
progress opens up the future.

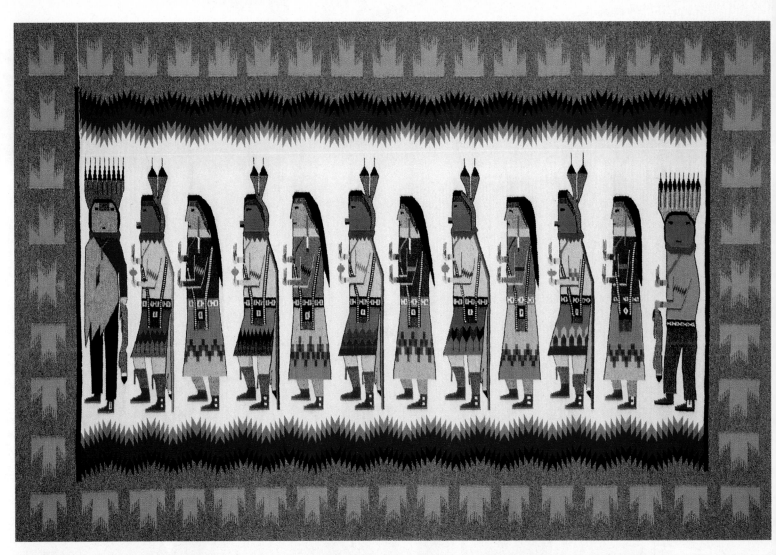

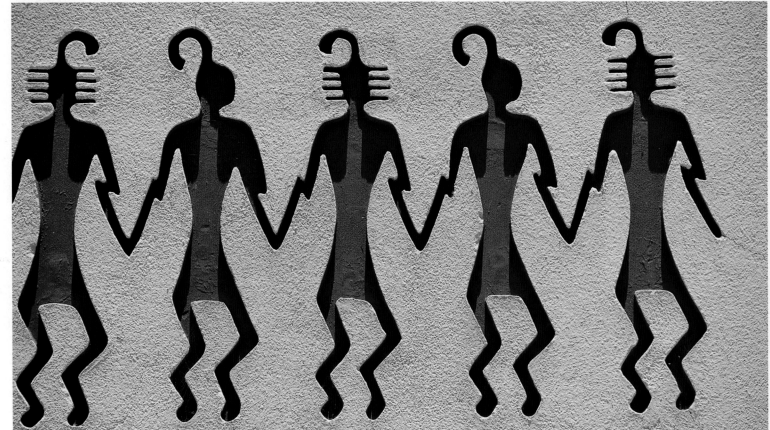

Throughout history, dance has been the rhythm of life, shimmying its way into art—and the modern lab—since the petroglyphs of prehistoric times.

ike the swirling symbols carved into prehistoric rocks throughout the area, there are plenty of spins to be had at the Arizona State Fair, which rolls into town each autumn. With its huge midway, loads of exhibits, livestock auctions, and big-name concerts, the event draws as many as 900,000 thrill-seekers annually.

© RICHARD CUMMINS / PHOTOPHILE

© J. PETER MORTIMER

G reater Phoenix comes aglow every year during the holidays when even the saguaros in suburban Ahwatukee get in on the act.

ince the glory days of Route 66 in the 1940s and 1950s, tourism has been a mainstay in Arizona's economy, with countless mom-and-pop motels dotting the landscape.

If you ever plan to motor west, you can no longer take the highway that's the best. Although portions of historic Route 66 exist in Arizona, Interstate 40 is the modern path across the state.

hether you're cycling through South Mountain Park or navigating the highways in a vintage car, the lure of the open road is powerful amid the scenic splendor of Greater Phoenix.

acing fever permeates the Phoenix area, where the need for speed can be sated at the Firebird International Raceway near Chandler (OPPOSITE TOP) or the Turf Paradise horse-racing track in Phoenix (TOP). For some airborne titillation, check out the area's ATV and motocross races.

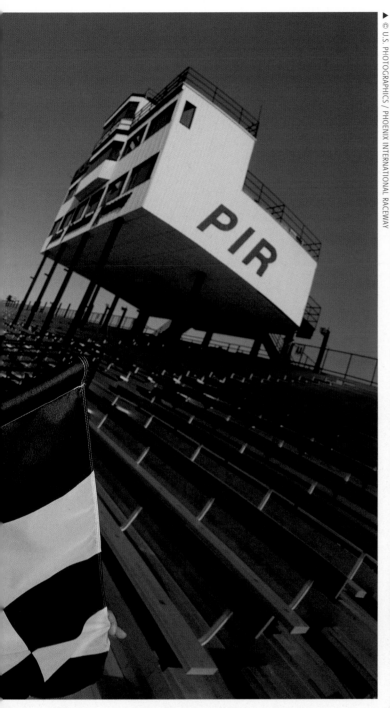

Many a checkered flag has fallen at the Phoenix International Raceway (PIR), operated by President Buddy Jobe (CENTER). Former Le Mans racer Bob Bondurant (OPPOSITE LEFT)—owner of the Phoenix-based driving school that bears his name—no doubt influenced some of the drivers who roared around the PIR track. But while the flag may signal the end of an arduous race, the journey for the Valley of the Sun is just beginning to unfurl, ensuring the area will forever remain a desert in bloom.

▲ © DAVID H. SMITH

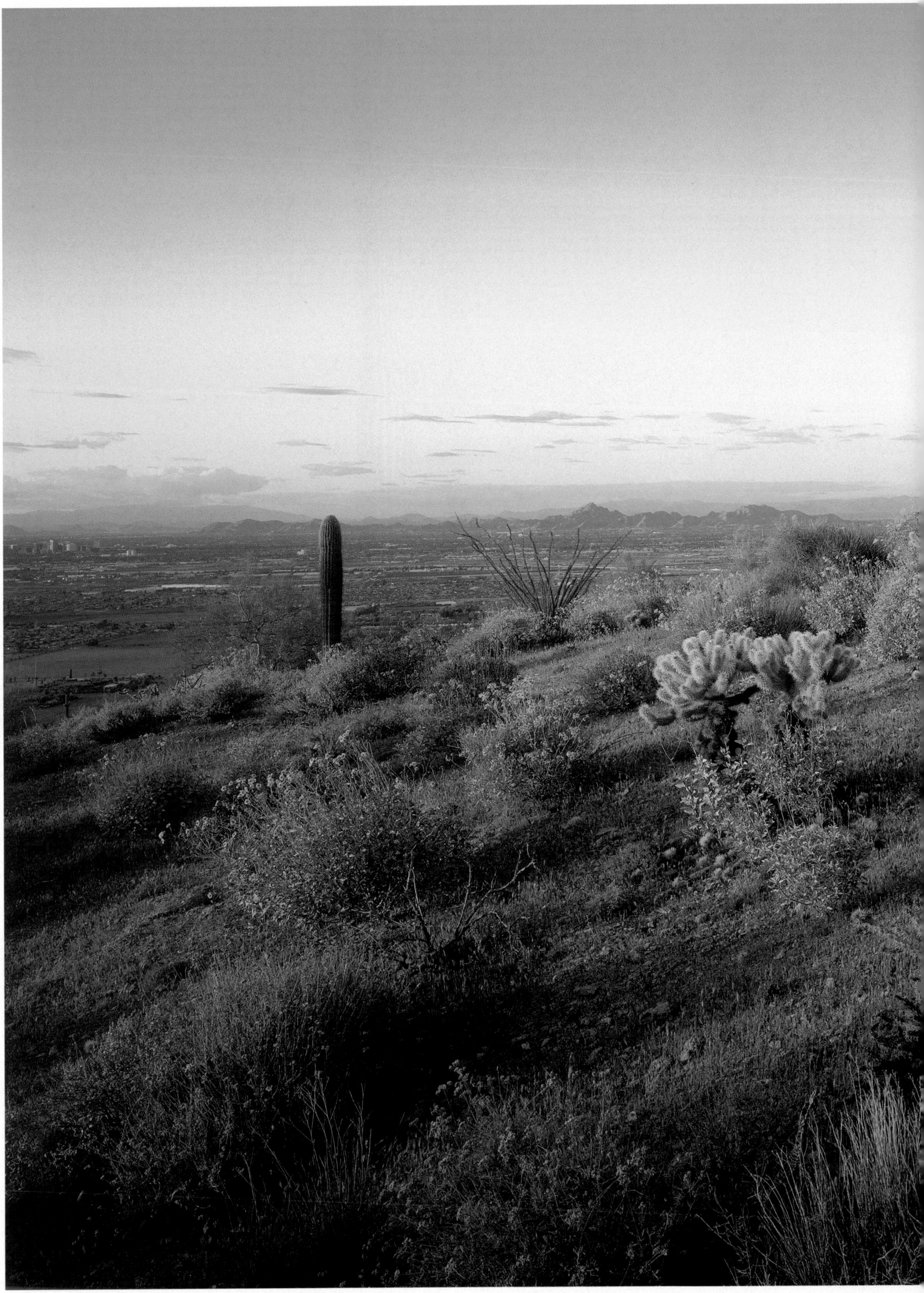

PHOENIX

PROFILES IN EXCELLENCE

A look at the corporations, businesses, professional groups, and community service organizations that have made this book possible. Their stories–offering an informal chronicle of the local business community–are arranged according to the date they were established in Greater Phoenix.

Achen-Gardner, Inc. ❦ Affiliated Cardiologists of Arizona ❦ America West Airlines ❦ Apollo College ❦ Arizona Federal Credit Union ❦ The Arizona Republic ❦ Arizona State Savings & Credit Union ❦ Arizona State University ❦ Avnet, Inc. ❦ Cable Systems International Inc. ❦ City of Phoenix ❦ Co-Sales Company ❦ Cox Communications, Inc. ❦ CSK Auto Corporation ❦ DEI Professional Services ❦ Delta Diversified Enterprises, Inc. ❦ Desert Schools Federal Credit Union ❦ EFData ❦ Equity Residential Properties Trust ❦ Ernst & Young LLP ❦ Fort McDowell Casino ❦ Gila River Indian Community ❦ Grand Bay Hotels & Resorts ❦ Greater Phoenix Chamber of Commerce ❦ Greater Phoenix Economic Council ❦ Grubb & Ellis Company ❦ Hermosa Inn ❦ Homestead Village Scottsdale ❦ Humanities and Sciences Institute ❦ Industrial Refrigeration & Boiler Company ❦ Joanne Bradley/Arizona Golf Properties and Luxury Homes ❦ KNXV-TV, Channel 15 (ABC) ❦ Linthicum Constructors, Inc. ❦ Mastercraft Companies ❦ Mayo Clinic Scottsdale ❦ MCO Properties Limited Partnership ❦ Milne Scali & Company ❦ Murro Consulting Inc. ❦ Ottawa University ❦ PacifiCare of Arizona, Inc. ❦ Paradise Valley Community College ❦ Perna Luxury Real Estate ❦ Phoenix International Raceway ❦ Phoenix Suns/Arizona Diamondbacks ❦ Powertrusion 2000 International, Inc. ❦ Primary Electric Company ❦ Ridenour, Swenson, Cleere & Evans, P.C. ❦ Rio Salado College ❦ Rowland Companies ❦ Sacks Tierney P.A. ❦ Saddleback Handcrafted Homes ❦ Salt River Project ❦ Schuck & Sons Construction Company, Inc. ❦ Scottsdale Village Square ❦ Southwest Gas Corporation ❦ Sperr and Associates/Architecture ❦ Sterling Human Resources International ❦ STMicroelectronics ❦ SunAmerica Securities, Inc. ❦ Sun Destinations Scottsdale, LLC ❦ SuperShuttle International, Inc. ❦ Tosco Marketing Company ❦ The Tribune ❦ Turner Construction Company ❦ University of Phoenix ❦ U S WEST ❦ Wells Fargo in Arizona

1859
Gila River Indian Community
1877
Wells Fargo in Arizona
1881
City of Phoenix
1885
Arizona State University
1888
Greater Phoenix Chamber of Commerce
1888
U S WEST
1890
The Arizona Republic
1891
The Tribune
1903
Salt River Project
1905
Co-Sales Company
1936
Arizona Federal Credit Union
1939
Desert Schools Federal Credit Union
1951
Arizona State Savings & Credit Union
1957
Tosco Marketing Company
1958
Ernst & Young LLP
1960
Sacks Tierney P.A.
1963
Industrial Refrigeration & Boiler Company
1964
Phoenix International Raceway
1966
Schuck & Sons Construction Company, Inc.
1968
CSK Auto Corporation
1968
Mastercraft Companies
1968
Phoenix Suns/Arizona Diamondbacks
1970
Affiliated Cardiologists of Arizona
1970
MCO Properties Limited Partnership
1971
Delta Diversified Enterprises, Inc.
1973
Grubb & Ellis Company
1975
Joanne Bradley/Arizona Golf Properties and Luxury Homes
1976
Apollo College
1976
University of Phoenix
1977
Ottawa University
1978
Rio Salado College
1978
Scottsdale Village Square
1979
KNXV-TV, Channel 15 (ABC)
1980
Ridenour, Swenson, Cleere & Evans, P.C.
1982
Achen-Gardner, Inc.
1982
DEI Professional Services
1982
Sterling Human Resources International

GILA RIVER INDIAN COMMUNITY

For some, the Gila River Indian Community represents a cherished cultural heritage. Others see it as a section of arid land in south-central Arizona straddling Interstate 10. And still others know it as 24-hour gaming entertainment at the two casinos rising from the desert south of the South Mountains of Phoenix. The community's values and traditions trace back to the Akimel O'odham, or "river people," who farmed the land, and the Pee Posh, a Yuma tribe of farmers and pottery makers who had a different language, but

who migrated east and settled near the Akimel O'odham. Now the two are more commonly known as the Pima and Maricopa tribes. The 19,000 members of the two tribes, 14,000 of whom live in the area, call the Gila River Indian Community home.

Recognized under the Indian Reorganization Act of 1934, the Gila River Indian Community's seven districts are served by tribal administrators in Sacaton, Arizona, located in the southeastern section of an area that encompasses 372,000 acres just south of Phoenix, Tempe, and Chandler. A governor, a lieutenant governor, and a 17-member, multigenerational tribal council continually work to balance what's best for the community and the Sonoran Desert environment. In the past several years, with a focused economic development strategy leading to steadily increasing industrial, retail, and recreational development activities, their efforts have dramatically moved the community from federal dependence toward self-sufficiency.

Focused Development

"Three industrial parks are located on the reservation, and the Lone Butte Industrial Park, housing high-tech firms, research and development, and retail services, including a major Home Depot warehouse, is considered the most successful Indian industrial park in the nation," says Carol Jackson, Gila River Indian Community public relations director. In addition, Gila Heritage Park is a theme facility operated by the community, telling the story of more than 2,000 years of American Indian life within the Gila River's desert basin. Gila River Telecommunications, Inc., another community-owned business, provides the community with state-of-the-art telephone service and other telecommunications needs with its 117 miles of fiber-optic cable and 342 miles of buried copper cable.

Tourist and scenic attractions bring visitors to the community, where they learn about its ancient heritage at the Gila Indian Center and at the Casa Grande Ruins in Coolidge, which preserves the remains of an ancient Hohokam farming village, as well as a fascinating, four-stories-high pueblo built in the 13th century. "We invite the public to join us in the festivities of the Mul-Chu-Tha Fair, with its parade and All-Indian rodeo in February," Jackson says.

In 1968, traditional garden plots were transformed into Gila River Farms, with a manager and farm board dedicated to creating employment opportunities and a profit base for the community. Today, this modern agricultural showpiece includes four different ranches and has a $10 million budget. To stimulate year-round employment and a dependable cash flow, the farms diversified their cotton operations to also include durum wheat, barley, alfalfa, citrus, olives, pistachios, melons, catfish, and tilapia. Independent farming operations cultivate another 22,000 acres for total agricultural product value of more than $25 million.

The community's newest and perhaps most visible economic development ventures are Wild Horse Pass and Vee Quiva gaming casinos that employ nearly 1,700 people, 85 percent of whom are community members. Vee Quiva offers live poker, live keno, slots, and a 500-seat bingo hall in an intimate, 66,000-square-foot setting that is designed to interpret elements of the community's rich heritage in a fresh and respectful way. At Wild Horse Pass, a larger, 167,000-square-foot facility

In 1968, traditional garden plots were transformed into Gila River Farms, with a manager and farm board dedicated to creating employment opportunities and a profit base for the Gila River Indian Community (left).

Tourist and scenic attractions bring visitors to the community, where they learn about its ancient heritage at the Gila Indian Center (right).

Profits from the Wild Horse Pass and Vee Quiva gaming casinos support education scholarships, a fire department, and a police force; build homes and improve existing ones; and update the community's infrastructure.

also inspired architecturally by the community's heritage, customers find Arizona's largest live poker room, a $50,000 live keno jackpot, slots, and a 1,500-seat bingo hall.

Profits from the casinos support education scholarships, a fire department, and a police force; build homes and improve existing ones; and update the community's infrastructure. A new health clinic is planned, and the tribe manages the community's 20-bed hospital.

Encouraging Education

Educating the next generation is a high priority at Gila River, beginning with a Head Start program and five elementary/middle schools. Another 1,250 students live in the community, but attend public or private schools away from the reservation.

Two Boys and Girls Clubs have opened, the first ones in Arizona in a Native American community; and a youth council has been formed to prepare the younger generation to serve in the tribal government. A scholarship program encourages students to continue their education beyond high school.

Much of the community's heritage is shared by word of mouth, with little written history, although Richard Ramon's calendar stick, created in 1994, marks a moment that was felt around the world. However, it was the 1945 flag raising on Mount Surabachi in Iwo Jima by community resident Ira Hayes, a Pima marine made famous by a now-familiar Associated Press photo, that focused worldwide attention on Gila River.

The tribe's vision for future land use includes resorts, golf courses, and a

possible site for a football stadium. The proposed Huhugam Heritage Center, celebrating the Akimel O'odham and Pee Posh heritages, is envisioned as a focal point for preserving and acknowledging the traditional relationship between the people, the land, and the sky. Future development is guided by the community's desire for continued self-sufficiency, even if the current gaming compact with the state is not renewed in 2002, when it comes up for review. Hoping to recapture some of the $40 million earned annually by community members—and now spent in Phoenix, Chandler, and Casa Grande—the Gila River Indian Community is looking to develop everything from supermarkets to department stores to automobile dealerships to help maintain its well-earned self-sufficiency.

WELLS FARGO IN ARIZONA

n 1998, the new Wells Fargo in Arizona was created by the Wells Fargo/Norwest merger, the latest of more than 500 mergers chronicled throughout the California-based bank's 147-year history. Regional President Jon R. Campbell, a 21-year Norwest Bank executive who came to the Valley in 1993, leads the Arizona operation, which has more than 7,300 team members, making it one of the state's largest employers. The merged banks provide Arizona customers with more than 315 full-service locations, 550 ATMs, 190 financial service

stores, and the state's largest in-store supermarket banking network.

"Customers, team members, and community involvement continue to be our top priorities," Campbell says. "We're blending the best in service with the best in products and high technology, and we're excited about the superior organization emerging from our combined practices and resources."

Leading the Banking World
The new organization leads the nation in mortgage lending, commercial real estate lending, agricultural lending, Internet banking, and in-store banking facilities. In addition, it ranks first in lending to small businesses, third in the number of ATMs in the United States, and seventh in assets among U.S. bank holding companies. As

a nationally chartered bank, the new Wells Fargo has more than 5,700 financial services stores in Canada, the Caribbean, Latin America, and all 50 U.S. states.

Wells Fargo operations in Arizona create a microcosm that illustrates the logic and operational synergy of the union between Wells Fargo and Norwest. Both organizations recognized the challenges of banking as a stand-alone industry and the emergence of a fiercely competitive, $1.9 billion financial services industry. They both were trying to regain corporate lending market share from investment banks and consumer savings from mutual funds, and they were developing similar financial service models in order to compete.

Norwest brought its recognized dominance of the community banking model to the table, and Wells Fargo con-

tributed an alternative-banking-channels model with supermarket locations and forward-looking PC and Internet banking services.

In Arizona, Norwest had plenty of community banking sites and was known for its friendly, one-on-one approach to banking customers. Its customers, however, were asking for more convenience and banking options. With more supermarket locations than any other banking operation in the state and an established Internet banking technology for both individuals and businesses, Wells Fargo had the convenience and options. Yet, its customers wanted a more well-rounded network with a bigger focus on one-to-one banking. So the marriage between the bank with the stagecoach logo and the one represented by a covered wagon was made.

Founded in 1852, Wells Fargo was an important symbol of the pioneering spirit in Arizona. The Wells Fargo Express office, shared with Arizona Stage Co., was established in Phoenix at the corner of Central Avenue and Jefferson Street.

Long-Term Benefits

"This new, geographically diverse banking franchise focuses its resources on delivering service and long-term benefits to our customers, our stockholders, our communities, and our team members," Campbell says. The new Wells Fargo has almost 20 million customers, deposits of more than $130 billion, and 90,000 team members throughout the organization.

Technologically, the bank has long been a leader, beginning with its first electronic transaction by telegraph in 1864 during the gold rush. Today, the new Wells Fargo continues making innovative inroads that could revolutionize the way consumers and businesspeople use on-line financial services.

In fact, on-line banking is Wells Fargo's fastest-growing service. It allows customers to log onto their accounts any time of the day or night. They can transfer money between accounts, see if certain checks have cleared, invest and trade, and pay bills, assured of privacy and security with each transaction. WellsNet Information Express brings the power of the Internet to commercial banking customers.

Company treasurers, chief financial officers, and controllers can access detailed information about their accounts and transactions, even when they are traveling or working at home.

Tailored to Specific Needs

Telephone banking is designed to provide 24-hour access to financial services. Wells Fargo telephone banking centers receive more than 10 million calls a month from customers who can complete more than 150 different transactions through a personal representative or by Touch-Tone phone.

Customers who use any one of the bank's ATMs also can bank 24 hours a day, including accessing individual retirement accounts, certificate of deposit accounts, and Wells Fargo proprietary mutual fund accounts. They can even buy stamps. All Wells Fargo ATMs offer instructions in Braille for visually challenged customers. Whenever it's necessary to bank in person, the Five-Minute Max pledge gets each customer through teller lines in five minutes or less, or a $5 credit is posted to his or her account.

As the new Wells Fargo approaches the 21st century, it faces the challenge that confronts businesses around the world to ensure that its computer systems can recognize the dates of the new century. Its bankwide Year 2000 Project Team is assessing existing systems and applications, and they're upgrading and thoroughly testing them when necessary. Before they are finished, they estimate they will have reviewed millions of lines of computer code to prepare for providing financial services in the next century.

The new Wells Fargo's top-notch service and technology are joined by a third element to create one of Arizona's best financial services organizations— community involvement. Wells Fargo and Norwest have contributed millions of dollars to Arizona causes and projects, and the organization is particularly focused on community redevelopment, lending, and investment. Its chief areas of involvement and contribution are economic development and kindergarten-through-12th-grade education. Involvement in these two areas will continue into the next century as well.

After the 1998 merger with Norwest, the new Wells Fargo in Arizona has more than 315 financial services stores and more than 550 ATMs throughout the state. The new Wells Fargo has more than 7,300 team members, making it one of the largest employers in Arizona.

CITY OF PHOENIX

Like its legendary namesake rising out of the ashes, Phoenix has emerged as one of the bright new cities of the 21st century. Clean industries such as software, financial services, and high technology are flourishing wildly in a friendly business oasis that complements an outstanding quality of life. Phoenix has magically transformed itself several times in its history. The city's modernization began in 1867, when Jack Swilling of Wickenburg, Arizona, stopped to rest his horse at the foot of the northern slopes of the

White Tank Mountains and looked down across the expansive, fertile farmland of the Salt River Valley. Swilling moved into the Valley and organized existing water channels into the Swilling Irrigation Canal Company, in the process laying the groundwork for a community that would become incorporated in 1881 as the City of Phoenix with a population of approximately 2,500 people.

Today, Phoenix ranks as the sixth-largest city in the United States, home to 1.3 million inhabitants. Its booming, diverse economy has been unfurling in spectacular fashion for more than 10 years. The high-technology industry in particular has prospered in the Phoenix area, making it a world-class center for electronics, aerospace, and semiconductor manufacturing.

Although high-tech companies have been the largest source of job growth in Phoenix in the last decade, they are not the exclusive source. The city is a leading industrial, wholesale, and retail center in the vast stretch between Dallas, Denver, and the California coast. Tourism also enjoys a solid, steady growth rate.

A Wealth of Local Resources

The local energetic spirit and business climate have prompted major businesses to establish headquarters in Phoenix,

including Fortune 500 companies such as Phelps Dodge and Avnet. Employers cite the local environment, schools, public service, and cost of living as excellent incentives for businesses and individuals thinking of relocating. Further enhancing Phoenix's pro-business environment and appeal is a large, eager, educated, and qualified workforce.

Keeping pace with growth in Greater Phoenix is the newly expanded Phoenix Sky Harbor International Airport. The world's 16th-busiest airport welcomed more than 30 million passengers in 1997, while handling more than 345,000 tons of

cargo. International flights include more than 100 direct or nonstop departures to more than 20 destinations worldwide.

Quality of Life

"Businesses and people are moving here for a variety of reasons, but the one common characteristic virtually always mentioned is the great quality of life Phoenix offers," says Phoenix Mayor Skip Rimsza. "As the city has grown, the city council and I have made a major commitment to renew our neighborhoods and implement wide-ranging programs to protect and revitalize them. Neighborhoods are not just the heart of our city, but its very soul."

One area where strong neighborhoods are making a comeback is downtown. In just a decade, Phoenix's once sleepy

The downtown Phoenix skyline is constantly changing thanks to a robust economy and a thriving, vibrant business atmosphere.

Whether it's playing golf or hiking the many trails found throughout the Phoenix Mountain Preserves, the lush Sonoran Desert provides wonderful views and outdoor activities.

▲▲ BOB RINK

downtown neighborhoods have changed the scene from ghost town to boomtown. On any given night, downtown is filled with people going to the symphony; professional baseball, basketball, and hockey games; the theater; and convention activities.

Historic Heritage Square, Phoenix Museum of History, Phoenix Civic Plaza Convention Center, Phoenix Symphony Hall, Herberger Theatre Center, and the recently completed, $47 million Arizona Science Center all are within a five-block radius in downtown Phoenix. Also nestled in the heart of the city are the Burton Barr Central Library, Phoenix Art Museum, Phoenix Theatre, Union Hall, and the newly refurbished Orpheum Theatre.

Another downtown attraction domi-nating the skyline is Bank One Ballpark—home of Major League Baseball's Arizona Diamondbacks—which opened in the spring of 1998. The 48,500-seat, state-of-the-art stadium features a retractable roof and includes natural grass, shops, restau-rants, a swimming pool, and picnic areas.

Next door is America West Arena, where approximately 2 million patrons attend more than 300 events each year. The $100 million, 20,000-seat facility was

developed as a public/private partnership by the City of Phoenix and is home to five professional sports teams: the NBA's Phoenix Suns, NHL's Phoenix Coyotes, Women's National Basketball Association's Phoenix Mercury, AFL's Arizona Rattlers, and Major League Soccer's Arizona Sandsharks.

City Manager Frank Fairbanks says, "More than $1.5 billion in public and pri-vate investments has been made to the

downtown area since the 1980s, creating an economic engine that offers significant employment, entertainment, retail, and residential opportunities. It is truly the heart of the Greater Phoenix area."

The work of the city council, the city staff, and the many citizen volunteers has earned Phoenix much recognition over the years, both nationally and internationally. In addition to four All-America City titles, Phoenix won the 1993 Carl Bertelsmann Prize, a prestigious international competition that recognizes the best-run city govern-ments in the world. Phoenix shared the prize with Christchurch, New Zealand, for its highly efficient and customer-oriented programs.

Development of Phoenix since 1950 has been, perhaps, the most remarkable of all. At that time, Phoenix encompassed an area of 17.1 square miles with a population of 106,000 that placed it 99th among American cities. Today, the city covers nearly 470 square miles.

Blessed with energetic and interested citizens and civic leaders willing to give their time to solve the tremendous chal-lenges of a growing economy, Phoenix faces an era of limitless opportunities for steady development in the years to come.

The City of Phoenix provides a wealth of sporting, leisure, and cultural attractions.

U S WEST

U S WEST has a rich history in Arizona dating back more than 100 years to the very first telephone service in the territory. Today, it is much more than the local phone company. ❧ From telephony and the Internet to digital television and on-line services, U S WEST is working to make life better for millions of customers in Arizona through integrated solutions, innovative new products, and superior service. "U S WEST is all about simplifying the way people communicate, now and in the future," says Bill Stack, general manager, U S WEST-Arizona.

Investing $1 million a Day

With more than 190,000 miles of fiber-optic cable and 2.6 million telephone lines connecting customers throughout Arizona, U S WEST is wired for the future. Each day, it adds nearly 600 telephone lines and invests an astounding $1 million in new equipment and facilities—from high-speed digital networks that provide quick access to the Internet, to self-healing networks that ensure reliable service. All told, the company has invested more than $4 billion in equipment and property in Arizona.

Part of this investment has gone to building facilities that are second to none in the industry, including more than 200 central offices that ensure reliable service throughout the state. Perhaps U S WEST's greatest investment is its workforce of more than 7,300 employees, who provide integrated communications solutions to approximately 1.6 million business and residential customers.

NOBLE STUDIO, INC.

As the largest telecommunications company in the state, U S WEST has the unique capacity to provide one-stop shopping by bundling a broad range of products and services, including local; long distance; wireless; and data, voice, and video.

Innovative Technology

U S WEST Choice TV & Online is the first technology of its kind to integrate digital television, telephony, and high-speed Internet access using existing telephone lines. "This one-of-a-kind service was launched in Phoenix first, making the Valley more connected than any other place in the nation," says Stack.

U S WEST also was the first to deploy the next generation of wireless telephone service. Advanced PCS offers unprecedented one-number integration, allowing customers to use the same number as their home or office phone.

As high-speed data services explode into the 21st century, U S WEST is working to make Web tone as readily available as dial tone. U S WEST MegaBit Services offers high-speed data connections up to 250 times faster than the typical dial-up modem—all over existing phone lines.

In addition to advanced products and services, U S WEST customers benefit from upgrades in the telecommunications network. One such enhancement is Network 21, a $32 million, self-healing network that instantaneously identifies phone line disruptions, and reroutes phone calls and data transmissions.

Community Minded

As a business leader, U S WEST takes its role in the community seriously. Each year, the company contributes more than $3 million to support education, arts and culture, economic development, and health and human services in Arizona. Beyond corporate giving, the Arizona workforce volunteers more than 9,000 hours at more than 50 charitable organizations annually.

Through research and development and strategic marketing alliances, U S WEST is positioned to stay in the forefront of technological advances. In the years to come, U S WEST will continue to focus on the needs of its customers and provide them with solutions to improve their lives.

U S WEST Choice TV & Online is the first technology of its kind to integrate digital television, telephony, and high-speed Internet access using existing telephone lines (top right).

From telephony and the Internet to digital television and on-line services, U S WEST is working to make life better for millions of customers in Arizona through integrated solutions, innovative new products, and superior service (bottom right).

With more than 190,000 miles of fiber-optic cable and 2.6 million telephone lines connecting customers throughout Arizona, U S WEST is wired for the future.

NOBLE STUDIO, INC.

Anticipating and responding to the rapidly changing needs of the community is nothing new to Arizona State University (ASU). After World War II, enrollment increased exponentially each year, and in the 1960s, new colleges and schools were added to expand offerings befitting university status. Today, extraordinary growth in Arizona is challenging the resourcefulness of the fourth-largest university in the country. ❦ ASU accepts both the challenge and responsibility of being the model

ARIZONA STATE UNIVERSITY

metropolitan research university for the next century. By matching university talents and expertise with the vision of community leaders, ASU provides indispensable research and support to address the major issues affecting the quality of life in the Valley of the Sun and throughout the nation.

The university has three anchor campuses and an extended campus in the Greater Phoenix metropolitan area. ASU Main, the original campus founded in 1885, enrolls more than 44,000 students from 50 states and more than 120 countries. ASU West, located in and primarily serving northwest Phoenix, has approximately 5,000 upper division and graduate students; ASU East, in Mesa, is the university's newest anchor campus, serving more than 1,000 students. ASU Extended Education brings university services into the community at more than 50 locations through flexible programs, technologies, and schedules.

Quality Graduates

ASU graduate programs consistently rank among the best in the nation in *U.S. News & World Report*'s listing of America's Best Graduate Schools, including those in the Colleges of Business, Education, and Law. *The Student Guide to America's 100 Best Colleges* and *Money* magazine rate ASU as one of the 100 best education values in the United States and one of the top public schools for in-state students in the country, respectively.

ASU is a Truman Scholarship Honor Institution, one of only 17 schools to be selected nationwide. The ASU Honors

College, with an enrollment of almost 2,000, is one of the largest and most sought after honors colleges in the country.

A Vital Member of the Community

ASU actively seeks community partnerships that promote economic development, address metropolitan issues, provide linkages with K-12 education, and develop innovative approaches to solving problems of concern to both the university and the community.

The ASU Research Park, established in 1984, facilitates technology transfer through university and industry relationships. Park tenants consist primarily of research and development organizations, company regional or national headquarters facilities, and pilot production operations. Tenants include Motorola Flat Panel Display, Motorola University West, Iridium of North America, VLSI Technology, and Walgreens Healthcare Plus.

The university also provides Greater Phoenix and the state of Arizona with some of the best performing arts and fine arts venues in the world. Gammage Auditorium, on ASU's main campus, is a Frank Lloyd Wright-designed landmark center for the performing arts, seating 3,000 and regularly attracting the nation's finest performers and productions. The Sundome Center for the Performing Arts in Sun City West is America's

largest single-level theater with more than 7,000 seats. ASU's Kerr Cultural Center in Scottsdale offers smaller-venue cultural events.

ASU is also involved in local television programming. KAET, Channel 8, an award-winning Public Broadcasting Service (PBS) affiliate, is operated by ASU and broadcasts 24 hours daily.

ASU is a member of the NCAA and the PAC-10 conference. With 21 varsity intercollegiate sports, ASU athletic teams consistently rank among the top 10 in the nation. For ASU, the future has never been brighter.

Clockwise from top:
The Arizona State University (ASU) Research Park brings education and industry together.

ASU's student population is one of the largest and most diverse in the country.

ASU's Nelson Fine Arts Center is a dramatic landmark.

THE DESERT IN BLOOM

GREATER PHOENIX CHAMBER OF COMMERCE

s the Greater Phoenix Chamber of Commerce celebrated its 110th anniversary in 1998, its focus remained much the same as it was in the beginning: To nurture the business community while creating an inviting city for people to work and live. Today, the oldest and largest business organization in the state finds its challenges are a little more complex, but a thriving business environment, solid infrastructure, dependable transportation, preservation of water, and effective schools are still topping the list of civic interests.

"People come to Phoenix for conferences, vacations, or to look for a new job, but they stay for the weather and the quality of life," says Valerie Manning, chamber president and CEO. "It's a place where you can make a difference," she says. "It's open and friendly, and filled with opportunity." Manning should know, having lived in Phoenix most of her life—watching the metropolitan area mature firsthand.

Sixth-Largest City
Ranked as the sixth-largest city in the country, Phoenix supports a chamber of more than 3,600 members (representing more than 310,000 employees), 90 percent of whom have fewer than 100 employees; 52 percent of its members have 10 or fewer employees. Accountants, lawyers, retailers, manufacturers, service providers, bankers, telecommunications representatives, and builders form the basis for a diverse, involved, and business-focused membership.

Following the lead of the organization's founding fathers, members work hand in hand with legislators and business leaders to shape public policy concerning core business issues, such as maintaining a business-friendly environment, reducing the overall tax burden, and minimizing government involvement. Specific items on the chamber's agenda include air quality, workforce readiness, and tax reform. As one of the fastest-growing areas in the country, growth has been added as an issue.

The chamber's successes include helping to reduce business personal property taxes, working with legislators to establish a clearer definition of independent contractors, and spearheading a process to improve the Valley of the Sun's transportation system. Recognizing the rapidly growing need for better-educated employees, the chamber has helped identify workplace skill standards, which are being incorporated into the K-12 school curriculum in communities across the Valley.

Focusing on Business
"Everything at the chamber focuses on the business community, its economic health, and the economy as a whole," Manning says. "Because we know that most of a community's economic wealth comes from existing businesses, we recognize that it's essential for our members' firms to remain strong so they can grow and thrive." In fact, 85 percent of all new job creation comes from existing businesses.

Arizona's middle market business picture is thriving, with a solid infrastructure supporting technology, a well-balanced manufacturing sector, a temperate climate, readily available transportation, a pro-business environment, and reasonable operating costs. Affordable housing and quality of life encourage a well-educated, qualified workforce to call Greater Phoenix home.

"There's a healthy competition between communities comprising the metro area, but it's really one market, and many companies find they can survive nicely serving customers here," Manning says of the cities included in this southwestern regional hub. Diverse styles of living with contrasting opportunities can be found in different parts of the Valley. Residents can live downtown and walk to work, or live near a nature preserve and walk to the wilderness.

Strategic Teamwork
The chamber, which operates like a business with strategically conceived product lines, recognizes the added value of using cutting-edge technology to support its many and varied programs. Its Web site at www.phoenixchamber.com provides cur-

Phoenix City Hall (top right)

"People come to Phoenix for conferences, vacations, or to look for a new job, but they stay for the weather and the quality of life," says Valerie Manning, chamber president and CEO. Ranked as the sixth-largest city in the country, Phoenix supports a Chamber of more than 3,600 members—representing more than 310,000 employees (bottom).

BOB RINK

all addressing the needs of the business community. For instance, the Presidents Roundtable provides a forum for executives to address workforce development and budget issues, while the Technology Roundtable addresses the often difficult task small employers face in managing the ever-changing world of technology. A mentoring program pairs executives from large and small member firms to share the benefits of everyone's best thinking.

As the Valley changes from a regional market to more global partnerships in the next century, the Greater Phoenix Chamber of Commerce is well positioned to provide leadership in serving its members and influencing the business community for many years to come.

"There's a healthy competition between communities comprising the metro area, but it's really one market, and many companies find they can survive nicely serving customers here," Valerie Manning, chamber president, says of the cities included in this southwestern regional hub. Diverse styles of living with contrasting opportunities can be found in different parts of the Valley. People can live downtown and walk to work (left), or live near a nature preserve and walk to the wilderness (bottom).

rent information on services, public policy issues affecting business, and resource materials. The organization's team-oriented culture makes membership services a priority for everyone on the 30-person staff, and recruitment and retention of members is a universal goal.

Each member firm can get answers to questions and solutions to problems from its assigned chamber customer development executive. Networking opportunities abound with Donuts & Dialogue in morning sessions, frequent after-hours events, and ambassadors helping new members make those important first personal connections.

An ongoing outreach program to determine how members rate doing business in Phoenix gives business owners a platform for their issues, and the feedback is used to help improve the Valley's overall

business environment. For instance, the city's building permit process now features permit by appointment, which expedites the issuance of permits; and the Venture Capital Conference has brought in more than $76 million to Arizona.

Outlook, an annual review of the economy and real estate market, provides businesses and real estate professionals an economic forecast into the next year, and the Mayor's "State of the City" Address speaks to community health while touching on major issues and opportunities ahead. Many important business connections are made at chamber events, large and small, that continue throughout the year.

Members Participate

Member participation is actively encouraged and chamber members serve on committees, councils, and task forces—

TODD PHOTOGRAPHIC SERVICES

THE ARIZONA REPUBLIC

In one of the fastest-growing metropolitan areas of the country, *The Arizona Republic* is the nation's fastest-growing daily newspaper, reporting newsworthy happenings and editorial comment to the Valley of the Sun's 2.4 million people. It has thrived from the beginning as a "newspaper first, last, and all the time," reporting on a busy, changing world that has gone from the horse and buggy to satellites circling the globe. As Greater Phoenix has changed from a fledgling frontier community on the desert to a magnetic Sun Belt destination,

the newspaper has fought for statehood, the observance of Martin Luther King Day, and the right of anyone to have his or her say.

"A newspaper is a history of a community, and we're that daily record," says Bill Shover, director of public affairs, describing the publication that traces its beginnings to May 19, 1890, when the first edition was published as *The Arizona Republican*. Paralleling the Valley's growth, the newspaper became the largest-circulation daily in Arizona in 1915, and has held that position since. In mid-1998, daily circulation was approaching 500,000, with Sunday editions at 634,000.

Today, most reporting is concentrated in central Arizona, with stringers making regular contributions from outlying regions. "Traditional news gathering processes don't change much, but our reporters have to be versatile to take advantage of different opportunities in the newsroom," Shover says. The paper claims two Pulitzer Prizes: one for the work of editorial cartoonist Reg Manning in 1951, and a second for the contributions of editorial cartoonist Steve Benson in 1993.

News on the Web

Today, news from AZCentral.com, *The Arizona Republic*'s sophisticated Web site, supports what subscribers find each morn-ing on their doorsteps. In addition, readers can check late-breaking news, traffic flow on freeways (updated every eight minutes), catch the latest sports or business news, look at the weather, or search the archives back to 1987. A 24-hour telephone service called Pressline goes beyond the day's headlines with recorded telephone messages ranging from ski reports to stock quotes.

Technologically, *The Republic* has been on the cutting edge from the first Linotype machine brought to the Arizona Territory in 1895, to the adoption of cold type printing and computer processing in 1977, to state-of-the-art composition and printing capabilities today. About 80 percent of the papers are printed at its modern, sophisticated satellite plant in Deer Valley, with the remainder produced at its Mesa facility.

Colorful, Innovative Leadership

Of the newspaper's owners over the years, certainly the most colorful and influential was Eugene C. Pulliam, who used both

"A newspaper is a history of a community, and we're that daily record," says Bill Shover, director of public affairs, describing the publication that traces its beginnings to May 19, 1890, when the first edition was published as The Arizona Republican (below).

Today, news from AZCentral.com, The Arizona Republic's sophisticated Web site, supports what subscribers find each morning on their doorsteps (right).

editorial and personal power to help mold the state in the boom days that followed World War II. He bought the newspaper in 1946 for $4 million, and led it from hand-set type and hand-drawn artwork to electronically generated type and computer graphics. He owned a total of four major dailies and a string of small papers in Arizona and Indiana under the umbrella of Central Newspapers, Inc.

"Pulliam was the last of the tough journalists, and he believed in front-page editorials and constant change in government," says Shover. As a student at DePauw University, Pulliam in 1909 was one of the founders of the prestigious national journalism organization, Sigma Delta Chi, now the Society of Professional Journalists. Locally, he helped initiate the Phoenix 40, now Greater Phoenix Leadership. An innovative as well as vocal crusader, he pioneered the op-ed page in 1964 and routinely gave his opponents space to air their views, a practice for which he received the coveted John Peter Zenger Award. When he died in 1975 at age 86, his wife, Nina, succeeded him, leading the paper as publisher and president for four more years.

Commitment to Excellence

The Arizona Republic's commitment to excellence begins with its employees, whose professional development is encouraged with training and educational opportunities. A profit-sharing plan gives every eligible employee a bonus if individual, departmental, and company goals are met, and annual awards recognize exceptional accomplishments. Scholarships, fellowships, and intern programs encourage students to study journalism, and reporters are actively recruited throughout the United States.

"We always have been committed to the development and support of this community, also," Shover says. "In 1998, we gave more than $8 million to local charities, much of it through the annual

Season for Sharing Campaign and The Arizona Republic Charities, which partners with the Robert R. McCormick Tribune Foundation in Chicago to match public contributions." Housed in *The Arizona Republic* Building, the $450 million Nina Mason Pulliam Charitable Trust, established to support charities in Arizona and Indiana, reflects the Pulliam legacy of generosity.

Under the guidance of Chairman Louis A. "Chip" Weil, marketing efforts at *The Arizona Republic* have been stepped up, and the organization is looking at new opportunities to acquire publications, beginning with acquisition of the daily newspaper in Alexandria, Louisiana, in 1996.

Nurturing Downtown

A conscious effort to nurture the growth of downtown influenced the newspaper's building of a 250,000-square-foot facility on East Van Buren Street next to its previous offices. *The Republic* continues to encourage downtown redevelopment with active support of projects such as the Arizona Science Center, renovation of the Orpheum Theater, the building of Bank One Ballpark, and development of Heritage Square.

As Greater Phoenix, now the nation's sixth-largest city, continues to grow, *The Arizona Republic* looks toward continuing prosperity in circulation and advertising revenues. "We're confident that we'll always have a place in this community, because people want more detail than they can get from a screen," Shover says. "We serve an urbane, sophisticated market, and we strive to discuss issues in depth, so that our readers will look to us to understand what those issues are."

A conscious effort to nurture the growth of downtown influenced the newspaper's building of a 250,000-square-foot facility on East Van Buren Street next to its previous offices.

Technologically, *The Republic* has been on the cutting edge from the first Linotype machine brought to the Arizona Territory in 1895, to the adoption of cold type printing and computer processing in 1977, to sophisticated composition and printing capabilities today. About 80 percent of the papers are printed at its 275,000-square-foot, state-of-the-art satellite plant in Deer Valley, with the remainder produced at its Mesa facility.

THE TRIBUNE

L ocal news stories are front page priorities at the *Tribune*, a regional newspaper publishing two distinct editions, one for the East Valley and one for Scottsdale and the Northeast Valley. Each day, the staff produces a comprehensive publication dedicated to being a vital contributor to the communities it serves, and always looks for the local angle, even in state, national, and world news. ❦ Today's *Tribune* bears little resemblance to one of its predecessors,

the *Evening Weekly Free Press*, founded in Mesa in 1891, the beginning of this continually published news organization. In 1996, Thomson Newspapers, Inc. purchased the *Tribune* and made a huge commitment to serve the eastern section of Maricopa County better than any other news organization. The commitment has taken various forms, including adding equipment and a significant number of staff members, and expanding the facilities. According to the Newspaper Association of America, Thomson Newspapers, Inc. is the 10th-largest newspaper company in the United States with more than 63 different newspapers and 1.3 million in circulation.

"Our priority is to provide readers an unbiased account of local news," says Publisher Karen Wittmer. "The *Tribune* is an integral part of the communities we serve and is dedicated to supporting those communities in a variety of ways." As CEO of Thomson's Phoenix Strategic Marketing Group, Wittmer also oversees the *Daily News-Sun* in Sun City.

Under Wittmer's leadership, the newspaper has invested significant resources into research to better understand the needs and interests of the area residents.

"Without input and feedback you can't expect to make sound decisions to serve your market," says Wittmer. Extensive research indicated what areas to focus local news coverage, and which interests to develop new sections that are relevant to the local lifestyle.

Get Out, a weekly entertainment and recreation guide, was added to the newspaper to give readers another compelling reason to pick up the paper. It is not the typical newspaper section. The staff that produces it is based in downtown Tempe, in the hub of the entertainment district. The editorial is upbeat, out of the box, and edgy. Readership is extremely high and the paper has continued to gain in advertising market share, the two elements every newspaper publisher wants to see products achieve. Reader feedback also indi-

cated an interest in "Desert Nesting," a home and lifestyle section featuring useful information about living in the Sonoran Desert. The booming economy—especially in the high-tech industry—created a niche for "Silicon Desert," the Monday business section.

The new sections are important reader services that provide a well-rounded product, but local news is and always will be the forte of the *Tribune* news staff. "We hire reporters who want to dig beneath the surface," says Wittmer. "The community demands that we're fair and accurate, but our reporters also have to have stamina and be fearless. Because we have an independent philosophy, we never get a chance to rest." *Tribune* reporters, a cross section of seasoned veterans and up-and-coming fresh talent, live in the communities where

The *Tribune*, where local news is first.

262

GREATER PHOENIX

they work, helping them keep their mission clear. Staff reporters are accessible, and Wittmer spends lots of time personally talking to readers, getting to know their opinions and needs.

Another step the *Tribune* has made to stay close to its readers is to have editorial offices throughout the community. With offices in Mesa, Scottsdale, Tempe, and Chandler, reporters keep up with news and events in the East Valley and Scottsdale.

"The dedication from the entire newspaper staff epitomizes the Thomson commitment to be the regional voice of local news. We encourage in-depth coverage of breaking stories and investigative reporting," says Wittmer.

Once considered sleepy bedroom communities, eastern Maricopa County, which is the *Tribune*'s market area, is now home to more than 900,000 people and is growing faster than nearly any other community in the country. This means increased readership for the newspaper, which has a daily circulation of well over 100,000 and is the second-largest daily newspaper in the state.

The *Tribune*'s non-heatset lithographic printing process at the newspaper's Mesa base of operations consumes 50 to 70 tons of newsprint daily. The plant is also home of one of the largest commercial printers in the Valley, specializing in printing newsprint publications.

In addition to the *Tribune*, a number of other services and publications are produced by Thomson's Phoenix-based marketing organization. The multimedia division is responsible for *Value Clipper*, a four-color coupon magazine direct-mailed

to 900,000 households throughout metropolitan Phoenix. A unique monthly tabloid targeting children, *curiocity for kids* is a colorful source of information distributed to younger readers. InfoLink is an audiotext system that provides 24-hour information via phone lines on a large number of topics. School Line is a division of InfoLink and provides local schools and teachers with voice mail. Parents can check the messages and get information on homework, field trips, etc. Parents can also leave messages on the system for the teachers. As the Thomson organization looks at growth, it considers new niche publications and services to add to this thriving collection.

The *Tribune* also supports community events and organizations through corporate sponsorships and volunteerism. The *Tribune* was one of three founding companies of Kids Voting, now a national program designed to

foster awareness of the political system and the importance of every vote. The editorial staff is frequently recognized for reporting and photography achievements in industry competitions. "The honors are great to receive, but doing the best job for our readers is our primary goal," say Managing Editor Jim Ripley, who focuses the news staff on the needs of his local readership.

"We recognize that the *Tribune* is in one of the fastest-growing markets in the country," Wittmer adds. "Thomson Newspapers is here by choice, and we are committed to continually providing quality news publications to our readers and aggressively meeting the needs of the marketplace." Whatever it takes, *Tribune* readers can be assured of having the news they need—with an emphasis on how it affects them locally—delivered to their door each morning.

The *Tribune* is a complete news source for readers in eastern Maricopa County.

SALT RIVER PROJECT

For nearly a century, the Salt River Project has supported life in the Valley of the Sun with low-cost, reliable water and electric power. It also has helped Greater Phoenix become a bustling, prosperous, cosmopolitan area. Named after the Valley's major tributary, the Salt River Project (SRP) is the nation's third-largest public power utility and the Phoenix area's largest water supplier; it's also the oldest multipurpose reclamation enterprise in the country. In 1937, the Salt River Valley Water Users' Association worked

with the legislature to create the Salt River Project Agricultural Improvement and Power District, a political subdivision of the state of Arizona, which ultimately became responsible for operating the area's power generation and distribution system. Together, the two are known as the Salt River Project.

SRP provides electric power to nearly 700,000 customers throughout a 2,900-square-mile service territory in central Arizona. At the same time, it administers water rights in a 240,000-acre area, operating a delivery system of dams and canals for both residential and industrial customers. The utility employs 4,200 people and generates annual revenues of $1.5 billion.

The SRP story is linked closely with the history of Arizona. The utility's service territory is situated in a large alluvial valley where an ancient people known as the Hohokam began to settle as early as 200 B.C. As the Hohokams' culture developed, they used stone hoes to dig as many as 250 canals that carried water from the Salt River to their vegetable and cotton fields. Why they moved out of the Valley 1,400 years later and abandoned their settlement is unclear, but they laid the groundwork for SRP's 131-mile canal system in use today.

A History of Progress

The modern story began with the city of Phoenix, which got its start in 1867 as a hay camp for the U.S. Cavalry stationed at Fort McDowell. John Y.T. Smith, a farmer from the Midwest, was contracted to harvest and

haul hay that was growing wild along the Salt River near what is now 40th Street. John W. "Jack" Swilling signed on as his wagon driver. Smith, Swilling, and others soon realized the ancient Hohokam water system could be cleared to carry water to grow valuable crops for the military post, and the first canal, known as Swilling's Ditch, was dug.

As the town's population grew, so did the canal system, but water-handling methods were crude and diversion into various canals was inconsistent. Often the rock and brush dams that farmers built to

divert water into their canals were washed out during heavy rains. There was no way to store excess water from spring runoff, and during summer months the river might dwindle to a trickle. During dry spells, conflicts arose among settlers over water rights.

To find a way to regulate the river's erratic flow and to eliminate constant bickering over the Valley's water, the Maricopa County Board of Trade named a committee to investigate the feasibility of a water-storage system. A future dam site was designated in a narrow canyon

Clockwise from top:
The Salt River Project's (SRP) Information Systems Building is the cornerstone of the Papago Park Center, a dynamic, multiuse urban center that is centrally located in an attractive Valley setting where business, cultural, and educational opportunities abound.

Machines and heavy equipment are used to maintain SRP's canals, where once the work was done by hand.

In the late 1880s, SRP's Arizona Canal offered Phoenix families a change of scenery and a place to picnic. Today, the Arizona Canal flows through a busy city, living up to the oft-quoted phrase "Phoenix grows where the water flows."

Construction of Theodore Roosevelt Dam, one of the nation's first large-scale reclamation projects, was the first project of SRP, one of the oldest companies in the Phoenix metropolitan area.

where Tonto Creek flows into the Salt River 85 miles east of Phoenix, but funding was a serious problem.

A solution finally came in the form of the National Reclamation Act of 1902. Under the act, an agreement with the government was signed two years later by the Salt River Valley Water Users' Association, which ensured repayment of a loan for the construction costs of the dam. It also enforced collection of each installment of these payments from individual landowners who were association members and who collectively had pledged 200,000 acres of their land as collateral. The association also took responsibility for equitably distributing the water collected in the reservoir behind the dam.

President Theodore Roosevelt, who recognized that reclamation would dramatically change the economy of the West, was among the distinguished citizens who gathered to dedicate the structure upon its completion in 1911. The highest masonry dam in the world, Roosevelt Dam was an amazing technological feat for the time. It stretched more than a thousand feet across the mouth of the canyon and was 184 feet thick at the base, 16 feet wide at the crest, and 284 feet high. It formed a lake 30 miles long and four miles wide, storing enough water to supply the Valley's needs for more than five years.

"While the original concept of Roosevelt Dam was solely for storage and water control, it soon became apparent

that hydroelectric power could be developed as a by-product of the falling water to help support the association," says General Manager Richard H. Silverman. In 1907, a permanent, 900-kilowatt unit was installed, and the first electric power reached westward to the city of Phoenix.

More SRP dams followed to help regulate water released from Roosevelt Dam and to provide hydroelectricity. Today, reservoirs on the Salt and Verde rivers store more than 2 million acre-feet of water for Greater Phoenix. SRP delivers 930,000 acre-feet annually. (An acre-foot equals 325,850 gallons—enough to supply a family of four for a year.)

In 1907, the powerhouse that would help control Theodore Roosevelt Dam was being constructed.

In Touch with the Changing Economy

Cotton crops, hay fields, and citrus groves have given way to high technology, tourism, and service companies, but thanks to the vision and dedication of these early leaders who saw the benefits of reclaiming sun-scorched desert lands, plentiful water and power have been meeting Arizona's needs continually for nearly a century.

In 1950, the City of Phoenix contracted with SRP to pay the annual assessment for urban acreage that no longer was irrigated. In turn, SRP delivers water—to which this urban acreage is entitled—to the city of Phoenix. The city acts as an agent for the landowners within its boundaries,

handling the treatment and delivery to the landowners.

Always mindful of the need for conservation in the dry Sonoran Desert, where the average annual rainfall is 7.6 inches, SRP began a long-range program in the early 1950s to modernize the canal and lateral water distribution system. Eventually, major canals were lined with concrete and many smaller lateral canals were put in underground pipes to help control seepage and evaporation. In 1974, SRP completed installation of its first water supervisory control facilities, an advanced system permitting remote operation and monitoring of canal gates, and automatic gauging of water levels anywhere on the system.

"While water reclamation was the catalyst that opened the West to 20th-century development, the demands of technological progress spurred SRP's growth as a power provider," Silverman

says. Through the years, the utility increased its capacity and diversified its means of power generation by also producing electricity from coal and diesel oil, always incorporating new methods as they were developed.

Continued Growth and Innovation

Today, SRP and its partners generate power from plants in Arizona, Colorado, Nevada, and New Mexico, with a diverse fuel mix of coal, nuclear, hydro, natural gas, and oil. This diversity allows SRP to take advantage of favorable markets and provide power to customers at the lowest possible cost.

Rededication of the Theodore Roosevelt Dam in 1996 celebrated completion of a nine-year, $430 million reconstruction project that gave the original structure a face-lift and increased water storage capacity to 517 billion gallons (or

1.6 million acre-feet). Now a 357-foot-high dam that remains the major source of water for Greater Phoenix, it features improved flood control and damage safety capacity both to meet future water needs and to protect SRP's fast-growing residential and business base.

For thousands of Arizonans and many of the state's visitors, water means recreation. Reservoirs formed by dams on the Salt and Verde rivers hold valuable water for use in metropolitan Phoenix, but they also provide opportunities for fishing, waterskiing, boating, picnicking, camping, and swimming within the Tonto National Forest. Water used for fun and relaxation also produces hydroelectric power at four of the dams on the Salt River.

SRP also participates in the Granite Reef Underground Storage Project, a cooperative effort that brought together the resources of six cities and the Salt River

Clockwise from top:
In the desert, water is precious and SRP's canal system brings this valuable resource to metropolitan Phoenix. The network of canals also provides attractive settings for fishing, jogging, bicycling, and horseback riding.

Water spills from the originally constructed Theodore Roosevelt Dam, a grand structure that has been the key to the Valley's sustained economic growth.

Theodore Roosevelt Dam as it looks today, after it was raised, strengthened, and rededicated in 1996.

SRP employees are active in their communities and their volunteer efforts have made the difference in the lives of many families. Employees have contributed their time and talent to such charitable organizations as Habitat for Humanity, which is dedicated to providing affordable housing for working families of modest means.

Pima-Maricopa Indian Community to develop a large underground water storage facility for the Salt River Valley. The site has a capacity to recharge up to 200,000 acre-feet of water annually.

SRP continues to provide innovative products and services for its electricity customers. General business customers—typically those with annual energy consumption of up to one megawatt—are the cornerstone of Arizona's thriving economy. SRP's Business Energy Manager, a suite of Internet products and services, is designed to help consumers reduce their electric bills, provide advice on equipment and technologies, answer energy-related questions, and offer opportunities to purchase products on-line at www.srpnet.com.

Home Energy Manager provides a similar service for residential customers that allows home owners to perform an audit of their energy consumption using their actual energy usage information stored in SRP's on-line billing system. "We encourage all of our customers, whether they're commercial, industrial, or residential, to use high-efficiency appliances and to shift to off-peak energy use as an alternative to our increasing power sources," Silverman says.

SRP's Select Business Locations program helps companies that are expanding or relocating to Greater Phoenix save time, effort, and expense in finding the right location. Using its expertise in energy and water, SRP has identified 16 key locations throughout the metropolitan area for commercial and industrial development, adding information on demographics, amenities, and business-related opportuni-

ties. The locations are considered ideal for a quick move-in.

Scottsdale's Waterfront Project represents SRP's vision of multiple-use development of its 131 miles of canals. The project will landscape the banks with bridges, pedestrian walkways, and terraces, which will then be dotted with cafés, shops, and parks. To maintain the canal, thousands of white amur—or grass carp, as the fish are commonly known—have been introduced into the waterways to control moss and weeds. The fish can eat nearly three-fourths of their weight in vegetation every day, reducing the need for chemicals and mechanical labor to rid waterways of aquatic weeds while saving thousands of dollars a year in labor-intensive cleaning.

Committed to the Community

Because its electric customers and its water shareholders are still its sole interest, SRP's

commitment to community involvement remains strong as always. "While SRP supports many organizations financially, we're most proud of the 24,000 hours volunteered by our employees in the past five years, averaging 36 projects annually," says Silverman. SRP employees serve on boards, work in homeless shelters, help in schools, and conduct food, clothing, and toy drives—always striving to make Greater Phoenix a better place to live.

Through the years, SRP has combined the best interests of both the community and the utility, and its future remains interwoven in this philosophy. Community partnerships are built into SRP's history, its experience, and its willingness to take risks and blaze through uncharted territory. And as the industry changes, SRP will always remain focused on its customers values and how it can best serve the community.

Saguaro Lake, 41 miles from downtown Phoenix, is one of six lakes on the Salt and Verde rivers formed by reclamation dams that SRP operates.

CO-SALES COMPANY

s the state's largest independent broker of dry groceries, frozen foods, and perishable products, Co-Sales Company plays a behind-the-scenes role in supplying supermarkets throughout Arizona. Based in Phoenix with a talented, diverse staff, the company also maintains operations with resident personnel in Tucson, Las Vegas, Albuquerque, El Paso, and Southern California. ❦ Co-Sales represents more than 80 food manufacturers, who produce more than 1,500 food items. As a conduit of the food

industry, the company regularly interacts with more than 500 retail grocery stores. Today's challenging, competitive environment finds the locally owned and operated company succeeding with an innovative sales force, supported by state-of-the-art computer technology.

As the southwestern market continues to grow and change, Co-Sales is dedicated to keeping pace with these changes by using its advanced technology, and by continuing to nurture honest, ethical relationships with both the manufacturers it represents and the customers to whom it sells.

Founded in 1905, Co-Sales has helped change the look and feel of Arizona's territorial grocers (top).

With the move to a new headquarters in 1995, Co-Sales not only doubled its office space, but practically doubled its volume of business at the same time. The building is centrally located in downtown Phoenix and was designed with two goals, comfort and productivity (bottom).

A History of Innovation

Co-Sales, one of the oldest companies in Arizona, was founded by Henry Winchester and Tasso Coe in 1905 as Winchester-Coe. At the turn of the century, the industry was unrefined and food was delivered to the market very differently than it is today. Products were ordered and delivered to individual stores prior to the inception of chain stores and wholesalers.

Monumental change came to the food industry after World War II, with the onset of dual-income families, life in the suburbs, processed and frozen/refrigerated foods, and supermarkets. Instead of selling to individual stores, the company began working with chains

and wholesalers, creating economies of scale through concentrated purchasing. As retail and wholesale operations became integrated, more emphasis was placed on supporting the retailer, forging links with more direct connections, and passing the savings to the consumer.

The company has evolved through the years, incorporating as Co-Sales in 1955. Don Cox joined Co-Sales in 1962 and became its eighth president in 1976, helping to focus on the vision that has made the organization what it is today.

In 1986, Co-Sales began a series of acquisitions of food brokerage companies, solidifying its position as a significant presence in the industry.

Three Elements to Success

"There are three key elements to our success," says Cox. "We have created a positive and supportive company structure, and hire and work to keep the best people we can find; we continually invest in leading-edge technology to maximize our efficiency and productivity; and we focus on our core grocery business."

Rick Bordwell, senior vice president operations, and Jeff Nelson, senior vice president sales, provide the daily direction of the company. An encouraging, nurturing atmosphere with shared responsibility has produced a cohesive organization where independent, entrepreneurial thinking and hard work are rewarded.

The company leverages its marketing experience with its considerable knowledge of the food industry—and keeps up with consumer buying habits—to introduce products that are likely to appeal in taste and quality to the southwestern market. Sophisticated market research plays an increasingly important part in ensuring a product's success. Co-Sales purchases specific product category information from national syndicated data companies. Subsequently, this information is used for data analysis to produce fact-based sales presentations to meet manufacturers' objectives.

Personal service drives Co-Sales Company, with each new food product presented to every buyer. The corporate office is equipped to prepare the manufacturer's product for the buyers to sample and evaluate. In addition, Co-Sales provides buyers with computer-generated schematics, suggesting how best to display and present products on the supermarket shelves and food cases.

Community Contributions

In addition to perpetuating the business and making it profitable, Co-Sales also emphasizes the recognition and support of the community it serves.

Co-Sales takes pride in being a local concern, and its personnel consider involvement in their community an impor-

tant part of their everyday lives. Employees volunteer to help with local causes, particularly those involving youth and the less fortunate, with many of their management personnel serving on advisory boards.

Co-Sales also enjoys the respect of national food industry leadership and has been chosen to serve on a number of broker advisory boards. These selective positions encourage communication and provide unbiased feedback on current and future sales, marketing, and merchandising decisions. Co-Sales' participation helps manufacturers understand brokers' concerns and capabilities, and it facilitates problem solving and the ability to focus on industry specific issues. Locally, Co-Sales is active in a number of Arizona food industry associations.

In an industry that is ever changing, through acquisitions and mergers, Co-Sales is well positioned to meet these challenges with a creative, stable workforce, and envisions a positive, prosperous future.

Co-Sales is one of the few remaining independent food brokers in Arizona. The key to the company's success is its passion for the food business, its dedication to service, and its ethics.

Co-Sales realizes that sophisticated market research plays an increasingly important part in ensuring a product's success.

Arizona Federal Credit Union

Arizona Federal Credit Union (AFCU) was established in 1936 as a financial cooperative of people helping people. The credit union began with savings accounts and loans, and today has grown into an organization with assets of more than $500 million, providing a vast array of financial services to its members. ❧ Originally serving City of Phoenix employees, AFCU now serves municipal employees in Apache Junction, Carefree, Chandler, Fountain Hills, Glendale, Mesa, Paradise Valley, Peoria,

Arizona Federal Credit Union (AFCU) was established in 1936 as a financial cooperative of people helping people. The credit union began with savings accounts and loans, and today has grown into an organization with assets of more than $500 million, providing a vast array of financial services to its members.

Phoenix, Queen Creek, Scottsdale, Tempe, and Youngtown. Major employee groups are also served, including Tosco Corporation, TRW Vehicle Safety Systems, Insight.com, Rural Metro, PetsMart, and many others. Additionally, a community charter provides membership eligibility for anyone who lives or works in the Ahwatukee/South Tempe area. Overall, AFCU has more than 115,000 accounts, serving 75,000 households.

While members might initially be attracted by AFCU's no-fee checking accounts, they also are secure in knowing that their institution is financially sound and is ranked among the top of its industry by independent agencies and regulators. The credit union offers competitive loan rates, and pays higher-than-average dividend rates on a variety of savings products. In addition, accounts are insured to $100,000 by the National Credit Union Share Insurance Fund. Members enjoy the close, personal attention found in the credit union's branches, and many also take advantage of AFCU's continuing education efforts through newsletters, seminars, and on-line communications.

"This is a dynamic organization, and we're always looking for new opportunities and ways to improve what we can do for members," President and CEO Ronald L. Westad says. "Because we're a not-for-profit cooperative, we can focus our efforts on maximizing benefits to our members by providing access to low-cost financial services and quality financial education."

Progressive Services

In 1998, a new, 80,000 square-foot operations center in East-Central Phoenix was completed, allowing all administrative and support services to join together under one roof. The improved coordination of services and improved efficiency resulting from this consolidation are expected to benefit members for years to come. The freeway-convenient location also houses one of the credit union's 15 branches, offering lobby, drive-through, and ATM services.

For those members wanting the convenience of self-service, AFCU offers C.U. Online, a virtual credit union that allows access to account balances, fund transfers, and automated bill payment via personal computer. On-line visitors can also get information on AFCU services, use retirement savings and mortgage calculators, and even apply for loans on the credit union's Web site, at www.azfcu.org. Plus, Arizona Federal was one of the first to offer a 24-hour, seven-day-a-week LoanLine allowing members to apply for loans and credit cards over the phone, with an answer by the next business day.

The AFCU vision continues to revolve around helping people help themselves through education and improved services. A survey of 40,000 member households in Phoenix found that 92 percent of the respondents rated Arizona Federal as equal to or better than other financial institutions. "We believe that this significant response is a clear indication of the difference between

Arizona Federal Credit Union

The AFCU vision continues to revolve around helping people help themselves through education and improved services.

our credit union and other financial service providers," says Westad. "This survey really brings our credit union to life and will help guide our planning for the future."

Focus on the Community
Arizona Federal's member-ownership structure creates a unique relationship between the credit union and the communities it serves, as community involvement is often a natural by-product of AFCU's

service efforts. In addition, Arizona Federal regularly supports member involvement in community service organizations through the sponsorship of major programs and through Community Partners, a nationally recognized grant program that directs financial gifts to organizations for which the credit union's members volunteer.

AFCU's plans for growth include a continuing commitment to locate branches where members live and work—even on-

site at employee locations whenever possible. Growth is specifically targeted at serving members statewide, a goal initiated in 1996 with the establishment of a branch in Tucson.

As it strives to be the total financial solution for its members, AFCU continues to offer new and improved value-added services aimed at guiding its members toward effective financial decisions that will provide benefits for many years to come.

AFCU's plans for growth include a continuing commitment to locate branches where members live and work—even on-site at employee locations whenever possible.

From the beginning, Desert Schools Federal Credit Union's philosophy has focused on being a caring institution, mindful of the special needs of its members and the communities it serves. At the same time, the financial cooperative also works diligently to provide its members with lower costs for financial services and higher interest rates on their deposits. "We are dedicated to the individual and the family, and we have programs for everyone from children to senior citizens," says Larry

Knoll, president and CEO. "We're not concerned about being the largest financial institution in town. We're more concerned about taking care of our members." The credit union, in fact, is the largest locally owned financial institution in Arizona, and Knoll attributes this status to listening to its members on a one-on-one basis and providing for their personal needs.

Growing from $78.75 to $1 Billion
Fifteen school employees planted the first seeds of the credit union in 1939 with a contribution of $5.25 each, not long after the Great Depression had left its permanent mark on the nation's economy. Their vision was to create a not-for-profit cooperative to help the average person save money and afford a better life, and they called it the Arizona Education Association #1 Federal Credit Union. From this simple idea, and $78.75 in deposits, the credit union has grown to more than 185,000 members, steadily increasing by 10,000 to 15,000 new members a year. In 1972, the name changed to the Desert Schools Employees Federal Credit Union, later dropping the word "employees." A volunteer board of directors, which oversees a business with

more than $1 billion in assets, continually works to blend the personal attention of the original credit union with the complete menu of financial services available today from a growing, thriving organization.

Membership comes from the educational community and from selected businesses mostly located in Maricopa, but also in Gila, Navajo, and Apache counties. Senior citizens who are more than 50 years of age and live in Maricopa County, as well as children, also can join. The typical member is in his or her early 40s and has used the credit union's services for eight or nine years.

Desert Schools offers a wide array of financial choices, including accounts for checking, savings, money markets, and IRAs. A variety of loans including auto, home equity, mortgages, education loans, and VISA® credit cards are also offered. Transactions can be made at one of the 15 offices in Maricopa County Monday through Friday or at night depositories, drive-through windows, and ATMs located valleywide. Members can also pay bills and transfer funds from one Desert Schools account to another electronically from their home computers.

Secrets of Member Satisfaction
Continually paying attention to personal relationships and updating financial services lead to satisfied customers, and the credit union still grows by word of mouth, says Knoll. "Each year, we revisit the schools and meet with all the new hires," he says, "and time and time again we hear the best testimonials from longtime employees who tell how they got their first loan for a refrigerator, or washer and dryer or automobile. They remember that we have been there for them through good times and bad."

Desert Schools' culture is built around community service, particularly involving schoolchildren. "We reach more than 20,000 students each year with 750 presentations explaining credit, how to balance a checkbook, and money management tools," Knoll says. "One of our employees single-handedly visits more schools annually than most states claim for their entire program." These visits also explain and encourage credit union career opportunities.

Desert Schools' pilot program provides grants to students who are at risk of dropping out of school for financial reasons.

Desert Schools Federal Credit Union encourages children from birth to 13 years old to join the Desert Kids Club to learn about money management.

Desert Schools Federal Credit Union has earned national honors for leading the country in presentations made in elementary through high schools that help prepare students for the future with financial understanding.

The program provides support for basic clothing and supplies to school-recommended eighth-grade graduates through their high school years if they have demonstrated a desire to complete their high school education and could not otherwise do so.

Children from birth to 13 years old are encouraged to join the Desert Kids Club to learn about money management, and teenagers can graduate to Trendsetters as they get older. Desert Schools' Community Service Award Program allows students who contribute 100 hours of service to learn the joy of giving their time while becoming eligible to win one of the many $1,000

scholarships awarded annually. Through Desert Schools' affiliation with Southwest Student Services, students can save on government student loans and access a wide variety of college funding information. College students, 18 years or older with a good credit history and proof of income, can qualify for their first VISA card. Desert Schools has received the Louise Herring Award for Credit Union Philosophy in Action because of these special programs offered to members.

New corporate offices in a sleek, technologically advanced building, rising at the corner of 48th and Washington streets,

will bring many factions of the now scattered administrative staff and back-office departments together. Future services administered from the new facility will continue to focus on member satisfaction, providing benefits for savers and borrowers, and will include more innovative financial services.

Since May 2, 1939, Desert Schools Federal Credit Union's philosophy has focused on customer service and its members' pride of ownership. As Desert Schools moves toward the future, the spirit and vision of its 15 founders are certain to remain.

Senior citizens who are more than 50 years of age and live in Maricopa County, as well as children, can also join the credit union.

ARIZONA STATE SAVINGS & CREDIT UNION

n a time when many financial institutions are merging and changing the services they offer, members of the Arizona State Savings & Credit Union find comfort in the organization's unwavering dedication to member satisfaction. ❦ By the numbers, the Arizona State Savings & Credit Union is impressive. Chartered in 1951 to serve state employees, the organization began an era of expansion in 1975 by reaching out to include university personnel, company groups, and communities. Today, its 20 full-service offices are open to more than 100,000 shareholding members throughout the state—growing by approximately 1,500 a month. With more than $500 million in assets, it is the largest state-chartered credit union in Arizona.

Personal Touch

"We like to think we're doing things right," says President R.C. "Dick" Robertson of the nonprofit cooperative. "We keep fees and loan interest rates low, share savings dividends high, and provide many convenient services that don't have fees at all." While the credit union's members appreciate these and other financial advantages, it is the personal touch that keeps them loyal year after year. "We base everything we do on member satisfaction," Robertson adds. "We always remember that our bottom line is our members."

Based on a philosophy of helping people who want to help themselves, the credit union makes loan decisions by looking at what it calls the three Cs— character, capacity, and collateral. And because of its nonprofit status, along with its close, personal relationships with members, the Arizona State Savings & Credit Union has significant flexibility in granting loans. "We're decentralized, and all of our offices have common capabilities and authority to make decisions," says Robertson. "Members know that our managers in Safford, for example, have as much ability to make a loan as we would in the central office."

The organization's dedication to members and the community, as well as its exceptional leadership within the credit union movement, has not gone unrecognized. In 1996, the Arizona State Savings & Credit Union was selected from among 12,000 others nationwide to receive the Roy F. Bergengren National Award, the highest honor bestowed on a credit union for exceptional achievement.

Success through Strong Leadership

Since he assumed the role of manager in 1959, Robertson has carefully guided the credit union's growth and success, always looking for ways to do things better. The lessons in teamwork that he learned on the athletic field in high school and college helped him build a cohesive organization of 210 employees that is now recognized nationally and internationally for its excellence. Closer to home, Robertson is also well known for his instrumental role in persuading state legislators to adopt progressive credit union laws that have brought membership availability to thousands of Arizonans.

Over the years, Robertson's vision and contributions have garnered recognition for the Arizona State Savings & Credit Union that reaches far beyond Greater Phoenix and the state. He is the only person to have served as the chief elected officer of the Credit Union National Association (CUNA), CUNA Mutual Group, and the World Council of Credit Unions. In 1998, Robertson was honored nationally through his induction into the Cooperative Hall of Fame in a ceremony at the National Press Club in Washington, D.C. While remaining on the forefront in the development of credit unions around the globe, he has always brought what he learns back home to continually improve

"We like to think we're doing things right," says Arizona State Savings & Credit Union President R.C. "Dick" Robertson of the nonprofit cooperative. "We keep fees and loan interest rates low, share savings dividends high, and provide many convenient services that don't have fees at all."

services and opportunities for members in Arizona.

Always Improving

Originally chartered as the Arizona State Employees Federal Credit Union, the organization was subject to federal law for its first two decades of existence. In the 1970s, Robertson recognized the potential benefits of operation under a state charter, which would take advantage of the fact that Arizona's credit union laws were among the most modern in the nation. He led the reorganization to become a state-chartered cooperative and was appointed statutory agent in 1972. Today, federal share deposit insurance continues to cover $100,000 per member account, with individual retirement accounts (IRAs) and deferred compensation accounts separately insured

to $100,000 each. A strong risk management program, bonding, and insurance assures the safety and soundness of the savings and credit union.

The credit union continues to make improvements in other areas as well. For example, in-house education and training through Arizona State Savings & Credit Union University gives employees the competencies to handle their ever changing jobs, and provides a thorough understanding of the organization's philosophy, strategies, and business objectives. Every employee is involved in the program, and is encouraged to expand his or her horizons both personally and professionally.

Additionally, advanced technology helps simplify day-to-day business and maintain the level of service to which members have become accustomed. A high-speed telecommunications network ties together

three major hubs in Arizona—Greater Phoenix, Flagstaff, and Tucson—with Dallas-based EDS, the largest provider of data processing information services for credit unions nationwide. Integrating information and making it available to all offices ensures instantaneous response time, and delivers more personal, individualized services to members faster and better than ever before.

But no matter how advanced the credit union becomes—even as members embrace PC financial services from home—the personal touch will remain important. Each day, the organization evaluates its performance to determine how members' needs were met and how they can be delivered even better the next day. With that kind of commitment in place, the Arizona State Savings & Credit Union is well positioned to serve its members statewide for another half century.

In a time when many financial institutions are merging and changing the services they offer, members of the Arizona State Savings & Credit Union find comfort in the organization's unwavering dedication to member satisfaction.

Tosco Marketing Company

The story of Tosco Corporation is one of tremendous growth over the past several years. Tosco is a Fortune 150 company based in Stamford, Connecticut, with $12 billion in annualized revenues. It is traded on the New York Stock Exchange as TOS. Tosco operates through two separate divisions, Tosco Refining Company and Tosco Marketing Company, which is based in the Greater Phoenix area. Tosco Marketing Company is the retail marketing arm better known in the Valley of the Sun and around the world as Circle K convenience stores and 76 gasoline.

The Name Behind the Brands

Today's Tosco is a dynamic blend of several very different companies. Tosco and Circle K have combined forces to create a company that today sells approximately 4.7 billion gallons of retail transportation fuels and more than $2 billion worth of convenience store products annually. Sixty-five hundred of Tosco's 27,000 employees work in Arizona, as part of a national retail network of approximately 4,800 fuel and convenience stores in 31 states and more than 3,000 Circle K-branded stores in seven foreign countries. Consumers in Arizona know Tosco by its brands: Circle K, 76, Exxon, and ProWash.

"Our family of leading brands includes some of the most recognizable names in retail today," says Bob Lavinia, president of Tosco Marketing Company. "Our goal is to be the customer's preferred choice for total retail convenience. By taking the strong equity of Circle K and pairing it with 76 or Exxon in Arizona, we've created a powerful consumer offering."

Tosco's Arizona origins can be traced to 1957, when El Paso-based Kay's Food Stores expanded into the state. The company's now-familiar red-and-white Circle K logo depicted an Old West branding iron. Twelve stores opened by the next year with the company venturing into New Mexico as well. In 1962, the corporate headquarters was built at 28th Avenue and Camelback Road, and the following year the company went public.

In 1964, Circle K opened its 100th store, and the company began producing ice in five automatic ice machines under the name Crystal Clear Circle K. As gasoline, dairy products, and money orders were introduced, the company grew. In 1966, the 200th store opened in Tucson. By that time, Circle K had almost 900 employees, and merchandise sales had reached $27 million. Five years later, the company opened a fast-food kitchen in Phoenix, and began manufacturing and delivering sandwiches to Circle K stores as part of its new Food Service Division.

Expansion at Home

Circle K made its mark in the southwestern United States with customers who had come to rely on the neighborhood stores as quick, convenient places to purchase the necessities as well as the niceties of life. As growth continued at home, the company moved west into California and, in 1975, opened its 1,000th store.

Circle K grew to 2,185 stores in 1983, nearly doubling its size by purchasing 960 UtoteM stores and expanding geographically from 12 to 19 states. The next year, 435 Little General Stores were acquired, predominantly in Florida, along with 21 Day-N-Night stores, and merchandise sales surpassed the $1 billion mark for the first time. Growth continued in 1985 with the purchase of 449 Shop-N-Go stores in Florida and Georgia and a new international headquarters in Phoenix.

When the company expanded into Arizona in 1957, the first Circle K logo was adopted to emphasize the company's western image (top).

The company's Arizona headquarters sits on a 12-acre campus in Tempe (bottom).

Circle K and 76, two well-known brands, have proven to be a strong marketing combination (top).

Since being designated as NASCAR's Official Fuel in 1954, 76 branded gasoline has been used in every race in every car on the NASCAR Winston Cup circuit (bottom).

The picture took a downturn in the late 1980s, however. Major oil companies, armed with prime real estate holdings, gained a foothold in the convenience store market, realizing tremendous opportunities to supplement strong gasoline sales with other merchandise. Circle K fell victim to softening merchandise and gasoline margins, and in 1990, filed for protection under Chapter 11 of the U. S. bankruptcy code.

A new, consumer-driven management team closed many of its unprofitable stores and led Circle K out of bankruptcy, announcing the sale of the company in 1993 to Investcorp, an international investment bank. At that time, Circle K operated 2,500 stores in 28 states. Two years later, back on solid financial footing, Circle K went public on the New York Stock Exchange.

From Shale Oil to Transportation Fuel
Meanwhile, Tosco was founded in Nevada in 1955 to develop and license technology for the extraction of oil from shale. The company acquired the Avon Refinery from Phillips Petroleum in Martinez, California, in 1976. As shale oil proved to be commercially nonviable, and the company's focus shifted to refining and marketing, Tosco restructured its operations as well.

Thomas D. O'Malley, formerly vice chairman of Salomon Brothers Inc., became Tosco's chief executive officer in 1990, leading the way to acquiring the Bayway Refinery from Exxon in Linden, New Jersey, in 1993. Later that same year and on into 1994, Tosco acquired the BP Ferndale

Refinery in Washington State, along with a network of BP franchise service stations in Washington, Oregon, and northern California, and Exxon stations in Arizona.

Tosco was growing into a major force in the petroleum industry, and in 1996, acquired the Trainer Refinery in Pennsylvania, its associated wholesale marketing assets, and a 500-site jobber system in the Northeast from BP.

Joining Oil and Convenience Stores
Additionally in 1996, Tosco purchased The Circle K Corporation. The combination of the two companies leveraged assets and talents, positioning the new Tosco to lead the way in a competitive, changing marketplace where the consumer is focused on strong brands delivered in a well-priced, convenient environment. Tosco's solid oil industry background and supply system for gasoline joined Circle K's marketing expertise and convenience store supply and distribution network; the result was a dynamic organization offering consumers high-quality gasoline and retail merchandise.

The company's fuel retailing capabilities were strengthened further, 14 months later, when Tosco acquired the West Coast refining and marketing assets of Unocal's 76 Products Company in April 1997. This purchase made Tosco one of the nation's largest independent oil refiners and marketers of petroleum products, and the largest operator of company-controlled convenience stores. Today,

Tosco owns a total of seven refineries, including two in the East, one in Washington State, and four in California.

As Tosco Corporation brought the experience of the convenience store and gasoline sales together in one company, Tosco Marketing Company became the official name for the retail marketing division in order to encompass the broad retail network and the strength of its diversified brands.

More Than a Building

Today, a new, 280,000-square-foot, four-story headquarters building sits on a 12-acre campus at the corner of Washington Street and Priest Drive in Tempe, bringing Valley employees together for the first time under one roof. The state-of-the-art complex includes office space for 1,300 Tosco employees representing marketing, refining, and shared services. Employees have on-site access to a host of services, including a fitness center, credit union, cafeteria, gift shop, dry cleaner, and child care facility for 102 children.

"This new campus represents more than building blocks and efficient operations," says Lavinia. "It's a place where we can finish bringing together the cultures of the diverse businesses that were merged successfully in a short period of time."

For example, on the third floor, a highly qualified group of commercial managers daily buy crude and sell wholesale

Tosco licenses the Exxon brand in Arizona.

petroleum products for the company's operations, dealing with markets all over the globe. A unique shared services division led by Rich Reinken, vice president of Tosco Corporation, provides the operating divisions of the company with key back-office services, including human

resources, credit card processing, information technology, accounting services, and building services. "The shared services concept allows Tosco to be flexible and efficient. It also positions us to absorb future acquisitions as we continue to grow," Reinken says.

With Tosco's acquisition of the 76 gasoline brand came a 100-plus-year heritage of quality and performance.

They're Everywhere

The 350 neighborhood Circle K convenience stores in Greater Phoenix offer the usual high-quality, top-selling merchandise customers have come to expect, plus special items such as the Diamondbacks Dog, the hot dogs available only at Circle K and Bank One Ballpark. Circle K's familiar lizard promotes Thirstbuster fountain drinks, and a poll in the *Arizona Republic* selected Circle K coffee as the Best of the Year in 1997. Additional convenience items such as phone cards, lottery tickets, and money orders are also available for Circle K's busy customers.

In conjunction with NASCAR's 50th anniversary in 1998, Tosco gained a new affiliation with NASCAR when Circle K was named its official convenience store. This alliance is intended to make the stores real pit stops, with special promotions, licensed NASCAR merchandise, and fast, friendly service. Since being designated as NASCAR's Official Fuel in 1954, 76 branded gasoline has been used in every race in every car on the NASCAR Winston Cup circuit. Co-branded 76/NASCAR Motor Oil is used in NASCAR competition and is also available

to consumers. Each October, Phoenix International Raceway hosts the Arizona segment of the NASCAR Winston Cup, America's fast-growing spectator sport.

Melding Cultures

New Circle K locations are opening and more established ones are being upgraded as Tosco's imprint on the company takes hold. New technology, such as pay-at-the-pump, is quickly becoming a standard feature at all locations. The company is also developing strategies to further enhance and streamline the customer's experience.

Productive and efficient employment practices contribute to Tosco's highly motivated employee base. New hiring and training practices in the retail business have reduced turnover and improved productivity. The company is focusing on career development and training programs for store employees, all of whom qualify for benefits and retirement plans.

"We know our store employees make a critical difference in this company," Lavinia says. "They're the ones who are in touch with our customers every day."

Supporting the Community

Tosco has almost 5,000 employees in Maricopa County, and the company reinvests in the community by contributing both time and money to neighborhood causes. Circle K's support of United Cerebral Palsy (UCP), which provides services for people with disabilities, is entering its 15th year. Special fund-raising events and a national customer canister program raise more than $2 million annually for the charity.

Tosco also supports Greater Phoenix community outreach and crime prevention programs, as well as the Boys and Girls Clubs. In 1998, the Valley's Clean Air Campaign recognized Tosco Marketing Company with a special award for its support of the Clean Air Campaign and Valley Bike Week.

Tosco's fast-track growth is likely to continue through acquisitions. Through it all, the company's goal is to provide quality products and services to its customers at competitive prices, have employees work in a safe and challenging environment, and make meaningful contributions to the communities where it operates.

Convenience, friendly service, and competitive prices are a signature of Circle K/76 sites.

ERNST & YOUNG LLP

five hundred dollars may not seem like much today, but at a 7 percent inflation rate through the years, $500 in 1894 can translate to approximately $768,000 in 1998. That is about how much Arthur Young put into his Chicago-based accounting firm which, in 95 years' time, would evolve into Ernst & Young LLP, the premier professional services firm in the world. ❧ Today, Ernst & Young's office in downtown Phoenix demonstrates the firm's worldwide commitment to the highest standards of quality, integrity,

and client satisfaction. Ernst & Young's business advisers are leaders in serving companies that make up an extensive array of industry fields, including electronics, computers, manufacturing, distribution, consumer products, health care, and real estate. Each is impacted by the experience and expertise of Ernst & Young professionals.

Presently, Ernst & Young's Arizona office has almost 300 personnel serving clients in Phoenix and Tucson. Overall, the firm employs more than 29,000 in the United States and more than 80,000 internationally.

A History of Client Satisfaction
Ernst & Young began more than a century ago from the wisdom and foresight of Arthur Young. Several years later, 21-year-old Alwan Ernst established his management consulting firm, Ernst & Ernst, in Cleveland.

By 1913, the 16th Amendment became law, establishing an income tax for the first time in history. The landmark decision paved the way for the Young

and Ernst firms to generate incremental business—while keeping them busy tracking tax developments to better service existing clients.

By 1976, Ernst teamed up with the English firm of Whinney, Smith & Whinney to develop business in overseas offices. In 1989, this firm joined with Young's, forming what many industry observers would later say was a natural partnership.

They took their own expertise, as well as that of their employees, and merged them to form a more powerful company that would provide greater client service. Ernst & Young was well on its way to becoming one of the largest, most prestigious companies of its kind in the world.

In subsequent years, Ernst & Young grew dramatically, never wavering from its principles and goals. The firm consistently maintained an ability to change with the times by keeping itself in tune with technology for the professional services industry—all for client satisfaction. Nearly nine decades later, Ernst & Young is continuing to make its mark in the professional services arena.

Arizona Presence
The firm first established a presence in Phoenix in 1958 with the opening of an Ernst & Ernst office. A Tucson location was later added to serve the budding business communities of Arizona. Like the firm's other locations throughout the world, the Arizona offices focus on public companies, health care, real estate, and entrepreneur-

Ernst & Young LLP began more than a century ago from the wisdom and foresight of Arthur Young.

As a direct result of Ernst & Young's efforts to support entrepreneurs, the firm created its Entrepreneur Of The Year program. Launched in 1986 in Milwaukee, the program honors entrepreneurs whose ingenuity, hard work, and perseverance have created and sustained successful, growing business ventures.

ial services as top priorities heading into the millennium.

The public arena is constantly changing, and Ernst & Young's up-to-date understanding and knowledge of national and international public finance administration practices provide tremendous value-added benefit to public companies, regardless of size and industry.

In the health care sector, Ernst & Young provides a full range of audit, tax, and consulting services to hospitals, nursing homes, managed health care organizations, physician group practices, home health agencies, and other health care companies. The firm was the only Big Five company to be chosen among the 30 most influential decision makers in health care by the *Phoenix Business Journal*.

The Ernst & Young Kenneth Leventhal Real Estate Group is considered to be the preeminent professional service provider to the real estate industry. The combined resources of real estate expertise with Ernst & Young's audit, tax, and financial advisory services result in a practice that is unsurpassed in providing a full range of real estate consulting.

The Entrepreneurial Services Group consists of a dedicated group of professionals who specialize in helping fast-growth companies plan for the future, develop operating strategies, attract capital, and enter new markets. The firm's business advisers are specially trained and have several years of experience working with high-growth companies in industries such as electronics, computer hardware and software, manufacturing, distribution, and consumer products.

Entrepreneurial Honors

As a direct result of Ernst & Young's efforts to support entrepreneurs, the firm created its Entrepreneur Of The Year program. Launched in 1986 in Milwaukee, the program honors entrepreneurs whose ingenuity, hard work, and perseverance have created and sustained successful, growing business ventures.

The first Phoenix Entrepreneur Of The Year program took place in 1989, and since then it has honored such entrepreneurs as grocery chain owner Eddie Basha, sports team owner Jerry Colangelo, auto dealership magnate Lou Grubb, and MicroAge cofounders Alan Hald and Jeff

McKeever. The historical impact that these visionaries have had on Phoenix is immeasurable and defines the entrepreneurial spirit.

Ernst & Young also cares about the communities in which it does business. The company contributes significantly to supporting education, health care, community housing, and other causes. Among associations the firm has supported are Habitat for Humanity, United Way, Junior Achievement, American Red Cross, Boys and Girls Clubs, and YMCA.

By providing professional services, creating business opportunities, and supporting causes for communities, Ernst & Young is an integral part of the Arizona market. Arizona Managing Partner Joe DeSplinter sums it up best when he says: "Ernst & Young has been the fastest-growing professional services firm over the past three years. I believe this is a direct result of the commitment we have made to providing outstanding services and value to our clients, our people, and our community."

Indeed, Ernst & Young is a leader among professional services organizations in delivering value, ideas, solutions, and results that clients care about and need. Ernst & Young has the industry experience and technical skills to tailor ideas and solutions for clients needs, thus delivering measurable results. With its size and global reach, Ernst & Young has the breadth and depth of resources to serve any company, any size, wherever it does business.

Arizona Managing Partner Joe DeSplinter sums it up best when he says: "Ernst & Young has been the fastest-growing professional services firm over the past three years. I believe this is a direct result of the commitment we have made to providing outstanding services and value to our clients, our people, and our community."

Among associations the firm has supported are Habitat for Humanity, United Way, Junior Achievement, American Red Cross, Boys and Girls Clubs, and YMCA.

SACKS TIERNEY P.A.

When a national hospital chain was facing the difficult challenges of state and federal regulations, the health care team at Sacks Tierney P.A. guided them through the intricate process. When a California-based real estate company needed assistance in negotiating its nationwide real estate transactions, Sacks Tierney was its law firm of choice. And when an Arizona Native American tribe faced sovereignty issues and a constitutional challenge in financing

construction of a hotel on reservation land, Sacks Tierney successfully resolved the litigation and closed the transaction. These situations are typical examples of the legal matters with which Sacks Tierney helps clients on a regular basis.

"First and foremost, we are dedicated to the success of our clients," says Robert G. Kimball, chairman of the firm's executive committee. "The firm was founded upon that goal, and it is crucial that we always keep that goal in sight."

"The practice of law is an intensely complicated and demanding profession, requiring absolute devotion, extensive experience, and finely honed skills. We have always recognized that in order to successfully represent our clients, the firm must recruit, develop, and retain high-caliber lawyers," states founding member Seymour Sacks. In furtherance of that objective, the firm collectively holds degrees from 18 law schools, including Arizona State, University of Arizona, Harvard, Yale, Stanford, Chicago, and Michigan, and has baccalaureate or advanced degrees in disciplines ranging from the practical to the esoteric, including taxation, business

(From right) Robert G. Kimball, chairman of Sacks Tierney's executive committee; founder Seymour Sacks; and named shareholder David C. Tierney dedicate themselves to providing their clients with quality legal services.

management, hydrology, geography, psychology, romance languages, anthropology, and philosophy. Many Sacks Tierney lawyers are State Bar Certified Specialists.

Giving Back to the Community
The lawyers at Sacks Tierney recognize that being a good lawyer goes far beyond

the boardroom and courtroom. The firm's history of community service is distinguished. Former members of the firm include several local and federal judges; one member is a former director of the Civil Aeronautics Board and several lawyers serve as pro tem judges. Each lawyer is actively committed to serving the local bar

Both corporate and real estate clients throughout the Valley look to Sacks Tierney for legal services from the acquisition and development phase of projects through sale.

associations and contributing to the local community. Sacks Tierney lawyers hold leadership positions in professional organizations such as Valley Leadership, Valley Partnership, Scottsdale Chamber of Commerce, Scottsdale Leadership, Greater Phoenix Black Chamber of Commerce, American Arbitration Association, National Association of Women Business Owners, Arizona Women Lawyers Association, and State Bar of Arizona. They also serve in leadership roles in many community organizations including the Arizona Arts Council, Arizona Mental Health Association, Valley Boys and Girls Clubs, Arizona Coalition for Tomorrow, American Heart Association, Foster Care Review Board, and the local Ronald McDonald House, operated by Accent on Kids, Inc.

Laying the Foundation

In 1960, Seymour Sacks, a Harvard law graduate, moved his young family to Phoenix after having served with the Department of Justice in Washington, D.C. Recognizing a need to meet the growing legal demands of business coupled with the dream of building a law firm of the finest legal talent, Sacks formed a law firm. In 1970, Sacks was joined by David C. Tierney, another Harvard law graduate just home from the Peace Corps in Barquisimeto, Venezuela.

Building for the Future

The firm has flourished along with the Arizona economy. It has grown from three to 30 lawyers and has recently relocated its principal offices to Scottsdale, while maintaining a satellite office in Phoenix. Today, the firm provides a broad range of services essential for today's business clients. Sacks Tierney's practice has expanded to include expertise in commercial, real estate, employment, taxation, health care services, and Indian law. In order to provide its clients with multistate and multinational expertise and to support its growing practice, Sacks Tierney is a member of Commercial Law Affiliates, an extensive worldwide affiliation of carefully selected, highly qualified law firms.

"At Sacks Tierney, we are responsive to our clients. We strive to understand their needs and to address and anticipate their concerns so that we can provide the best possible results," says shareholder Tierney. "Our team approach provides our clients the extensive experience and specialization that is typical of larger firms, while maintaining the personal attention usually found only in smaller firms. It is

Health care providers throughout the Valley rely on Sacks Tierney for their legal needs (top).

As Arizona tribes diversify and develop economically, they face many issues. Sacks Tierney has provided innovative solutions that have permitted ongoing development (bottom).

our selective growth and personalized client service that will enable us to maintain our long tradition of providing excellent legal services to our clients."

In today's competitive legal environment, the true meaning of "quality legal services" can only be defined by effectively and efficiently meeting the needs of the client. This is most evident when clients are confronted with crisis and the assistance they seek is from their attorney.

Sacks Tierney hopes that, because its lawyers care, they will meet these crises with intelligence and passion.

As the firm approaches its 40th anniversary, Sacks Tierney takes pride in its reputation for tenaciously and successfully pursuing its clients' goals. A dedication to its founding philosophy positions the firm to successfully guide clients confronted with business opportunities and challenges into the future.

INDUSTRIAL REFRIGERATION & BOILER COMPANY

ndustrial Refrigeration & Boiler Company has been keeping Greater Phoenix cool for more than 35 years. As a fully integrated design/install refrigeration, boiler, and process piping contractor, the company provides complete system engineering, installation, retrofitting, and continuing maintenance service to meet customers' needs. ❧ Recognized as Arizona's leading expert in the design of industrial refrigeration systems, the company's registered professional engineering staff is often called upon by private consultants to provide

design assistance in creating innovative cold storage and processing solutions. Industrial Refrigeration is also well known for servicing and maintaining boilers in hotels, office buildings, and large apartment complexes. Whenever possible, the environmentally conscious company promotes the use of ammonia systems for cold storage and comfort and process cooling, eliminating the use of less environmentally safe refrigerants.

Stressing Service

Since 1981, when President James Gerdes joined the company, Industrial Refrigeration's annual revenues have increased steadily, from $1.2 million to more than $7 million in 1998. Gerdes credits the company's continuing success to its ability to provide full service to customers—beginning with its engineering and design expertise, and continuing through the construction process, service, and maintenance. An experi-

enced engineering staff designs projects with state-of-the-art computer-aided design (CAD) tools, constantly looking for ways to improve installation quality while reducing costs to the customer. The use of CAD systems can significantly improve piping layout, and promotes prefabrication of piping systems in the company shop prior to field installation, thus reducing both installation time and operating costs. Every step of the way, multidirectional communication keeps everyone who is contributing to a project in the loop, so information and suggestions can be exchanged and implemented.

"Our engineers are able to discover exactly what design refinements will improve system performance and reliability, while they're supporting service and construction activities," Gerdes says. "This team approach saves our customers significant costs in system installations, while providing optimum operating efficiency and maintainability over other systems." Longtime customers, primarily heavy commercial and industrial accounts returning time and again, have come to depend on Industrial Refrigeration for listening to their needs and then doing the job right. They also value the company's computerized service dispatch, available around the clock, seven days a week.

Clockwise from top:
Industrial Refrigeration & Boiler Company has been serving the Southwest since 1963.

Industrial Refrigeration sets the industry standard for customer service.

The company's staff provides value to customers through professionalism, effort, and integrity.

◄ DUANE DARLING

◄◄ DUANE DARLING

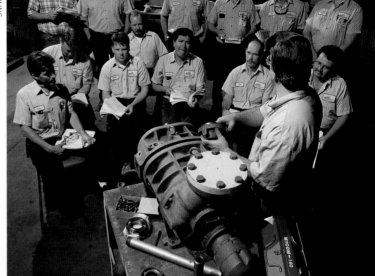

▲ DUANE DARLING

Many of Industrial Refrigeration's customers would be totally incapacitated if their systems went down even for a short time. These companies count on a quick response to safeguard the quality of their products. In anticipation of any emergency need, Industrial Refrigeration stocks a large supply of parts, in order to be able to respond immediately to a customer call. "Our service people come back and tell us what is—and what is not—working," Gerdes says. "When a customer has a problem, we don't just fix it, we take notes. Then our engineers can work to avoid similar problems in the future."

A Demanding Business

A typical project is a 100,000-square-foot distribution facility with multiple temperature zones, requiring a mile to a mile and a half of closed piping systems. "This is a demanding business, and our employees need to have electrical, mechanical, and pipe fitting skills, as well as a thorough understanding of refrigeration systems," says Gerdes.

To help employees learn and grow with the company, weekly meetings are conducted on safety and on new equipment in a modern, on-site classroom; and manufacturing representatives are invited in several times a year to discuss the use and installation of new products. The company also has helped design curricula for a program in conjunction with Gateway Community College for entry-level trainees who can work in the company while pursuing an associate's degree. Continuing education is encouraged through company-paid books and tuition, as well as flexible work schedules; in fact, more than half of the firm's 40 employees are enrolled in college classes.

Caring for the Community

Taking care of the surrounding community is an important part of the company's concern, as well. An annual Santa Party for neighborhood children, started in 1987, provides more than 1,500 young people and adults with a day of fun, festivities, and holiday treats, including a petting zoo, moon walks, mariachi singers, pony rides, an elephant, and, of course, Santa's sleigh.

Industrial Refrigeration sponsors local soccer and baseball teams, and participates in the city's Jobs for Valley Youth program. Area young people are offered jobs on the condition that they participate in company-sponsored education programs and go to college at company expense. The company also has donated equipment and installed refrigeration systems for the Society of St. Vincent de Paul, and maintains the systems free of charge.

The Future

As Industrial Refrigeration looks down the road, its focus is on maintaining steady growth. Although the company is licensed in California and New Mexico, Industrial Refrigeration was started as an Arizona company, and its work is predominately in the Valley. "We make sure that projects we bid on make sense for us and fit into our strategic business goals," says Gerdes. "While we are currently enjoying a growing construction market, we have been through a few up-and-down cycles of the construction industry. The development of engineering and support staff as well as skilled tradesmen will propel Industrial Refrigeration & Boiler Company to lead the industry. We are looking beyond today to what will bring healthy, stable growth in the long term."

To help employees learn and grow with the company, weekly meetings are conducted on safety and on new equipment in a modern, on-site classroom; and manufacturing representatives are invited in several times a year to discuss the service and installation of new products.

An experienced engineering staff designs projects with state-of-the-art computer-aided design (CAD) tools, constantly looking for ways to improve installation quality while reducing costs to the customer.

▲ DUANE DARLING

PHOENIX INTERNATIONAL RACEWAY

Phoenix International Raceway (PIR)—a world-class, one-mile, paved oval known in racing circles as the Jewel of the Desert—hosts the most varied menu of motorsports in the country, ranging from Indy cars to stock cars, and from motorcycles to pickup trucks. Based on history, schedule, competition, and the nature of the track, PIR is considered one of the top five tracks in the country, along with the Indianapolis Motor Speedway, Daytona International Speedway, Talladega Superspeedway, and Charlotte Motor Speedway.

Legendary driver Parnelli Jones set the pole with the fastest qualifying speed of 114.822 mph at the track's very first race in 1964. Although racing times are faster today, PIR has always maintained the tone of competitive excellence that was set with this first race.

Today, Phoenix International Raceway (PIR) has grown into a 70,000-seat facility that hosts more than 100,000 race fans during a single day of racing.

"It's a great track because it's fast, and the layout encourages passing and lots of action," says Scott Simpson, director of advertising and promotions. "It's known as the world's fastest one-mile oval for a reason. Everybody's been here, and many have come and won." Indy Racing League stalwart Arie Luyendyk currently holds the track record of 183.599 mph, which was set during a qualifying round in March 1996.

A Full Calendar of Racing

Each year from October through April, four major annual events keep racing action strong at PIR. Assisted by Arizona's beautiful weather, three marquee events—the NASCAR Winston Cup Series Dura-Lube 500 in October, the Skoal Bandit Racing Copper World Classic in January

Monument Hill, the zero-zero point of Arizona, overlooks the world's fastest one-mile oval and provides a great general admission view of PIR events.

and February, and the Indy Racing League Phoenix 200 in March—draw hundreds of thousands of fans to the track's oval layout. The American Motorcyclist Association's Cruise America Superbike Challenge in February is raced on the 11-turn, 1.51-mile road course.

Before each of the three marquee events, drivers, car owners, and sports celebrities participate in a charity golf tournament held at the Wigwam Resort to

raise money for PIR Charities. In addition to these fund-raisers, the track sponsors the annual Diamond Ball—a West Valley celebration to benefit a number of local nonprofit organizations, including Phoenix Children's Hospital and Midnight Basketball, a south Phoenix program to keep children off the streets through sports.

Much of the credit for PIR's current success can be traced directly to the dedication and tenacity of Emmett "Buddy" Jobe, who bought the track on September 15, 1985. He methodically worked to improve the schedule, increase parking and seating, and build fan-friendly structures, such as the pedestrian bridge across the track at turn four, which allows fans a crossing while on-track activities are under way. Jobe's efforts brought the first Winston Cup Series race to the track on November 6, 1988, attracting a record 60,000 spectators to

the track. Today, more than 100,000 fans regularly attend the annual event, filling the reserved grandstands and the terraced hillside general admission area.

Jobe sold the track in 1997 to International Speedway Corp. (ISC), a leading publicly held motorsports entertainment company traded on the Nasdaq exchange. Jobe now serves as president of PIR and is a vice president of ISC, which also operates the Daytona International Speedway.

"ISC gives us the additional leadership, knowledge, and resources to grow more quickly and to reach our fullest potential," says Jobe. Since the ISC acquisition, PIR has enjoyed a number of improvements, such as the addition of a 5,000-plus-seat grandstand at turn two—topped by six additional luxury suites—bringing total reserved seating capacity to more than 72,000. In addition, a five-lane bridge across the Gila River immediately north of the track, which is currently being constructed by the State of Arizona, will provide greater access to the track.

A Boost for the Local Economy

Major racing events at PIR may last up to four days, but many people start arriving a week ahead of time to camp, party,

barbecue, and renew old acquaintances. Motor sports fans travel great distances to see a good race, and most of the states in the Union are represented at these events. This translates into tax and revenue dollars for Greater Phoenix, attracting 350,000 visitors annually and generating $246 million into the local and state economy through racing, testing, vehicle manufacture, dealer promotions, and motion picture/television filming.

A study done by the Arizona State University College of Business predicts that the annual economic impact generated by PIR will rise to $316 million by

2000. The track generates the equivalent of 4,590 full-time jobs, including a year-round track staff of 35 and an average of more than 900 temporary employees hired for each racing event. Jobe recognizes the West Valley as a thriving, growing area. "We're proud to be a part of what's happening here," he says. Jobe predicts that in the future, the sports facility will also become home to festivals, concerts, and car shows during the off-season, giving people even more reason to venture to PIR to enjoy themselves where the Gila and Salt rivers meet at the base of the rugged Estrella Mountains.

PIR—a world-class, one-mile, paved oval known in racing circles as the Jewel of the Desert—hosts the most varied menu of motorsports in the country, ranging from Indy cars to stock cars, and from motorcycles to pickup trucks.

Major racing events at PIR may last up to four days, but many people start arriving a week ahead of time to camp, party, barbecue, and renew old acquaintances. Motorsports fans travel great distances to see a good race, and most of the states in the Union are represented at these events.

Schuck & Sons Construction Company, Inc.

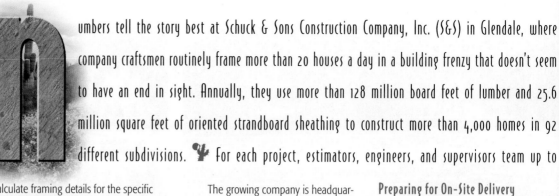

Numbers tell the story best at Schuck & Sons Construction Company, Inc. (S&S) in Glendale, where company craftsmen routinely frame more than 20 houses a day in a building frenzy that doesn't seem to have an end in sight. Annually, they use more than 128 million board feet of lumber and 25.6 million square feet of oriented strandboard sheathing to construct more than 4,000 homes in 92 different subdivisions. ❦ For each project, estimators, engineers, and supervisors team up to

calculate framing details for the specific home model, and then compute standardized production plans that can be precut and partially assembled in the yard prior to delivery to the construction site. Before one board is touched, however, an in-house design team using state-of-the-art computer technology electronically tests all possible configurations to determine the most efficient one for the job at hand.

The growing company is headquartered on a concrete-covered yard in Glendale that once was a farmer's cantaloupe field. Today, lumber is king, and through its sophisticated assembly system, specialized equipment, and extensive inventory, S&S can supply its customers with any size order of preassembled trusses, doors, mouldings, shelving, stair parts, locks, and hardware.

Preparing for On-Site Delivery

A tour through the plant finds more than 320 employees testing and grading lumber, assembling trusses, prehanging doors, cutting framing packages, and creating more-intricate assembly pieces, such as pop-outs, stairs, and arches. For each home being constructed, S&S delivers complete packages bundled and labeled for use, ready to be coordinated and then attached to the new foundation. In addition to materials for homes, S&S has specialized, commercial equipment to fabricate trusses for warehouses, shopping centers, and office complexes up to three stories tall.

Large quantities of ungraded framing lumber are bought by the railcar load directly from mills and delivered to the company's own railroad siding, allowing S&S to pass the resulting savings on to its customers. To guarantee that they consistently receive the highest-quality materials, the company was the first truss plant in the country to install MSR (machine stress rated) equipment. MSR testing certifies that each piece of two-by-four and two-by-six lumber is mechanically checked for strength, visually inspected for defects, properly graded, and physically stamped.

A Hot Market

Well-known builders throughout the Valley of the Sun—Del Webb, Continental Homes, Shea, Courtland, Robson Communities, and Pulte—are S&S customers who appreciate the value and quality of buying preassembled materials. "It's a hot market and growing," says Craig Steele, president and CEO of S&S, "and I don't anticipate the extreme peaks and valleys we've seen in this industry in the past."

S&S employs more than 650 craftsmen who make up 125 framing and trim carpentry crews to assemble the packages on-site. Responding to the needs of a constantly changing market, the company has created its own in-house apprenticeship program, and maintains ongoing training to ensure a consistent, qualified workforce. Well-practiced teams completely frame a typical 2,200-square-foot house in an average of four to five days. An in-house registered engineer provides professional expertise to the company and is an added

State-of-the-art component saws add to Schuck & Sons Construction Company's (S&S) efficiencies (top).

S&S buys its lumber direct and takes delivery by rail (bottom).

resource available to customers for problem solving.

A fleet of 250 vehicles, all equipped with mobile phones and two-way radios, ensures on-site/on-time delivery anywhere in the Valley. More than 40 vehicles are equipped with digital communications equipment to receive text messages and track equipment in the field for quick response.

Ingenious Vision

The company's comprehensive systems are built on the vision of its founder, the late Kent Schuck, a carpenter who not only understood the intricacies of framing, but also had the ingenuity to leverage the advantages of preassembly. A one-of-a-kind unit-saw, which he designed and built for cutting full bundles of framing in one pass, is still an integral part of S&S' innovative assembly process.

In 1990, Schuck's wife Jackye took over as president, teaming up with Steele and doubling the size of the business. The Schuck family sold controlling interest to the company's employees in 1997 through a stock option plan, giving everyone an opportunity to benefit from the company's success. Steele became president, and Schuck's son Keith remains active in the business as vice president of operations.

They are charter members of the MSR Lumber Producers Council and active in the National Association of Home Builders. Locally, S&S shares its expertise and resources by contributing time and materials to Christmas in April to help refurbish homes for underprivileged people. The company participated in the construction

of a wing to the Sojourner Center for Battered Women, and was a major contributor of time and materials to Boys Hope Girls Hope of Arizona, a downtown Phoenix facility for young people at risk, spearheaded by Del Webb.

Excellence Recognized

Each year since Arthur Anderson has been compiling a list of the top 100 Arizona companies, S&S has been included. Nevertheless, the company is continually identifying new ways to improve already efficient operations. "Our reputation in the marketplace for being dependable and innovative is the best in the country," Steele notes with pride. "Company representatives

come from all over to see how we do things here."

The next step for the employee-owned operation is to expand geographically from established regional markets in Arizona, Nevada, and Southern California, and company management is looking at Colorado, Texas, and a number of locations in the East where they anticipate a continuing demand for preassembled residential and commercial materials.

"To grow, we're going to have to look beyond our current capabilities and to other markets for opportunities," Steele says. Wherever the business is, S&S will find it and will undoubtedly come up with ways to do it better.

CSK Auto Corporation

Customers never hear the word "no" at CSK Auto Corporation, which sells retail automotive parts and accessories in more than 800 stores throughout the western United States. Its 10,000 associates pride themselves in locating even the hardest-to-find car part, and the company's forward-looking use of technology helps in locating and delivering whatever customers need. CSK offers a broad selection of national brand-name and private-label automotive products for both domestic and import automobiles, vans, and light trucks. Each store typically carries between 13,000 and 16,000 stock keeping units (SKUs) with an additional 200,000 items available on a same-day delivery basis to a majority of its locations. Store orders are filled electronically and delivered several times each day.

Associates take the company's slogan, The Place to Start for Parts, seriously. Each conveniently located store has testing equipment that can help customers test parts in the parking lot to determine if they need a starter, alternator, or battery in their car. The traditional paper parts catalog has been replaced by instant access to the company's electronic parts catalog listing items from the tiniest pin to complete engines. CSK's Priority Parts operation electronically handles approximately 96,000 inquiries each week.

Open around the Clock

Stores offer extended hours each day, and a depot store in Phoenix is open around the clock. "Even if it's two in the morning, you can call and we can help you," says CSK President Jim Bazlen. A centralized call center assists when store personnel are not free to answer, and call-center associates can respond to store-specific questions, including parts availability and pricing. This allows sales associates to give their undivided attention to customers in the store, while call-in customers are served quickly and efficiently as well.

Training for new associates begins with a two-day class, with others offered through CSK University, dedicated to the continuous improvement of store associates through on-the-job training and formal classroom instruction. Associates also are encouraged to take the annual Automotive Service Excellence (ASE) test so they can better serve customers.

Combining Resources

CSK Auto Corporation brings together three successful regional auto parts businesses into one strong company based in Phoenix. Each has exceptional name recognition and an established, loyal customer base of its own. In March 1998, the company went public on the New York Stock Exchange, trading under the symbol CAO.

Checker Auto Parts was founded in 1968 by Valley Distributing Company, when the first Checker store was opened in a country-and-western dance hall on Glendale Avenue, west of the Black Canyon Freeway. Checker has grown to more than 250 stores in Arizona, Colorado, Idaho,

CSK's corporate headquarters on the corner of 7th Street and Missouri Avenue in central Phoenix is home to 600 corporate associates.

New stores are designed around convenient locations, combining a clean, attractive appearance with strong brand identity. CSK will add over 150 new units in 1999 alone.

Montana, New Mexico, Nevada, Texas, Utah, and Wyoming.

Schuck's Auto Supply's first store—opened in 1917 by Harry Schuck in Seattle—carried motorcycle and bicycle parts. The oldest of the three chains, Schuck's has more than 150 stores in Idaho, Washington, and Oregon. Kragen Auto Parts was founded in San Jose by Al Kragen in 1947. California and Nevada are served by almost 400 Kragen stores, including 82 in the Los Angeles market that were acquired from Trak Auto Corporation in 1997.

CSK's Hot Shot delivery system—which can deliver parts within a half hour—is becoming increasingly attractive to commercial customers, who now constitute about 16 percent of the company's growing business. These include repair shops, fleet owners, municipalities, military installations, and national accounts.

Saving Time and Money

Strategically located warehouses and technologically advanced distribution systems use bar coding, radio frequency scanners, sophisticated conveyors, and equipment to move products from centralized facilities to the stores. These automated systems reduce distribution costs while saving time in getting items to the customer. The company's two main distribution centers are located in Phoenix and Dixon, California.

Because stores are located in the western states, business is naturally sensi-

tive to extreme weather conditions. "We may be the only ones who look forward to Arizona's sizzling summers and Montana's freezing winters," says Bazlen. "We know that means increased business, particularly with battery sales." A special Heat Beater battery has been developed for sale in this market.

Supporting the Community and the Environment

Community involvement shows in CSK's sponsorship of major sports teams such as Coyotes Hockey in Phoenix and a National Hot Rod Association (NHRA) car on the 30-event NHRA drag racing circuit, which includes the Checker, Schucks, Kragen Nationals held at Firebird International Raceway. The company also actively supports Boys and Girls Clubs of America, and works with technical schools in various markets to help educate students interested in the automotive industry.

CSK initiated an oil recycling program in 1990 in the Phoenix market that is now being implemented in more than 675 stores in 12 states. Last year, the company received an Environmental Award of Excellence from First Recovery—one of the nation's largest oil collection and recycling companies—for collecting more than 10 million gallons of used oil from customers. CSK was the first company to reach the 10 million-gallon mark since the program's inception.

"We had more than $1 billion in sales in 1998, a 19 percent increase over the previous year," says Bazlen, "and we anticipate increasing that number even more by building our commercial business, opening new stores, and acquiring additional stores." In an ongoing effort to be the best-known and preferred auto parts store in the western states, CSK will continue to invest in technology to streamline services and ensure quick, friendly attention to meeting customers' needs.

The company's NHRA drag racing team is highly popular among its target audience of automotive do-it-yourselfers.

MASTERCRAFT COMPANIES

astercraft Companies' quality is based on one simple philosophy: A good part starts with a good mold. President Arle Rawlings has led Mastercraft Companies—during its 30 years in the business—to a position of leadership in the design, engineering, and production of the highest-quality plastic injection and die cast molds available, earning the company a stellar reputation in the industry. It follows naturally that the company then molds the best precision components possible for a variety of quality-conscious, demanding customers, located primarily in the western United States, with about half in Arizona.

Mastercraft began in 1968 as a tool-making company dedicated to serving the injection molding industry with 800 square feet of space and two employees. The company grew over the next decade to 10 employees, and eventually expanded to custom injection molding in a 23,000-square-foot facility. In 1992, Mastercraft moved into its current home, which includes two manufacturing buildings. First, molds are designed, created, and qualified for production in a 21,000-square-foot facility. Then, when samples have passed the stringent testing processes, the action moves to a 37,000-square-foot neighboring building that houses equipment for production and quality control checks, as well as the corporate offices.

Manufacturing Millions of Components

The company manufactures millions of components for hundreds of products for more than a dozen Fortune 500 customers, from parts for medical diagnostic instruments to electronics and telecommunications connectors to critical parts for automobile air bags. Quality control checks follow each part from the beginning of the custom design through the manufacturing process to the final inspection of the finished product.

Making a mold has always required thinking in reverse, but the engineering methods have changed considerably through the years. Once molds were designed on the drawing board, and then were created manually. Today, the business is totally computer based, with specification files downloaded from the Internet. Mastercraft's new clean room demonstrates the firm's dedication to staying ahead of the technological curve with the equipment and know-how to serve each and every customer's special needs.

The engineering-grade plastic materials that the company molds require more precise quality control checks than the usual consumer products, and the ability to meet critical conformity requirements time and again has earned the Phoenix company a solid reputation for excellence. No matter how difficult the challenge or how sophisticated the part, Mastercraft has the ability to provide the tooling that conforms to critical specifications. "Our 20 closed-loop injection mold presses are equipped with statistical process controls to reduce process variations and eliminate defects before they occur," Rawlings says.

Using Concurrent Engineering

The company's unique ability to build tools using concurrent engineering—beginning the toolmaking process without final designs in hand and creating the tool as the final design is completed—gives it an edge over many other mold makers. By using the same database as the customer, weeks can be shaved off the lead time normally required for the mold-building process, and the final product can meet the precision requirements most customers require. As

Clockwise from top:
President Arle Rawlings has led Mastercraft Companies—during its 30 years in the business—to a position of leadership in the design, engineering, and production of the highest-quality plastic injection and die cast molds available, earning the company a stellar reputation in the industry.

Many complex molded components go into this controller for a medical infusion pump for Mastercraft customer Abbott Critical Care.

Mastercraft's two-building complex, which totals 58,000 square feet, sits on a beautiful campus in Phoenix.

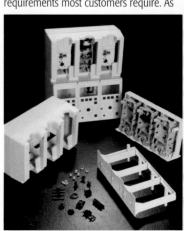

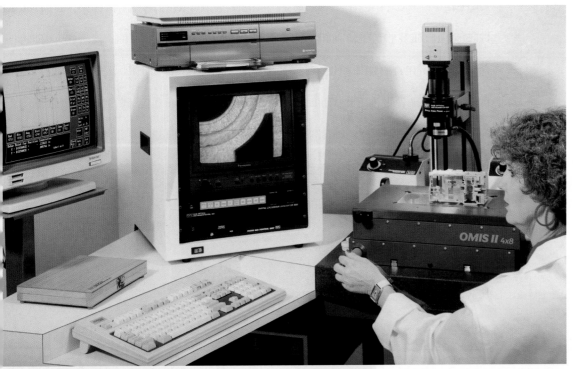

mold making, a thorough knowledge of engineering thermoplastics processing, and a dedication to providing high-level service and quality awareness. Mastercraft recognizes their contributions with generous benefits—including a biyearly bonus tied to longevity and company profitability—for everyone after six months of employment. The company supports an internal certified apprenticeship program to educate and encourage tool makers entering the business, and also explores ways to be more proactive with schools to let students know about the many opportunities available in manufacturing.

Rawlings looks to grow the $10 million company to $15 million or $20 million, most likely from acquisition of a strategically compatible company, and by expanding into international markets. With Mastercraft's recognized leadership in its field, the company is sure to build on its success well into the next century.

a result, more orders than ever are coming in for tougher, more complex parts.

Among its customers, Mastercraft counts many Fortune 500 companies that have come to rely on its experience and expertise in creating molds that other mold services may not be able to produce. For example, when no one wanted to bid on a job creating a mold for a part requiring more than 900 dimensions that was needed by Abbott Critical Care in Mountain View, California, the company came to Mastercraft. By combining computer-aided design and manufacturing experience with complete dimensional inspections of each component of the mold throughout the process, Mastercraft was able to meet Abbott's accuracy requirements, with the first completed part produced from the prototype mold.

Mastercraft's extraordinary success in combining the latest design engineering technology with the integrity of old-world

craftsmanship has been rewarded with special recognition from its customers. Abbott Laboratories honored the company for its custom injection molding as one of its critical suppliers, and Flextronics named Mastercraft its supplier of the year for consistent excellence of parts for products Flextronics supplies to IBM.

ISO 9001 Certified

Becoming ISO 9001 certified to meet international quality standards is a step Mastercraft Companies took with a view toward future globalization of the business. "Our customers appreciate the exercise we went through to gain certification, and it puts us at a different level in their eyes," Rawlings says. "It also helped us improve our overall operating procedures."

The company's 110 employees team up to provide a cohesive blend of mold design and engineering expertise, skilled

PHOENIX SUNS/
ARIZONA DIAMONDBACKS

There was a time when it seemed as though someone quietly rolled up the sidewalks in downtown Phoenix each day at 5:30 p.m. as workers made their way home to the suburbs. Today, however, downtown Phoenix is a thriving sports mecca, and Phoenix Suns basketball at America West Arena and Arizona Diamondbacks baseball in Bank One Ballpark have played key roles in changing the city's scenario. Sharing the sports spotlight and dedication to supporting a dynamic downtown from America West Arena

are Phoenix Coyotes hockey, Arizona Rattlers arena football, and Phoenix Mercury women's basketball.

It is difficult to think of either baseball or basketball in Phoenix without including the catalyst behind this sports vision—Jerry Colangelo, the Suns' managing partner, and president and CEO of the Arizona Diamondbacks. Colangelo is a former player and coach who understands the game and how to reach out to fans, and he's the man who made Major League Baseball in Phoenix and Bank One Ballpark possible. His never-say-never attitude came with him from Chicago in 1968 when he arrived as a 28-year-old general manager (the NBA's youngest ever) for an as yet unnamed expansion basketball team, destined to become the Phoenix Suns. In 1987, he put a partnership together to buy the franchise, and then settled into working to get a new playing facility, the America West Arena. The Suns' 31-year tradition of excellence both on and off the basketball court speaks for itself.

A Civic Enterprise
When it came time to raise money for the Diamondbacks, Colangelo's track record

encouraged plenty of takers. All three major local banks are involved, as well as every major corporation in Arizona, making Bank One Ballpark truly a civic enterprise.

It was Colangelo's success with the Suns that encouraged community leaders to seek him out to bring Major League Baseball to Phoenix, and he responded by putting his expertise and reputation on the line to build a team for Arizona. On March 31, 1998, 28 months after ground was broken on the $354 million stadium, 50,179 fans

(including 36,000 season ticket holders) filled the ballpark for the first of the season's 81 games.

Truly Unique Facilities
Back when Abner Doubleday was inventing baseball, he surely didn't have this kind of playing field in mind. Bank One Ballpark's 1,100-foot-high, retractable roof, which operates on the same technology as a drawbridge, opens in less than five minutes to let in the desert sky. It's the best of baseball in a natural grass setting with all of the modern conveniences, including a mile of concession stands offering ballpark fare. It's the only ballpark in the country with a swimming pool and hot tub for 35 guests in the right-center-field bleachers, allowing a carefully placed home run to really make a splash. To keep it affordable for everyone, 500 $1 tickets go on sale two hours before each game at the stadium. The Bank One Ballpark is owned by the Maricopa County Stadium District and operated by the Arizona Diamondbacks. Operating the facility requires more than 3,000 full- or part-time employees.

While Bank One Ballpark is intended only for baseball, America West Arena is a multipurpose facility considered by many to be one of the finest indoor venues in the country for an ongoing stream of ice shows, concerts, rodeos, monster truck competitions—even the Ringling Bros. and Barnum & Bailey Circus. It seats 19,023 spectators for basketball and all seats have an unobstructed view. A private practice

In 1995, Jerry Colangelo hired talented manager Buck Showalter to lead the Diamondbacks, more than two years before they took the field. This bold move is indicative of Colangelo's proactive decision making (top).

The America West Arena opened in 1992, spearheading a furious round of new development in downtown Phoenix (bottom).

PHOENIX SUNS

▼ ▲ BARRY GOSSAGE/PHOENIX SUNS

The Suns and the Diamondbacks are generous partners in the community, not just for their economic impact, but also for the vitality and spirit they bring to Greater Phoenix. Their games are seen and heard across the nation, and names of athletes sporting those familiar purple and orange Suns uniforms are nationally known and recognized.

beginning in 2003 illustrates the innovative thinking of an organization that continues to grow. U S WEST will also be the sponsor for a five-story addition to America West Arena to open in 2000, adding 130,000 square feet of entertainment, dining, office, and retail space to the sports complex.

Fans can depend on Colangelo's winning tradition and visionary business strategies to keep professional sports in the spotlight in Arizona for many years to come.

It was Colangelo's success with the Suns that encouraged community leaders to seek him out to bring Major League Baseball to Phoenix, and he responded by putting his expertise and reputation on the line to build the Arizona Diamondbacks.

court allows the Suns to work out even when other events are booked in the main hall.

More Than Athletic Teams

Colangelo is the first to point out that successful sports programs are more than a team of athletes and a stadium. His is a well-oiled organization built on loyalty, and many of his key employees have been with him through the years. Supporting the sports teams is a larger team of marketing, public relations, and financial professionals; facilities managers; food service organizers; and an administrative organization

completing the behind-the-scenes tasks that make a night out at a ball game a rollicking good time.

The Suns and the Diamondbacks are generous partners in the community, not just for their economic impact, but also for the vitality and spirit they bring to Greater Phoenix. Their games are seen and heard across the nation, and names of athletes sporting those familiar purple and orange Suns uniforms are nationally known and recognized. Down the street a couple of blocks, the Arizona Diamondbacks also are making a name for themselves.

Giving Back to the Community

The Suns' gorilla mascot—usually seen bouncing across the basketball court—shows his serious side by encouraging elementary school students through reading programs or leading public athletic events such as an 8K competitive run to benefit Phoenix Suns Charities, which has given more than $3 million to community programs since 1990. More recently, Colangelo formed Diamondbacks Charities, which will focus on children and homeless issues, and potentially will contribute even more to the community.

An agreement between the Suns and U S WEST to provide digital TV and on-line service through existing phone lines throughout Phoenix for all 41 Suns home games and all home play-off games

▶ ▲ BARRY GOSSAGE/ARIZONA DIAMONDBACKS

AFFILIATED CARDIOLOGISTS OF ARIZONA

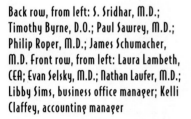

More than a quarter of a century ago, Affiliated Cardiologists of Arizona began as a group of dedicated medical professionals with a vision of helping patients requiring treatment for cardiovascular disease. Led by Dr. Nathan Laufer, managing partner, they have created one of the premier providers of cardiovascular services in the state, specializing in heart disease diagnosis and the latest coronary intervention treatments. A true team approach gives patients the benefit of the services of 10 board-certified physicians supported by an experienced cardiovascular nursing staff. Seven of the 10 physicians consistently have been named to *Arizona Business Magazine's* annual list of top cardiovascular doctors in the Valley.

Striving for Excellence

"We continually strive for excellence, and our mission is to treat all of our patients the way we would want our own family members to be treated," Laufer says. "We offer the most recent, cutting-edge technology available, and we make cardiovascular care as easy and accessible as we can make it."

Patients can be referred by their primary care physicians, or they can call directly and make appointments for treatment without a referral. There are two offices in downtown Phoenix and one in Maryvale. All preliminary evaluations and noninvasive diagnostic tests can be performed in the office, saving patients a trip to the hospital. The practice has patients ranging in age from 18 to senior citizens, with the most typical being males 62 years of age, although the number of women is increasing noticeably. Outreach into rural areas provides services to patients in Miami-Globe, Payson, Winslow, Holbrook, Page, Lake Havasu City, and Wickenburg, so they don't have to travel to Phoenix for each appointment.

The practice stresses the importance of detecting cardiovascular disease in the early stages, when patients often can benefit from a modified lifestyle and possibly prevent the need for some procedures. Anyone with a family history of heart disease or high blood pressure is encouraged to have baseline evaluations before any problems are apparent. The practice works with the Arizona Heart Association to educate the public on heart-healthy lifestyles and how to identify symptoms that precede an acute heart attack.

Committed to Research

Affiliated Cardiologists is heavily committed to pioneering cardiovascular research and developing new care techniques. Several of the physicians are nationally known for their roto-blader technique. One of the physicians has had great success in teaching the innovative roto-blader technique to other medical professionals. Also, one physician in the group founded the Cardiovascular Society of Arizona, a nonprofit organization dedicated to bringing world-renowned physicians to the Valley to teach the newest techniques and procedures associated with the treatment of cardiovascular disease.

As Affiliated Cardiologists grows, its staff continues to stress dedication to meeting and exceeding patient expectations. "You don't have to travel to other parts of the country to get the best cardiovascular care available," Laufer assures his patients. "We offer it right here in this community."

Back row, from left: S. Sridhar, M.D.; Timothy Byrne, D.O.; Paul Sawrey, M.D.; Philip Roper, M.D.; James Schumacher, M.D. Front row, from left: Laura Lambeth, CEA; Evan Selsky, M.D.; Nathan Laufer, M.D.; Libby Sims, business office manager; Kelli Claffey, accounting manager

From just one small office that opened in Oakland in 1958, Grubb & Ellis Company has grown to become one of the largest publicly traded, full-service commercial real estate firms in the world. ❧ In 1959, Hal Ellis joined the John M. Grubb Company, a residential real estate brokerage firm, to establish a commercial brokerage operation. The name Grubb & Ellis Company became official in 1961, and geographic expansion began two years later with the opening of residential brokerage offices in Contra Costa and

Marin counties in California. The company's growth continued throughout the 1960s with new offices in San Francisco and suburban Los Angeles. The next decade brought Grubb & Ellis to Honolulu, downtown Los Angeles, Orange County, San Diego, Colorado, and Washington State.

The Phoenix office opened in 1973. That same year, Grubb & Ellis became the second-largest real estate services firm in the western United States.

Rapid Expansion

During the 1980s, Grubb & Ellis added to its presence in the West. From 1981 to 1986, the company tripled in size. In 1982, it became the first real estate brokerage firm listed on the New York Stock Exchange.

In 1993, shareholders approved a $53 million recapitalization of the company's debt and equity, including $32 million of new equity investment by Joe F. Hanauer; the Prudential Insurance Company of America; and Warburg, Pincus Investors, L.P., Grubb & Ellis' largest shareholder. This infusion, along with a strengthened management team, has allowed the company to emerge as a major national force with global services and vision.

In January 1996, Grubb & Ellis completed the purchase of IBM's shares in their joint venture, Axiom Real Estate Management, Inc., making the company the sole owner of one of the nation's leading property and facilities management firms. Grubb & Ellis further strengthened its management capabilities in Arizona with the 1998 acquisition of Eagle Western Property Management, Phoenix's premier property management firm, now a part of the nationwide Grubb & Ellis Management Services (GEMS).

Neil Young, who joined Grubb & Ellis in 1983 as an industrial broker, became president and CEO in late February 1996 and chairman of the board in April 1997. That same year, two major common stock transactions enabled the company to retire all of its long-term debt.

Strong Infrastructure

Today, Grubb & Ellis has a presence in 90 markets throughout the United States and abroad, as well as an infrastructure that allows it to maximize its clients' real estate investments. Because the company is financially stronger than it has been at any time in its 40-year history, it is ideally positioned to meet the challenges of the rapidly changing real estate services industry. State-of-the-art research and computer capabilities, a professional marketing communications staff, and an in-house graphics department are some of the expanded services the firm now offers its clients.

Under the leadership of Ronald T. Bennewate until the end of 1998, and now with Managing Director and Senior Vice President Peter K. Bolton at the helm, the Phoenix office has consistently been among the top three in the nation. In 1998, it was the first recipient of the Grubb & Ellis President's Award for excellence not only in sales, but also in the implementation of innovative programs to provide outstanding service to clients.

The vision of the Phoenix office, as established by its own real estate professionals and staff, is to be the dominant, most respected commercial real estate services company in Arizona. "We believe in listening to our clients," Bolton says. "Our company can only be as good as the services we provide to them."

If history is any indication, Grubb & Ellis will continue its award-winning performance not only in Phoenix, but throughout the world.

Grubb & Ellis Company's Phoenix team includes (from left) Executive Vice President and Regional Managing Director Don Morrow, Research Services Manager George Gramm, Administrative Assistant Patti Martin, former District Manager and Senior Vice President Ronald T. Bennewate, Business Operations Manager Barbara Peterson, and Managing Director and Senior Vice President Peter K. Bolton.

EGLIN PHOTOGRAPHIC PRODUCTIONS

MCO PROPERTIES LIMITED PARTNERSHIP

Located on 12,060 acres of land on the northeast edge of Greater Phoenix, the small town of Fountain Hills was once part of the largest land holding in Arizona. Developed by MCO Properties Limited Partnership, the parcel was purchased by Robert McCulloch in 1968, and the town was designed by C.V. Wood Jr., who also designed Disneyland. ❦ MCO Properties is a subsidiary of Maxxam Inc., a publicly held Fortune 500 corporation and one of the nation's leading real estate management and development companies. With

properties throughout Arizona, California, Colorado, and Texas, MCO Properties strives to create developments that are as right for the land as they are for people. In Fountain Hills, MCO develops only about 60 percent of its land for residences and other uses, leaving the remaining rugged rock outcroppings and desert vegetation in their natural state.

Fountain Hills

The picturesque community of Fountain Hills, framed by mountain ranges, reservation land, and a large, natural regional park, is home to 17,000 permanent residents, and swells to 20,000 in the temperate winter months. Homes range from town houses to expansive custom estates surrounded by desert trees and the stately saguaros that fill nearby arroyos, with spectacular views of Four Peaks, Firerock, the Verde Valley, and the Superstition Mountains in the distance.

"It's a move-up housing market," says MCO Vice President Hank Lickman. "Of the people who buy homes in Fountain Hills with Arizona addresses, 80 percent are from Scottsdale and are moving out of dense subdivisions. With a total land size of approximately 12,000 acres, and an eventual population expected to be around 30,000, Fountain Hills has one of the lowest population densities in the Valley. They come for the incredible desert and mountain views, the open space, and custom housing." Home prices range from $175,000 to more than $1 million, and neighborhoods project the feeling of a small, friendly town in a major metropolitan area. The Beeline

Expansive custom homes reflect the individuality of Fountain Hills' diverse population (top).

The 18-hole championship SunRidge Canyon Golf Course is as challenging as it is beautiful. In 1996, it was named one of the Top 100 Golf Courses in the United States by *Golf Magazine* (bottom).

Highway and expanded Shea Boulevard place Fountain Hills commuters within a half hour of most places in the Valley.

A growing list of more than 500 businesses, professionals, and retail firms serve Fountain Hills residents, whose average age is 42. Students attend two elementary schools, campus-style middle and high schools, a private academy, and a charter school. There is also an active local theater company that performs several ambitious productions each year. A community center with a 500-plus-seat performing arts theater is on the town council's drawing board.

What really sets Fountain Hills apart from other communities, besides open desert living, is a giant fountain, the community's namesake, recognized by the *Guinness Book of World Records* as the highest fountain in the world. When it erupts 560 feet into the blue, desert sky, on the hour each day for 15 minutes between 9 a.m. and 10 p.m., it is five feet taller than the Washington Monument, 110 feet higher than the Great Pyramid of Cheops in Egypt, and three times as high as Old Faithful geyser in Yellowstone National Park. Towering over a 28-acre lake in the center of Fountain Park, it was designed as the centerpiece of the development, and it can be seen from almost everywhere in Fountain Hills.

Three high-pressure, 600-horsepower pumps recycle community water reclaimed by a state-of-the-art treatment system from the Fountain Park lake, flowing at a rate of 7,000 gallons per minute. At that rate, the typical backyard swimming pool would be completely filled in two or three minutes. Conscious of conserving Arizona's precious natural groundwater, Fountain Hills has long been a pioneer in the use of reclaimed water for its irrigation of parks and golf courses, and for other water features throughout the incorporated town.

Golfers find three challenging 18-hole public courses, including Fountain Hills Golf Club, Golf Club at Eagle Mountain, and nationally ranked SunRidge Canyon. Residents enjoy tennis, basketball, and sand volleyball courts; swimming facilities; lighted ball fields; playgrounds; an athletic center; and miles of jogging and biking trails. For more rugged individuals, neighboring McDowell Mountain Regional Park offers 22,000 acres of wilderness camping and hiking.

"We want people to see Fountain Hills as a place where we are building a community that is sensitive to the environment, instead of changing the environment to meet the needs of the community," says Lickman.

Supporting the Community

MCO's support of the unique community it has built is generous and far reaching. Employees help local elementary school children in an ongoing, one-on-one mentoring program, and family activities have included a free concert performed by the Phoenix Symphony Orchestra in Fountain Park. Other community events include the annual Turkey Trot at Thanksgiving with events for every age and ability, holiday parades, Fourth of July fireworks, a hot air balloon festival, and two of the largest juried arts festivals in the West. Along with the many community events, this small town is home to a large number of service clubs and organizations, which provide ample opportunity for volunteers.

In a region where great weather and quality of life are taken for granted, Fountain Hills manages to stand out. Authors Lee and Saralee Rosenberg list the community in *50 Fabulous Places to Raise Your Family*, and *Parenting* magazine considers it one of the 10 top family communities as well.

The 800-acre Firerock Country Club Community, a private, gated neighborhood planned south of Shea Boulevard, is the newest MCO project. Plans include 390 spacious, custom homesites and 288 luxurious attached units, built around Fountain Hills' first and only private 18-hole golf course.

MCO's master plan, initiated in 1970, will be completed by the future development of 1,500 acres in the northwest corner of the community bordering Scottsdale communities, which will be known as Eagles Nest and Eagle Ridge North.

Panoramic views of the high Sonoran Desert are framed by the distant Goldfield Mountains (top).

Fountain Hills is named for its landmark fountain, which, at 560 feet, is among the highest in the world, according to the *Guinness Book of World Records*. The impressive stream of snowy white water is five feet higher than the Washington Monument (bottom).

DELTA DIVERSIFIED ENTERPRISES, INC.

Delta Diversified Enterprises, Inc., one of the largest electrical contracting companies in Arizona, has had a hand in completing the electrical installations for many major projects that have been constructed around the Valley. The company's work is found in the Chase Credit Card back-office call center in Tempe, as well as in the Mayo Clinic in Scottsdale, Arrowhead Mall in Peoria, McDonnell Douglas Helicopter Company in Mesa, and Wigwam Resort in Goodyear. Projects range from a small improvement contract at Chapel Square in Phoenix to 20-story Phoenix Plaza Tower downtown.

Delta Diversified's experience includes almost every kind of heavy industrial electrical challenge imaginable, including health care, institutional, and commercial projects. The company is well known for its special expertise in the sensitive electrical installations required in clean rooms, where materials such as microchips for the fast-growing semiconductor industry are manufactured. The Valley's major high-technology companies and their suppliers are listed on Delta Diversified's client roster, and the company has wired clean rooms from as small as 5,000 square feet up to one of the world's largest Class 1 facilities containing 250,000 square feet.

Solid Management

A management staff averaging more than 14 years each with the company provides the foundation for pride of workmanship and the success that brings. President and majority owner L.R. Donelson, who joined the company in the early 1980s, is continually looking for ways to improve the services Delta Diversified provides and for growth opportunities in this thriving economic market. The company began operations in 1971 under the leadership of R.J. Berry, with a small workforce and the determination to build a quality electrical contracting business. As the company grew, leadership passed to his brother Ron H. Berry in 1978, and Ron's son Brad is a major stockholder actively serving the company as vice president/chief financial officer.

Today, Delta Diversified is licensed to do work in Arizona, Nevada, California, and New Mexico, and the firm has a branch operation in Las Vegas providing electrical contracting services to that area. The company's initial pride of accomplishment

Clockwise from top:
(From left) Vice President Leo Correll, President Larry Donelson, and Vice President/Chief Financial Officer Brad Berry continually look for ways to improve the services Delta Diversified Enterprises, Inc. provides.

Delta Diversified's team of craftsmen are known and respected throughout the Valley for quality workmanship and dependable, responsive service.

In its 1999 Best of Arizona Business edition, *Arizona Business Magazine* ranked Delta Diversified as the number one electrical contractor in Arizona.

MICHAEL WOODDALL

Clockwise from top left:
Custom nightscape lighting is just one
way Delta Diversified meets the special
needs of its customers.

As a leader in landscape lighting, Delta
Diversified has installed many innova-
tive exterior lighting designs in Greater
Phoenix.

remains a vital part of the everyday work life of Delta Diversified's 200 well-trained employees. Arthur Andersen's most recent annual list of Arizona's top 100 privately held companies ranked by revenue places Delta Diversified in the 93rd position with yearly income between $35 million and $40 million.

Serving the Customer

"We owe our success to good employees and our dedication to serving our customers to the fullest," Donelson says. "We've never walked away from a problem on a job, and we have never walked away from a customer who doesn't want us to return." He stresses that in this fast-moving economy where there is daily pressure to complete projects on schedule and on budget, a company's reputation for dependability and integrity takes on significantly greater importance.

Pride in craftsmanship runs throughout the company, and safety and work excellence are rewarded through a profit-sharing program reaching to every level to provide for each employee's future retirement. "We appreciate the people who share our pride in the business and work hard for this company, and it's only fair that we share the rewards," Donelson says.

Encouraging Industry Excellence

Delta Diversified encourages excellence in the construction industry through active participation in both the local and national divisions of the Associated Builders and

Contractors (ABC). The company is heavily involved, both personally and with financial support, with furthering craft training in local vocational schools sponsored by the ABC, and it also contributes to the National Center for Construction Education and Research.

Delta Diversified's headquarters also has innumerable plaques and photographs speaking to the company's dedication to supporting local activities in the surrounding communities. The firm has provided volunteer participation and funding to area YWCA chapters, the Boy Scouts, and many

local softball and football teams. Each year employees donate labor, tools, and materials to projects coordinated through Habitat for Humanity and Christmas in April, which provide less fortunate members of the community with housing and needed repairs to their homes.

As Arizona continues to build and grow, Delta Diversified, Inc. will look for increased opportunities to expand its reach throughout the state, developing methods along the way to provide quality workmanship more efficiently and to serve its customers better.

Since 1971, Delta Diversified employees have
worked more than 6 million man-hours
providing total electrical services to commercial, industrial, retail, institutional,
hotel/resort, and health care clients.

SPEEDFAM

native Arizonan with almost 25 years of experience as a full-time real estate professional, Joanne Bradley, president of Joanne Bradley/Arizona Golf Properties and Luxury Homes, fully understands the community of Scottsdale and its changing market conditions. Specializing in luxury homes in the north Scottsdale and Carefree areas, Bradley and her staff most often market custom-designed homes in exclusive, gated communities such as Desert Mountain, Desert Highlands, Estancia, and Troon

A native Arizonan with almost 25 years of experience as a full-time real estate professional, Joanne Bradley, president of Joanne Bradley/Arizona Golf Properties and Luxury Homes, fully understands the community of Scottsdale and its changing market conditions.

"I traditionally carry the largest inventory of golf course properties available through a listing agency," Bradley says. "Because I have been here since the beginning of most of these communities and I specialize in these areas, I'm knowledgeable about what each property offers, including club memberships and specific CC&Rs [codes, covenants, and restrictions]." She began in north Scottsdale as one of the first women to sell raw land in the early 1980s, before many custom developments existed.

Listed among the top 1 percent of brokers in the country, Bradley typically sells million-dollar, 5,000- to 7,000-square-foot residences to buyers who are looking for second or third homes in a secure, gated community. Many come from the Midwest and California, looking for new homes as well as resale properties. Most of her business is through referrals, and Bradley is known for her honest, candid assessments and increasingly successful track record.

Marketing Phoenix to the World

Bradley is always looking for interesting marketing techniques, and annually produces *Exclusive Arizona Golf Properties and Luxury Homes©*, a slick, four-color publication distributed to a targeted market of individuals owning real estate in high-end, exclusive communities, as well as to local hotels, concierges, and key businesses. She carefully selects publications such as *Unique Homes*, *Ritz Carlton Service*, the *Wall Street Journal*, *America West*, various golf magazines, and several European publications to advertise the exceptional properties she lists. Bradley is also developing a Web page to reach a global audience.

Bradley has been included in Who's Who in Luxury Real Estate, an organization that recognizes firms and individuals who have a reputation for exceptional knowledge and expertise in the marketing of high-end, luxury properties. She is a member of the Unique Homes Referral Network—which includes 250 member brokers marketing luxury real estate throughout the

United States and abroad—and the International Real Estate Federation, through which she annually travels to host cities to market properties to members gathered from 54 other countries.

In her own community, Bradley is active with the Creative Women of Pinnacle Peak and the Phoenix and Scottsdale chambers of commerce. As a member of the Kidney Foundation, she donates a portion of her commissions toward increasing awareness for donating organs. Bradley received a kidney transplant more

than 10 years ago and urges people to understand the benefits of donating organs—what she considers the "gift of life."

"More than 82,000 people come to Arizona every year, drawn by the lifestyle, the weather, and the rich Sonoran Desert," Bradley says, predicting that this trend will continue for the next three to five years and probably longer. And with her dedication, experience, and love for the community, Joanne Bradley will continue to satisfy the housing needs of Greater Phoenix's exploding population.

S mall classes, a nurturing faculty, and a quality education are the hallmarks of Apollo College. An educational institution whose doors opened in 1976, Apollo prepares some 4,000 students annually for medical and dental careers. "We like to say Apollo is where caring careers begin," says Margaret Carlson, president and founder. "We challenge our students to see how far their minds can take them." Students experience a blend of classroom instruction, guest lecturers, and field trips designed to provide a firsthand look at the

work practices and procedures of a large number of Valley-area hospitals with which Apollo is affiliated. Under teacher supervision, the students also assist at health fairs throughout the community, providing eye and hearing tests, blood screenings, blood pressure and cholesterol examinations, and back-to-school inoculations. In addition to these programs, a contract with the Navajo Nation offers training for students who complete their education to go back and practice in the outlying, rural areas.

Building Careers

Through its small, intimate campuses located in convenient proximity to the populations they serve, Apollo College makes it as easy as possible for students to get an education. Apollo has schools in Phoenix, Mesa, and Tucson, as well as

Portland, Oregon, and Spokane. An open-entry system allows students to complete some 16 nationally certified or registry-eligible programs offering diplomas and associate degrees. These features, combined with the school's formal graduation every three months and its flexible class scheduling, enable Apollo to attract students from across the United States. Financial aid in the form of federal and state loans and grants is also available to eligible students, and the college can provide for welfare-to-work candidates under the Job Training Partnership Act.

Typical Apollo College students tend to be very career focused, a quality that keeps them on track with their education. A significant number are retraining for second careers. In fact, Apollo boasts a 90 percent completion rate among its enrollees.

The Future of Health Care

With a growing elderly population among Greater Phoenix's 2.7 million inhabitants, there is an increasing need for health care providers. The field is one of the fastest-growing professions in the United States, and Apollo is training students to fill the area's rapidly rising number of available positions. Apollo's success rate for placing its graduates is very high.

At Apollo, more than 200 faculty and support staff ensure that students get personal attention all along the way. Help is readily available for personal, academic, vocational, or any other need. "If a career in health care is the path a student chooses," Carlson says, "our staff will find a way to help them get it."

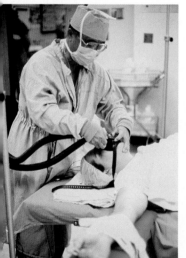

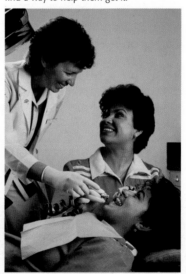

Founded in 1976, Apollo College prepares some 4,000 students annually for medical and dental careers.

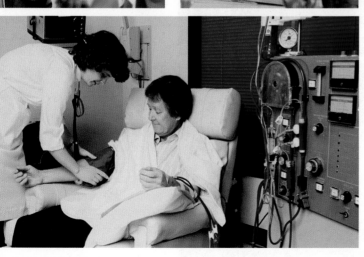

UNIVERSITY OF PHOENIX

The largest private university in the United States, the University of Phoenix offers a practical, real-world education to its students. Especially designed for working professionals, the university offers degree programs at more than 70 campuses in more than a dozen states, Puerto Rico, and British Columbia, and serves a rapidly growing enrollment of more than 60,000 students. 🌵 Educational trendsetter John G. Sperling, the university's chairman and CEO, founded the university in 1976, offering evening

classes to a select group of firefighters and police officers. As a professor at San Jose State University, Sperling saw firsthand the differences in needs and learning styles between a traditional, younger university student still deciding on a career and a working adult with professional goals and practical experience. Schools throughout the nation are now realizing what Sperling recognized early on—that working adults need a streamlined education process with concentrated curricula and flexible schedules, tailored to their special needs and responsibilities.

The university's dynamic learning model is based on classes of 15 to 24 students. These small classes encourage lively interaction and faculty members are trained to facilitate classroom discussion. Faculty members, who have master's or doctoral degrees, bring real-world experience to the classroom as they also are employed full-time in the area they teach.

Students also get practical experience in teamwork by participating in study groups of four to six students where they develop

Educational trendsetter John G. Sperling, the University of Phoenix's chairman and CEO, founded the university in 1976.

the cross-functional tasking, interpersonal, management, and collaboration skills demanded in today's workplaces. Study groups meet weekly, outside of the classroom, to work on case studies and projects. Most students stay with the same groups throughout their degree program, so relationships are developed and leveraged for maximum success.

"Even though we have grown into a large university, we still act small, striving to deliver service with a personal touch," says Larry Gudis, the University of Phoenix's Arizona senior regional vice president. "At the University of Phoenix, you're an important member of our university community, not a number." Every student is assigned an enrollment counselor to help work through the admissions process; then an academic counselor provides support and guidance through the student's University of Phoenix educational experience.

Making It Work

Convenience is the cornerstone of the University of Phoenix philosophy. Almost all administrative business can be conducted by phone, fax, E-mail, or the Internet. Multiple campuses are placed in prime, easy-to-reach locations, where students have a choice of attending classes close to work or home, and the university's library is a collection of on-line documents that can be accessed conveniently via the Internet.

Partnerships built over time with area employers help to provide tuition reimbursement and support for students. Companies that contract with the University of Phoenix to educate their employees on-site benefit from research and problem solving geared to their business, as well as from specialized instruction pertaining to their industry.

New curricula are developed as needed for nationwide use, and instruction

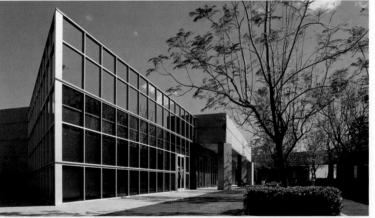

"Even though we have grown into a large university, we still act small, striving to deliver service with a personal touch," says Larry Gudis, the University of Phoenix's Arizona senior regional vice president. "At the University of Phoenix, you're an important member of our university community, not a number."

is always evolving and improving. The curriculum is continually updated to ensure its relevance, so that what students learn today can be applied in the workplace immediately. The university constantly surveys students and researches the market to assure that degrees are serving the needs of the organizations that will employ its graduates. Because it carefully monitors trends, the university can move quickly to offer cutting-edge curricula. The institution is recognized nationally for its award-winning assessment process, and students are surveyed at the end of every course for feedback on staff, faculty, textbooks, and the learning facility, providing an ongoing flow of information to guide change.

Serving the Local Community

The university's Greater Phoenix campuses, with an enrollment of more than 7,000 students, have two graduations each year, conferring degrees on about 800 students each time. "When you see the expressions at graduation, you know you're changing lives," Gudis says. "It's rewarding to look out across this community and see that our graduates are in responsible positions, using what they have learned here every day."

While 98 percent of the University of Phoenix's educational efforts are built around degree programs, professional certification is a rapidly growing area. Certificates are offered in call center management,

human resource management, essential skills of mediation, and more than 20 other areas.

The University of Phoenix, accredited since 1978, is the largest subsidiary of Apollo Group, Inc., a publicly traded company (Nasdaq: APOL). Despite tremendous growth in the nearly quarter century since its founding, University of Phoenix officials believe the school has not yet reached its full potential. As the demand for better-educated workers grows, university officials will expand course offerings and campus

sites in order to meet the needs of both students and businesses across the United States.

The University of Phoenix is accredited by the Commission on Institutions of Higher Education of the North Central Association of Colleges and Schools. The Bachelor of Science in Nursing Program is accredited by the National League for Nursing. The Master of Counseling/Community Counseling program is accredited by the Council for Accreditation of Counseling and Related Educational Programs.

OTTAWA UNIVERSITY

ince 1977, more than 15,000 students have experienced the excellence of an Ottawa University (OU) education in the Phoenix area. Widely respected as a private, nonprofit liberal arts university, OU Phoenix offers bachelor of arts and master of arts degrees, along with teacher certification and continuing education for certified teachers. Ottawa University was established in 1865. Its history goes back to 1837, when a missionary and printer, Jotham Meeker, and his wife Eleanor came to minister to the Ottawa tribe.

Reverend Meeker was interested in Native American languages and authored a dictionary of the Ottawa language. After his death, missionary work was taken over by John Tecumseh (Tauy) Jones, the son of a Chippewa, an honorary member of the Ottawa tribe, and the person often credited with the founding of the university.

The mission of Ottawa University Phoenix is to extend the university to adult students, to bring classes and instruction to the students, and to reduce as much as possible the barriers that inhibit adult students from completing their degrees or furthering their adult-educational interests. In keeping with this goal, OU Phoenix opened its Tempe instructional site in 1990 and its Scottsdale site in 1995, both accredited by the North Central Association of

Colleges and Schools Commission on Institutions of Higher Education. In addition, Ottawa has adult learning centers in Milwaukee, Kansas City, Malaysia, Hong Kong, and Singapore.

Flexible Options, Personalized Planning
OU Phoenix is committed to meeting adult lifestyle needs with quality and flexibility. Students are members of both the learning and instruction teams as real-life situations are addressed by the 28 full-time and more than 300 adjunct faculty members, all of whom bring real work experience to the classroom. By offering evening and weekend classes, adults with jobs and/or family responsibilities are better able to complete their degree requirements.

"It's the most-personalized education you could ever receive," says Provost Dr. Fredric Zook. "Each student has an individual faculty advisor who is committed to his or her overall success." The university's faculty members strive to help each student develop as a total person living up to one's full potential both in and out of the classroom. As Ottawa University grows throughout Arizona, it will continue to remain dedicated to providing a quality education tailored to fit the ever changing needs of its adult students.

Ottawa University of Ottawa, Kansas, is accredited by the North Central Association of Colleges and Schools Commission on Institutions of Higher Education, which is located in Chicago.

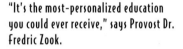

"It's the most-personalized education you could ever receive," says Provost Dr. Fredric Zook.

ompanies opening offices internationally need to learn a lot more than a new language to be successful. Cultural differences often dictate where to find the right executives and middle managers, what they expect in compensation and benefits, and what it takes to build long-term, loyal working relationships. Sterling Human Resources International offers valuable assistance to these companies through its locally staffed Asia-Pacific offices in Beijing, Shanghai, Singapore, and Hanoi, and the company is quickly

extending its reach as multinational organizations look to it for solid, trustworthy advice. Client needs have propelled Sterling Human Resources International from a local temporary employment placement company to an international adviser to U.S. Fortune 500 and mid-size companies with global aspirations. Over the last five years, Sterling's average annual revenues have increased at a rate of 15 percent, as the scope of the successful Phoenix operation has grown steadily to encompass the world.

Filling a Need

Sterling's Asian operations began as the first American human resources company to locate in Beijing, with its staff of one in 1992 growing to five members by the spring of 1996 and expanding to Shanghai a year later. The company offers a critical partnership to companies expanding to China,

helping to guide its clients through the complexities of overseas employment, expatriate regulations, and foreign investment in wholly owned and joint venture businesses.

"We staff each of our full-service offices with local nationals or American-born Chinese who are proven human resources professionals," says Robert Macdonald, founding president. "We train them and then we let them take over the operation with their knowledge of local standards and procedures, without imposing the Western view on how the office is managed."

Macdonald believes that every culture and every business has lessons to teach, and savvy companies take note and make adjustments to stay on the cutting edge. As companies extend their operations, local, firsthand knowledge can make the difference between success and failure, productivity and problems, and profit and

loss for U.S.-based firms. The Asian offices work very closely with each other, as well as with the Phoenix office.

Sterling represents major U.S. companies in the information technologies market doing business in the Asia-Pacific region, but also counsels financial services, marketing, human resources, and banking clients. Besides executive search consultation, Sterling also researches competitive intelligence and can provide on-site human resources services.

A strategic alliance has been signed between Sterling Human Resources International and Executive Asia of Hong Kong, increasing Sterling's international staff to 50, and more offices are being considered in Australia, India, and Japan in the 21st century. "We believe the timing is good to expand," says Macdonald. "We're looking at long-term growth, and we want to be positioned to be a player in the world economy."

Sterling Human Resources International has been propelled from a local temporary employment placement company to an international adviser to U.S. Fortune 500 and mid-size companies with global aspirations.

RIO SALADO COLLEGE

io Salado College may be located in the Phoenix suburb of Tempe, but its educational outreach is global. Behind Rio Salado's success story is a more than 20-year commitment to bringing learning opportunities directly to unserved or underserved students, anytime and anyplace. According to the college's mission statement, "Rio Salado College creates convenient, high-quality learning opportunities for diverse populations. We specialize in customized, unique programs and partnerships, accelerated formats and distance delivery. In all that we do, we pursue continuous improvement and innovation, and we challenge the limits of tradition."

Rio Salado College's administrative headquarters is located in Tempe (right).

Serving the Non-Traditional Student

From its founding in 1978, Rio Salado operated outside the traditional concept of a bricks-and-mortar campus, preferring to take its courses directly into the community by renting classroom space in public buildings, shopping centers, and existing schools. At the time, Rio Salado was highly unusual because it identified an untapped student market—adults age 30 and older who work and have family commitments.

Today, Rio Salado still targets non-traditional students whose schedules demand convenience and flexibility. Rio Salado meets their needs through a combination of traditional and accelerated formats, through on-site workforce training, and by offering many of its courses "anytime, anyplace" through distance learning. By delivering 250 different courses through formats such as the Internet, CD-ROM, computer disk, audio/videocassette, and mixed media, Rio Salado reaches diverse student populations throughout Maricopa County, nationally, and occasionally around the world.

An Educational Change Agent

Under the leadership of Dr. Linda Thor, who has served as president since 1990, Rio Salado has sharpened its role as an educational change agent while achieving impressive growth. Rio Salado has become the third largest—and the most cost effective—of the 10 colleges in the Maricopa County Community College District, the second-largest such district in the country. Its enrollment has steadily increased over the years, with more than 25,000 credit and 25,000 noncredit students currently attending classes.

The college offers more than 3,200 credit courses annually, with 125 of the 250 distance learning courses accessible through the Internet. Eleven Associate degree programs and 29 certificate programs are available. The courses are taught by Rio Salado's 500 adjunct faculty members, working professionals who are experts in their fields.

"We were established as a college without walls and have become a college without boundaries," says Thor. "We have eliminated geographical limitations, and we constantly are updating our use of the latest, most innovative methods to deliver instruction, counseling, schedules, registration—whatever our students need to succeed. Frankly, we see Rio Salado as a global institution, serving not only Maricopa County, but the Southwest, the nation, and the world."

Rio Salado has received numerous regional and national awards, plus significant news coverage from media such as the *New York Times*, the *Chronicle of Higher Education*, and National Public Radio.

The Rio Salado family includes the full-time faculty and administrative staff at Rio's Tempe headquarters; KJZZ-FM and KBAQ-FM radio stations; Sun Sounds Statewide Radio Reading Service; Rio School of Dental Hygiene; Rio Sun Cities Lifelong Learning Center; Rio Luke Air Force Base; Rio Paradise Valley Mall; Rio Phoenix at 7th Avenue; and Rio East Valley.

Accelerated Formats

Rio Salado offers accelerated learning formats, such as the Fastrack program for its military students at Rio Luke Air Force Base. Fastrack allows students to work full-time and still earn 12 credits per semester by taking classes in eight-week formats.

Another learning alternative is the Program for Adult Student Success (PASS), which allows active adults who work and have families to earn their Associate degrees more rapidly by attending class just one night each week and every other Saturday.

Rio also introduced self-paced learning to computer students through Open Entry/Open Exit classes. State-of-the-art computer lab facilities are available at five locations.

Partnering to Meet Needs

Many Rio Salado classes originate through partnerships with corporations and government agencies, with customized curricula designed to suit each organization's unique needs. Thor cites the Rio School of Dental Hygiene as emblematic of the school's

Today's students see technology as a powerful tool for achieving their educational goals.

determination to, as she puts it, "meet the needs of the community by partnering with employers." The state-of-the-art facility was financed through contributions from the Arizona Dental Association and Delta Dental Insurance. Funds were used to renovate an existing, 8,200-square-foot building near downtown Phoenix, where students undertake a 15-month program to become dental hygienists.

The Arizona law enforcement community's need for a higher-education partner also led to an unusual relationship between the college and the Phoenix Regional Police Academy, Arizona Law Enforcement Academy, Mesa Police Academy, and Maricopa County Sheriff's Department Reserve Academy. In this case, law enforcement professionals, who are Rio Salado instructors, design and teach Law Enforcement Technology (LET), complemented by Rio Salado's academic courses. In a typical year, the LET program graduates more than 500 cadets, making it the largest program of its type in the Southwest.

Technology in Education

Rio Salado is renowned for its innovative uses of technology. Not only did Rio Salado pioneer Internet courses, it also created an infrastructure that allows on-line access to all student services at http://www.rio.maricopa.edu. Students can register, order books, receive academic counseling, and apply for scholarships, all with the click of a mouse. A major benefit of Internet and other distance learning courses is that students can choose from 26 possible starting dates per year.

Military personnel at Luke Air Force Base are typical of the non-traditional students who benefit from Rio's on-line courses and services. When they are deployed to places such as Kuwait, Saudi Arabia, Japan, and Germany, they can continue their studies without interruption.

Students can conduct research on Rio's Cybrary, an electronic library with links to thousands of newspapers and magazines. They can also access OWL, an on-line writing lab, complete with a dictionary and thesaurus. For Spanish and math students, there's Beep-a-Tutor, which provides help over the phone upon request. Seven days a week, the Rio Helpdesk assists Internet students in downloading materials and answering any questions they may have about their on-line courses.

Rio utilizes the latest technological advances to deliver educational opportunities anytime, anyplace. By using integrated technologies, Rio is entering the millennium with such sophisticated global capabilities as satellite uplink, computer conferencing and collaboration, two-way multipoint videoconferencing, and interactive two-way audio/one-way video computer conferencing.

Serving Special Adults

Rio Salado has built its Adult Basic Education Program into the largest one of its kind in the state, serving 25,000 residents of Maricopa County annually. They take advantage of noncredit courses in GED (high school equivalency diploma), Adult Basic Education, or English for Speakers of Other Languages (ESOL). Learning is self-paced, and open enrollment is offered throughout the year.

Rio Salado initiated a Concurrent Enrollment program, which allows thousands of academically committed high school students to earn full college credit and gives them a head start on their college course work.

Rio Salado has also developed educational programs for the incarcerated and other adults considered at-risk in the educational world. Through the REACHOUT Project, funded by a generous grant from the Alfred P. Sloan Foundation, nearly 200 at-risk students have access to computers at labs in their neighborhoods, housing projects, and, in some cases, their own homes.

As Rio Salado has flourished, its achievements have been acknowledged by the North Central Association of Colleges and Schools, which has renewed Rio's accreditation for 10 years—the maximum possible.

With its flexibility in scheduling, an extensive menu of academic opportunities, and an arsenal of technologically sophisticated resources, Rio Salado College provides adults with every opportunity to sharpen their job skills and pursue their educational goals and dreams.

High-end technologies that have recently become a reality at Rio Salado include satellite uplink, two-way multipoint videoconferencing, and interactive two-way audio/one-way video computer conferencing (top).

Distance learning formats at Rio Salado include the Internet, CD-ROM, and mixed media such as audio/videocassettes (bottom).

SCOTTSDALE VILLAGE SQUARE

Many people may not realize that most of the 300 residents who call Scottsdale Village Square home have lived for more than 70 years—and some for as long as 100. The hustle and bustle of the attractive lobby, the unending schedule of interesting activities, and the van at the front door traveling to destinations far and wide attest to the fact that the passing years don't necessarily slow a person down. 🌵 "Progressive retirement centers today focus on the quality of life of the resident," says Colleen Sweet, Scottsdale Village's executive director. "Retirement communities are changing to meet the expectations of today's growing senior population," adds Sweet. "I believe, in time, as more people visit nursing facilities, they will find dramatic changes, discovering a stimulating and high quality of life with new methods focusing on wellness and preventive care that will eventually eliminate the phrase 'nursing home.' "

Scottsdale Village Square, which is owned by Scottsdale Residential Care Investors, offers an intimate collection of retirement living options clustered on a single campus. In this way, it can provide just the right care when it's needed, with easy transition from independent to assisted living as more care becomes necessary. Most of the 250-person staff has been associated with the facility for many years, and close bonds develop with the residents and family members.

Families are always welcome, and there is a guest apartment where they can stay overnight or where a potential resident can experience the community personally before deciding to stay. "Moving into a retirement facility can be stressful and emotional," Nikki Rowland, community relations director, says. "We try to help by looking at the positive aspects and doing what we can to alleviate most of that stress."

Enjoying Independence

All apartments have direct intercom connection to the front desk and 24-hour emergency call systems in the bedroom and bathroom. As residents require a helping hand from time to time, services can be added for as long as they are needed. These might include medication reminders, shower assistance, escorts to the dining room, or nonemergency nursing care.

Included on the spacious grounds are a swimming pool, a heated spa, and a nine-hole putting green. There are also many quiet places to just relax and enjoy the temperate Arizona climate.

In its accelerated thrust towards maximizing both the physical and psychological health of residents, Scottsdale Village began a comprehensive wellness program in 1997. Activities include tai chi, an ancient Chinese martial art used to heal the body and calm the mind, and music therapy, which can trigger memories and feelings to improve seniors' self-esteem. Therapeutic massage, which has been shown to reduce muscle tension, headaches, insomnia, and minor aches and pains, is also offered. Rounding out the wellness emphasis is a range of exercise programs, from water aerobics to chair and strength exercises for nonambulatory residents.

Stimulating retirement facilities? Although this may seem like an oxymoron, long-term care isn't what it used to be, when meals and television provided the chief stimuli. "Today's senior facilities

Scottsdale Village Square's front entrance welcomes visitors and residents alike into a truly unique retirement community (top).

Residents find a sense of tranquillity and as much freedom as their capabilities will allow in an environment designed to feel like home (bottom).

have more services and socialized activities," notes Sweet. "Our activities range from going out to happy hours, Friday night dances, participating in art shows, and performing in musicals. Our budget for activity staff has increased tenfold in the last decade. We used to have one activity director, and now we have 28 activity staff members."

Focusing on Wellness

The Village's award-winning Kiva is a carefully designed, fully licensed skilled nursing center for long-term or short stays. Residents as well as other seniors in the surrounding community find affordable, quality nursing care. Families can also obtain short-term relief care to fill in during an emergency, or to provide care while they're on vacation. Through Safenet, a community outreach project, Scottsdale Village Square can also take a variety of health services to a senior's own home.

Convenient doctor and dentist appointments can be made with health professionals who schedule visits to Scottsdale Village Square; and Nova Care, which has a therapy room and an office on-site, provides physical and speech therapy.

Sense of Tranquillity

Innovative programs at the Vistas, a progressive Alzheimer's and related dementia community, offer separate levels of specialized care based on the guidelines of the National Alzheimer's Association. Always with an individualized approach, the same care management team works with residents and their families throughout their stay as needs and care levels change.

Each separate area of the Vistas has its own dayroom and social and activity spaces with apartments that open into a safe, secure, and beautifully landscaped patio and garden. Residents find a sense

of tranquillity and as much freedom as their capabilities will allow in an environment designed to feel like home. Their personalized programs include group and one-on-one activities focusing on reminiscence, word association, and motor skills. Several years ago, a Vista North art project created a special greeting card to send to President and Mrs. Ronald Reagan. Use of the design expanded to note cards and T-shirts, and the Arizona Alzheimer's Association adopted it for the group's annual conference.

Solid Reputation

"We've been here for 20 years and have an established reputation," Rowland says, "and we have encouraged community

involvement from the beginning." The Village has strong ties with children from Tonalea Elementary School and the YMCA of South Scottsdale, who come in the summer to take swimming lessons in the pool and to volunteer. Some work at the front desk, run errands, talk with residents, or take the Village's dogs, Duke and Pepe, to visit around the campus.

Scottsdale Village Square was recognized by the Arizona Health Care Association with its prestigious Facility of the Year award both in 1991 and in 1996. Proud of their innovative programs, the owners of the Village constantly research new ways to make the senior facility even better, providing its residents with a safe, enjoyable community in which to live.

Clockwise from top left:
Residents and their families enjoy improving their game on the nine-hole putting green.

Art adorns the hallway walls for residents' enjoyment.

Vista North residents enjoy their beautiful surroundings while helping to prepare one of Scottsdale Village Square's weekly barbecues.

KNXV-TV, CHANNEL 15 (ABC)

howing its dedication to news, education, and entertainment in Greater Phoenix, ABC affiliate KNXV-TV, Channel 15 has a new home. The 70,000-square-foot facility—filled with modern technology, including a state-of-the-art newsroom—is the most recent television station to be built in Phoenix from the ground up. The facility has two studios 60 feet wide and 80 feet long, each with a 22-foot grid-height clearance. The new facility also includes a three-level parking structure for nearly 200 automobiles and a landing pad for

Chopper 15. The studio is designed to be compatible with the future of digital television.

Centrally located near Loop 202 and State Route 143, KNXV-TV can dispatch its reporters to cover news stories readily in any part of the Valley, either from the air or on the ground. "Location is critical because breaking news is a top priority and the strategic placement of our new facility will allow us quicker access to every corner of our coverage area," says Brad Nilsen, vice president and general manager.

Fast-Paced and Innovative

Signing on as an independent station in Phoenix on September 9, 1979, KNXV-TV was owned by New Television Corporation and originally broadcast from a 3,500-square-foot facility. The call letters NXV were chosen to stand for "News 15." The station adopted the slogan We're # Fun, and leased its prime-time hours to National Subscription Television, which featured first-run films, Arizona State University sporting events, National Hockey League games, and boxing matches. In 1984, a banner year for Channel 15, the station was sold to Scripps-Howard Broadcasting for $30 million.

As part of the Scripps-Howard family, KNXV-TV is in good company. Parent E.W. Scripps Company operates nine network-affiliated television stations; 20 daily newspapers; two cable television networks, Home & Garden and the Food Network; Cinetel Productions; and United Media, a worldwide syndicator and licenser of news features and comics (*Dilbert*, *Peanuts*, etc.).

The station became one of the first affiliates of the fledgling Fox network in 1986, and made history on April 5, 1987, as it helped launch Fox's first prime-time lineup. Toward the end of its eight-year association with Fox, the station was leaning toward creating an innovative local news format, and began in 1994 to prepare for its first news program.

Before the newscast was launched, the station learned it would be changing from Fox to an ABC affiliate, effective in early January 1995. To prepare for this change, the fast-paced "No Chit Chat, More News" newscast premiered at 10 p.m. August 1, 1994. News programs at 6 p.m., 5 p.m., and 11 a.m. soon followed. On January 9, 1995, the day ABC was officially on board, the fifth daily newscast, from 6 to 7 a.m., was added.

Dedicated to News

This dedication to news was not only appreciated by viewers, but was also recognized in 1998 by the Arizona Chapter of the National Academy of Television Arts and Sciences with 26 Rocky Mountain Emmy Award nominations for general news; newscast production; feature hard news story-same day; investigative reporting; photography; and sports. ABC 15 won 11 Emmy Awards.

The station was also honored for its coverage of local education issues as winner of the 1997 Arizona Education Association Presidential Award for Excellence in Education News Coverage. "Education First" airs every weeknight during *News 15* with stories dedicated to teachers, schools, and other educational topics. In *What's Up?*, an educational program designed to appeal to children from 8 to 12 years of age, the station visits Greater Phoenix museums, the zoo, sports organizations, businesses, and community activities. KNXV also has the exclusive broadcast rights to the Arizona State Spelling Bee, which sends its winner to the Scripps Howard national competition in Washington, D.C.

Even with its dedication to reporting local issues, KNXV still knows how to have

KNXV-TV Channel 15's 70,000-square-foot facility filled with modern technology, including a state-of-the art newsroom, is the most recent station in Phoenix to be built from the ground up.

The anchors for ABC's *20/20* include (from left) Charles Gibson, Sam Donaldson, Diane Sawyer, Barbara Walters, Hugh Downs, and Connie Chung.

fun. In addition to ABC's comedy and drama lineup, KNXV offers its own locally produced brand of entertainment. *Sonoran Grill*, a weekly cooking program, is hosted by "Mad Coyote Joe" Daigneault. He teaches viewers how to prepare gourmet grilled dishes, such as mesquite-grilled swordfish and roasted Cornish game hen with a prickly pear and chili glaze. Each show demonstrates grilling tips for novice and experienced cooks alike.

Serving the Community

Community service is a natural extension of KNXV's dedication to reporting happenings in the Valley. The station has teamed up with the Children's Miracle Network to raise funds for Phoenix Children's Hospital and is a major supporter of Check Out Hunger, the only statewide campaign to raise funds for all food banks. And, as part of the commitment to put education first, KNXV was one of the first participants in an innovative Washington School District bus advertisement program designed to raise funds to convert district vehicles to compressed natural gas. The station also proudly sponsors the Hon Kachina Volunteer Awards program, which has been in the Valley for 22 years.

With its new facility on North 44th Street in the Gateway Center, a dedication to the community it serves, and an affiliation with the ABC Television Network, KNXV-TV is a must-see in Phoenix.

Peter Jennings anchors ABC's *World News Tonight.*

RIDENOUR, SWENSON, CLEERE & EVANS, P.C.

Times were good in the early 1980s when the founding shareholders formed Ridenour, Swenson, Cleere & Evans, P.C. (RSC&E). They were determined to shape a firm with a different character. As Bill Ridenour says proudly, "We always have worked to provide a comfortable, informal environment for our clients, attorneys, and staff. Most partners and associates came to RSC&E from large firms, attracted by the personal and professional satisfaction that thrives in the unique atmosphere created

by the founders. The tangible result of this is seen by its clients in teamwork and a positive, can-do approach to legal problems. This atmosphere, along with high-quality, timely legal services, has helped us establish many valued, long-term relationships with our clients." It is hard to find many law firms that have a trail ride and cookout for a Christmas party, or have a luncheon in its office to congratulate and encourage one of its clients on the one-year anniversary of his quitting smoking.

RSC&E grew from the original firm to a 26-lawyer, full-service practice. Expertise was developed in the areas of real estate, lending, business planning and corporate matters, estate planning, tax, construction litigation, commercial transactions, mergers and acquisitions, personal injury defense, plaintiff personal injury and wrongful death, bankruptcy, health care, agriculture, and malpractice.

The firm has a well-earned reputation for providing excellent legal services, but it goes beyond in many situations. "We want to help in any way we can," says Ridenour. "Our clients really depend on

Agriculture is an important part of Arizona's economy and a specialty area for Ridenour, Swenson, Cleere & Evans, P.C. (RSC&E) (top).

Colorful sunsets provide the backdrop for Arizona's sophisticated business and legal climate (bottom).

us, listen to us, and take our advice to heart." Repeat business is the norm—creating loyal, ongoing relationships.

The firm takes deep pride in the fact that the close relationships developed with clients have, in many cases, pushed the firm's involvement beyond traditional lawyering into full membership in the client's decision-making or problem-solving team, or as a sounding board for new business ventures or actions. Clients have

learned that they can call an RSC&E lawyer to run something by him or her, and not automatically be billed for the time.

When asked what he believes sets RSC&E apart from other firms in the delivery of legal services other than the development of a relationship, Harold Swenson, one of the firm's founders, says, "There are many good firms that provide quality legal service as we do. What makes us different is our attention to cost. We avoid overstaffing a matter, and keep the focus on the problem and issues that make a material difference in the result. We have made a conscious decision to keep our fee rates below that of other firms providing similar services."

The firm encourages its lawyers to be involved with their families and community. Its lawyers devote substantial time and energy to more than 100 nonprofit and charitable organizations. This participation ranges from the coaching of Little League teams, to membership on the sheriff's search and rescue squad, to the provision of caregiving for the elderly and persons with AIDS, to volunteer legal services. All attorneys and staff are committed to family and community participation.

Corporate clients regularly put their trust in the firm for legal guidance. RSC&E has handled a $3.2 billion loan transaction with a consortium of more than 80 lenders; significant mergers and acquisitions, such as the recent sale of Valley Rental to RSC Rental Service Corporation; and securities work, including a rare going-private transaction for a bank client. The firm also

◄ RICHARD D. STRANGE

represents restaurants, automobile dealerships, commercial real estate owners, developers and managers, television and radio personalities, manufacturers, and other companies in a wide variety of business enterprises. RSC&E attorneys routinely advise clients on all legal aspects of business affairs—from employment issues to leases.

RSC&E is also deeply involved in banking and lending. It represents Johnson Bank, National Bank of Arizona, Bank One Arizona (trust department), Pacific Century Bank, Chase Manhattan Mortgage Corporation, Kennedy Funding, Inc., Stearns Bank Arizona, and the FDIC.

The firm has a varied clientele. RSC&E represents Farm Credit Services Southwest, one of the largest agriculture lenders in the Southwest, and a long list of farmers and ranchers, cotton gins, chemical suppliers, and other related agribusiness enterprises. Clients include the Duncan Family Farms in Goodyear, a unique farming venture engaged in "entertainment" agriculture, among other busi-

nesses. Arnott and Kathleen Duncan hold annual pumpkin fests, and the farm is a regular field trip for local schoolchildren.

RSC&E has been designated as approved outside counsel for the State of Arizona and Maricopa County, and also has represented Yavapai and Cochise counties, the cities of Phoenix and Wilcox, and the towns of Paradise Valley and Gilbert. The Arizona State Retirement System and the Arizona State Compensation Fund are major state clients of the firm.

The firm represents several large insurance companies, including State Farm, Allstate, St. Paul Fire & Marine, California Casualty, AMICA, and GEICO. Many of the

firm's shareholders are certified specialists in wrongful death litigation, and regularly handle complex insurance defense, product liability, and construction defect litigation, as well as coverage issues.

Looking at the long term, RSC&E doesn't strive to be the largest firm in town, and by design it never will be. The firm does want to keep fees fair and reasonable, and maintain its informal and nonintimidating atmosphere. At the same time, clients can depend on the highest-quality legal advice available anywhere. Success will continue to be measured by the ongoing relationships that bring clients back for legal counsel time and again.

Clockwise from top:
The firm is located in downtown Phoenix, the business and governmental center of the state.

RSC&E litigation attorneys represent clients before all levels of state and federal courts.

The firm's annual holiday party includes a trail ride and cookout.

MARLON DE CASTRO

ACHEN-GARDNER, INC.

A tourist driving past the manicured medians and detailed brickwork that create the ambience of downtown Scottsdale will rarely think about the company whose attention to detail and craftsmanship has made the area one of the most visited spots in the Southwest. Most people would also never imagine that this same company is responsible for major streetscape work in other Valley of the Sun hot spots such as Tempe, the home of the Fiesta Bowl, and beautiful downtown Phoenix, the vital heart of the capital city. Viewing these projects that have become part of the very fabric of life in the Valley of the Sun offers only a glimpse of the capabilities of a company that is one of the premier contracting services companies in Arizona. This company is Achen-Gardner, Inc.

A New Standard

Becoming a dominant force in the fiercely competitive Phoenix-area construction market requires more than raw building skill. When Sanders T. Achen and Douglas D. Gardner joined their talents to start their own contracting services company in the early 1980s, their visionary blend of cutting-edge technology and an "always exceed their expectations" business philosophy began a dynamic company that is now the pacesetter for construction in the Valley of the Sun.

Great Timing

Achen-Gardner began in 1982, just as an industrywide recession was ending. Economic expansion, along with phenomenal growth in the Phoenix markets in the mid-1980s, allowed the fledgling company to gain a major foothold in residential and commercial construction. However, a turning point came in the late 1980s, as the country plunged into another recession. In a daring move to retain quality employees and mitigate the weakness in the commercial construction market, Achen-Gardner diversified into the heavy highway industry. This critical decision began a new era for Achen-Gardner, as the new division became the cornerstone for a stronger, more diversified company.

In just 17 years, Achen-Gardner has expanded to cover a diverse scope of construction needs with its five divisions: General Engineering and Heavy Highway Construction, Commercial Building Construction, Subcontract Framing, Residential Development and Construction, and Heavy Equipment Leasing, which supplies and supports the other divisions. "We are unique because most firms are either home builders, commercial builders, or heavy highway constructors," says Gardner, company chairman. "Each of our divisions is larger than many stand-alone companies." With such broad capabilities, Achen-Gardner's dominant status is well deserved. Adds Gardner, "We're here for the long

Clockwise from top:
In just 17 years, Achen-Gardner, Inc. has expanded to cover a diverse scope of construction needs with its five divisions: General Engineering and Heavy Highway Construction, Commercial Building Construction, Subcontract Framing, Residential Development and Construction, and Heavy Equipment Leasing.

The heavy equipment division keeps each project running smoothly.

The engineering division gives Old Town Scottsdale a great new look.

term. We're building an organization and a legacy that we're proud of."

Excellence Is the Only Bottom Line

A major part of that legacy mind-set stems from Achen-Gardner's commitment to the highest standards of quality and customer service, the bedrock values of the company. Effectively serving clients requires quality personnel, hands-on management, and superior management control systems, all of which Achen-Gardner incorporates in every decision. Gardner puts it this way: "There is no secret to our success. Giving the customer the best job for their money is at the root of everything we do. They come to us the first time because of the price; they come back because we give them more than they pay for." Achen, company president, echoes Gardner with a profound understanding of the obvious connection between good employees and satisfied clients: "Our employees make it possible. We recognize that it is the field people who create much of our success. We can bid all day long, but if the project doesn't get done right and on time, no one wins. As managers, our style is to walk around, keep our eyes open, ask questions, and really listen. We are proactive so that problems are solved before they happen."

Greatest Asset

Although many companies strive for quality and customer service, Achen-Gardner sets itself apart by the way the company delivers on these values. At the heart of the company's strategy are people and relationships. By attracting and retaining the best staff, subcontractors, and equipment suppliers, the firm is able to deliver on customer service and enjoy repeat business in a way that few other companies can. A unique example of this is the way that Achen-Gardner seeks to foster and reward an entrepreneurial spirit among its employees. Says Achen, "We search for the best people, then give them the tools and authority to do their jobs well. Our division managers would probably be running their own companies if they didn't work for us. We provide excellent profit sharing and good benefits, but money in itself isn't enough. People also want increased opportunities. Our managers are entrepreneurs who don't want to take the big risk on their own, but who want an opportunity to reach their professional potential." This philosophy creates satisfied employees, and enables Achen-Gardner— through the retention of quality management and a skilled labor force who have many years of experience working together— to deliver consistent quality for its clients. Those hard-earned relationships lead to more and bigger projects in the future, keeping the wheels turning.

Giving Back: The Mark of Integrity

Sharing its success with the communities that have helped it grow, Achen-Gardner contributes to projects that help people in need. Working with the City of Casa Grande and Seeds of Hope, a non-profit organization, Achen-Gardner contributed labor at cost to a project called Casa de Ensueno, a subdivision for low-income families who contributed sweat equity until all the homes and a neighborhood park were completed. Annually, Achen-Gardner

also sponsors the Achen-Gardner/Chandler Horizon Rotary Club Hole-In-One Contest, which raises money for local East Valley charities and youth scholarships. Whether serving clients or their community, Achen-Gardner's work ethic means putting people first.

Out in Front for Good

In a society where consumers increasingly have to make a choice between the very best product and golden-rule customer service, Achen-Gardner's outstanding commitment in both areas is redefining the construction industry in Arizona. Add visionary leadership and ever increasing annual sales figures, and you have a solid company that will lead its industry into the 21st century, always ahead of whatever the future holds. "This company will go as far as we can take it," adds Gardner with enthusiasm. "We just provide the right tools and trust our team to make it happen."

Clockwise from top left:
Beauty and technology come together in a downtown Phoenix streetscape project.

The framing division makes sure every wall is perfect.

The Achen-Gardner management team includes (clockwise from top left) Jeff Coffman, Doug Gardner, Sanders Achen, Dennis Troggio, Dean Sandell, Lynton Leslie, and Kelly Huston.

When Achen and Gardner joined their talents to start their own contracting services company in the early 1980s, their visionary blend of cutting-edge technology and an "always exceed their expectations" business philosophy began a dynamic company that is now the pacesetter for construction in the Valley of the Sun.

DEI PROFESSIONAL SERVICES

DEI Professional Services features a team of skilled, experienced professionals who go wherever and whenever they are needed to provide their clients with technologically advanced civil engineering project services. This team is the backbone of DEI, helping it grow to the eighth-largest civil engineering and land surveying firm in Greater Phoenix. ❧ This multidisciplined firm provides a full spectrum of services, including planning, project management, surveying and mapping, flatland and hillside residential and resort design, commercial site design, sanitary engineering, water resources, transportation, and infrastructure design.

DEI has grown consistently since it was founded in 1982, and is annually ranked as one of the top 25 engineering firms in the Valley by the *Business Journal*. Today, the firm's staff of 60 is comprised of civil engineers, designers, draftsmen, surveyors, and an administrative support team, with a second office in Irvine to serve California clients.

DEI is strategically positioned to broaden the scope of its operations. Historically providing services within the Southwest, the firm now services clients nationwide.

Dedicated to a Team Approach

Strong dedication to a team approach works well for DEI. In fact, 90 percent of its business comes from repeat clients or referrals, enabling its revenue and staff to double in size since 1993. The firm prides itself on its experience and ability to respond to unusual challenges. Whether it is the rough terrain of a hillside residence or a sprawling commercial site with unique requirements in an urban area, DEI's team is there to serve. Clients include many state and county governments in the Greater Phoenix metropolitan area, as well as AlliedSignal Inc., Bank One, Del Webb's Coventry Homes, Opus West Corporation, MCO Properties Inc., Motorola, Inc., and Ryan Companies U.S., Inc., among others.

Keeping up with leading-edge technology and training employees to take the fullest advantage of these technological advances are ongoing goals at DEI. Technology is integrated into every phase of production, helping the firm provide efficient, cost-effective services. DEI's global positioning system, for example, can contour a surface as fast as a vehicle can drive over it. With automatic tracking stations, one person can do the work of an entire survey crew to collect map data and stake a construction site.

The firm's sophisticated in-house document management system can scan and print materials at a rapid pace, including information gathered by the global positioning system, making data available instantly to all team members anywhere. Clients also have access to the output via the Internet.

The Firm of Choice

"We strive to be the firm of choice for skilled employees, strategic allies, and clients whenever civil engineering services are needed," Peter Vesecky, P.E., R.L.S., president of DEI, says. "We believe that keeping on top of technology is a strategic key to attaining that goal, supporting our commitment to quality and excellence in everything we do."

As an example, each year DEI takes its special technological capabilities to the Professional Golf Association's Phoenix Open Golf Tournament, surveying measurements to determine the $15,000 winner of the Closest to the Pin competition on the 15th hole of the Tournament Players Club in Scottsdale. Combining high-precision electronic total stations with traditional trigo-

Clockwise from top right:
Equipped with advanced technology like the global positioning system and auto tracking robotic stations, DEI survey crews can rapidly collect mapping data and coordinates of features on any site.

At the Phoenix Open's Closest to the Pin competition, DEI combines high-precision electronic total stations with traditional trigonometry, thereby computing distances within .01-foot accuracy and within 60 seconds from the time the golf ball lands.

President Peter Vesecky (right) joined with employees and valued clients to host the firm's first annual golf tournament in 1995 to raise funds for the Chrysalis Shelter of Phoenix. Since that year, the tournament has become an annual event to support a worthy charity within the Phoenix community.

▲ M. ELLER

nometry, distances are computed within .01-foot accuracy without ever stepping onto the green and within 60 seconds from the time the golf ball lands. DEI also provides high-detail, color digital imaging to help tournament organizers create a format for event planning. Output from a global positioning system is coordinated with aerial photographs to determine the best places for tents, staging areas, television towers, ATMs, ice machines, and whatever else is needed for the world's best-attended golf event.

Always Improving

Always striving for excellence, DEI conducts both internal and external surveys, designed to improve the firm and the services it offers. Besides looking for ways to be profitable and to nurture a growing client base, Vesecky has worked to create an environment that attracts and retains some of the industry's best and brightest professionals. He actively encourages them to achieve personal and professional goals, and employees describe DEI's environment as one where each individual has the opportunity to succeed.

"Our approach values the contributions of each person assigned to a project," Vesecky says. "Innovative solutions thrive in this environment, and our professionals, technicians, and staff have an opportunity to grow as well."

The firm's management style encourages every team member to be responsible for quality, not just the person in charge of the project, so its commitment to client satisfaction is easier to fulfill. Vesecky himself exemplifies DEI's commitment to excellence. Throughout his career, he has been involved in the community and in his profession. He has served as an adjunct faculty member at Arizona State University, where he earned a bachelor of science degree in civil engineering and a master's degree in environmental/water resource engineering. He was president of the Arizona Society of Civil Engineers in 1995 and 1996. Vesecky is a Registered Land Surveyor in Arizona and a Registered Professional Engineer in Arizona, California, Colorado, New Mexico, Nevada, Utah, and Idaho. He serves as principal engineer or quality control manager on all DEI projects.

DEI Professional Services prides itself on adding value to client projects, and looks forward to continuing to serve its clients' needs, always searching for better ways to do what it already does well.

Clockwise from top left:
DEI has provided civil engineering, structural engineering, and land surveying services for several AlliedSignal Engines Division buildings in Arizona.

Specializing in both flatland and hillside residential developments, DEI provided the civil engineering, surveying, and construction phase services for the quiet hillside community of SunCor.

The six-story, 125-room Sumner Suites hotel enjoyed its grand opening in 1997, and is one of two Sumner Suites facilities for which DEI has provided civil engineering, structural engineering, and surveying services.

The Motorola Flat Panel Display is one of several Motorola manufacturing facilities for which DEI has provided its full spectrum of services.

The 2,300-acre community of Grayhawk includes two championship golf courses, residential developments, commercial sites, schools, a hospital, and a world-class resort. DEI provided the residential subdivision designs, roadway designs and improvements, clubhouse civil design, and drainage analysis for both golf courses.

AMERICA WEST AIRLINES

A winning formula that includes full service, low fares, dedicated employees, and strong community support makes America West Airlines one of the nation's celebrated success stories. The "hometown airline" of Greater Phoenix, America West is the nation's ninth-largest carrier and has coast-to-coast schedules that include more than 600 daily flights, serving major destinations across the United States and parts of Canada and Mexico. ☙ The airline operates an effective hub-and-spoke system that

serves more than 77 destinations, with hubs located in Phoenix, Las Vegas, and Columbus, Ohio. America West serves 75 destinations with convenient nonstop service, more than any other carrier flying out of the Valley of the Sun. A strategic alliance with Continental Airlines provides customers with expanded domestic travel options, while code sharing arrangements with Northwest Airlines, Air China, and the Taiwanese carrier EVA accommodate passengers who are traveling to Asia. America West also has an agreement with British Airways for international travelers going to Europe. In partnership with Mesa Airlines, America West Express serves smaller markets such as Flagstaff or Fresno and eight destinations in the Colorado ski country.

Full Service, Low Fares

"Offering full service—but still generating competition with low fares—is one of the great benefits this airline brings to business and leisure travelers alike," says C.A. Howlett, vice president of public affairs. "Phoenix has among the lowest average passenger fare per mile of most major hubs." Being an affordable and easy-to-reach destination encourages businesses, convention meeting planners, and tourists to look toward Greater Phoenix as a desirable place to visit or conduct business.

An annual flight study by *Frequent Flyer* magazine and J.D. Power and Associates has ranked America West Airlines the nation's number one carrier for customer satisfaction for flights of 500 miles or less two years in a row. "In addition to being

number one, we improved in nine of the 10 categories that contributed to the overall satisfaction rating, and we significantly improved our performance in the long-haul category," says Howlett.

America West also ranked first in baggage handling among the 10 major airlines in the *1997 Air Travel Consumer Report* published by the U.S. Department of Transportation. The airline's highly advanced laser baggage system can shuttle baggage to a flight departing Phoenix from one of its 35 gates in 11 minutes or less.

Growing Steadily

The airline is a wholly owned subsidiary of America West Holdings Corporation, a $2 billion aviation and travel services company trading on the New York Stock

America West operates a modern, fuel-efficient fleet of aircraft, equipped with state-of-the-art safety features. The carrier's fleet includes Airbus A320 and A319 and Boeing 757 and 737.

Exchange under the symbol AWA. The airline initiated service on August 1, 1983, with three aircraft and 280 employees, and has grown to 111 aircraft and more than 12,000 employees systemwide, with more than 8,500 based in the Valley. America West's payroll and direct and secondary expenditures bring more than $850 million into the local economy annually. Total economic impact, including passengers' spending, is $3.3 billion a year. America West also supports a wide variety of charitable organizations and civic activities in the cities it serves through financial and in-kind support to health and human services, arts and culture, education, and the environment.

America West is dedicated to continuing its growth as a safe, full-service airline that offers low, affordable fares. By 2002, the airline intends to have more than 300 flights a day scheduled at Sky Harbor International Airport, 80 percent of which will be increased frequency to major markets such as Los Angeles, Boston, Baltimore, Chicago, Atlanta, Dallas, San Francisco, and Washington, D.C.

As America West Airlines positions itself to move into the 21st century, it maintains a strong commitment to its customers, reaffirming its status as a national success story.

FlightFund, America West's frequent-flyer program, offers travelers a unique and flexible program featuring First Class upgrade and worldwide award travel. FlightFund has attracted and maintained the loyalty of frequent travelers since 1987.

PRIMARY ELECTRIC COMPANY

n 1983, two men, armed only with an entrepreneurial spirit, two pickup trucks, and very little money, put their experiences to work and added another page to the classic American business story. Thomas J. Said, CEO, and his retired partner, Nello Rosato, started Primary Electric Company with four people: Robert Hale, Ray Crouch, Jerry Shiflet, and Eileen Murphy, all of whom continue to be a part of the strength of the company. Since then, Primary Electric's income has grown to $30 million annually and the payroll now lists some 350

employees. In addition to providing commercial and industrial electrical services and engineering/system design, the company maintains 24-hour on-call service for commercial, industrial, and residential needs.

Wiring the Valley of the Sun

Primary Electric has been involved with a wide variety of major construction projects in Arizona. In the past five years, the economic growth in the Phoenix area has skyrocketed. This, coupled with excellent management skills, dedicated employees, and a superior knowledge of the trade, has allowed Primary Electric to maintain rank among the top five electrical contractors in the state. With opportunity knocking, Primary Electric is also preparing to take the industry lead with the highly anticipated projected Wall Street expansion of the Valley. Scottsdale Fashion Square, Factory Outlet Mall in New River, Wyle Distribution Facility, Estrella Community College Campus, Mayo Clinic, and the Phoenician Resort are but a few of the projects in the Valley that the company is proud to have completed so far. Primary Electric is looking to the future of the company by becoming a major presence in Arizona with the resources and flexibility to reach customers all over the state—from the new ABCO stores in Tucson to projects contracted by the company's Northern Division office in Flagstaff, such as the Grand Canyon Hotel and the Coconino County Jail.

Said expanded his horizons in 1993. With his brother, John D. Said, National Electric Corp. was formed to pursue new

opportunities by targeting a different share of the construction marketplace. Again, in 1994, this time partnered with Vincent E. Gagliardi, vice president of construction for Primary Electric, Primary Cabling was founded to keep in step with customer needs for data communications and fiber optics.

A powerful team is required to manage a successful business. For example,

under Said's progressive leadership and the continual evaluation of asset management by Susan Millard, CFO, Primary Electric averages a growth pattern of 30 to 50 percent annually.

Start with the Right People

As attested by Said, "We started out just to make a living and do a better job than most. We wanted people to come to work for us and stay forever, so that we could build a business with a good reputation and reasonably good future. But, in this business, as in many others, you have to prove yourself over and over again. It takes dedicated and trusted people, working for the company to do better at what they already do very well. I sincerely recognize that people are the company's single largest asset."

Finding the right people is the largest challenge faced by Primary Electric. According to Said, "Most of our new hires are young and just beginning careers in the electrical field. By developing our youth, we are putting more complete, well-trained

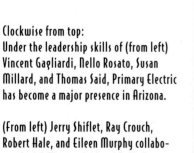

Clockwise from top:
Under the leadership skills of (from left) Vincent Gagliardi, Nello Rosato, Susan Millard, and Thomas Said, Primary Electric has become a major presence in Arizona.

(From left) Jerry Shiflet, Ray Crouch, Robert Hale, and Eileen Murphy collaborated with Thomas Said and Nello Rosato to create Primary Electric Company in 1983.

This Southwest Airlines hangar is just one example of Primary Electric's quality work.

journeymen and foremen out into the state of Arizona." Primary Electric Company's apprenticeship instruction begins with a basic in-house class on electricity, as well as on-the-job training continuing for 12 weeks. "At this point," states Said, "people know if the electrical trade is where they want to be and we can invest in their education. Everyone wins. We also bring in experts in the industry to instruct our journeymen and foremen on the latest products in the marketplace, such as lighting, fire/security alarms, and electrical distribution equipment."

Incentive programs and company benefits are always being tested and improved. Employees of the month receive a bonus for quality work. Safety and absentee programs provide monthly recognition.

The company's goal is to build personal relationships that last. A monthly newsletter communicates company happenings and accomplishments. Company-sponsored activities throughout the year stimulate the family tradition inherent to the business. In the fall there is a company picnic, and at Christmas, a dinner is held for everyone, with awards for outstanding employees. One highlight every year is called Kid's Day, when children and families of all the company employees are joined by homeless children in the Valley for a huge carnival.

Giving Back

Primary Electric Company and all of its employees support the Thomas J. Said Foundation. "This is a charitable foundation," remarks Said. "I had an idea and put it to

work; the other founders put my name on it." The Thomas J. Said Foundation buys a house each year and employees, along with their families, volunteer to renovate and furnish it, and then give it away to a needy family. Local radio personalities publicize the house so people can apply to be considered, and the new owner is given the key on the first Saturday in December. The foundation, like the business, is dedicated to encouraging and helping people who want to help themselves.

Always looking for ways to go to the next level, Said repeats, "It takes dedicated people doing better at what they already do very well. We want to go as far and as fast as our people can take us and still maintain standards of quality. We'll never stop growing and evolving."

STMICROELECTRONICS

The name may have changed over the years, but the core values of STMicroelectronics, a company with more than half a century of semiconductor manufacturing experience, are the same. Today's STMicroelectronics was formed in 1987 when Thomson Semiconducteurs combined forces with SGS Microlettronica, both of which trace their roots to pioneering semiconductor companies founded in the 1950s. Known for a time as SGS-Thomson Microelectronics, the worldwide entity changed its name to STMicroelectronics in May 1998.

The organization today is a global enterprise with 28,000 employees, nine advanced research and development units, 31 design and application centers, 17 manufacturing sites, and 57 sales offices in 23 countries. With net revenues of more than $4 billion in 1997, STMicroelectronics is the world's 10th-largest semiconductor manufacturing company.

STMicroelectronics offers a broad, balanced portfolio for a multitude of applications. Offering more than 3,000 different products to its customers, STMicroelectronics designs, develops, manufactures, and markets a broad range of high-growth applications in the communications, computer peripherals, consumer, automotive, and industrial sectors.

The 18-acre Arizona campus has become one of STMicroelectronics' major multi-product facilities for making eight-inch wafers, which individually yield hundreds of silicon chips for customers' specific needs (top).

STMicroelectronics chips are used in a variety of automotive applications (bottom).

Coming to Phoenix

The company's association with Phoenix began in 1980 when Pasquale Pistorio, then living in the city as worldwide marketing manager for Motorola Inc., was hired as chief executive officer to breathe new life into SGS-ATES Semiconductor Corp. As part of the company's subsequent expansion, the Phoenix facility was completed in 1983 to house a design center, as well as the U.S. sales and marketing group. Later, a 285,000-square-foot fabricating complex was added to produce semiconductor silicon wafers.

The 18-acre Arizona campus has since become one of STMicroelectronics' major multiproduct facilities for making eight-inch wafers, which individually yield hundreds of silicon chips for customers' specific needs. It is also the central shipping point for products packaged in Europe and the Asia-Pacific region, and distributed to customers across the United States.

Breadth of Customers and Products

More than 1,500 customers—including Chrysler, Delco, Ford, General Instruments, Alcatel, Ericsson, Bose, Hewlett-Packard, IBM, Motorola, Nokia, Nortel, Sony, Philips, Western Digital, and Seagate—look to STMicroelectronics for cost-efficient, well-designed semiconductor components that make their own products perform faster and better. The company's commitment to industry expertise through ongoing research and development supports a broad line of dedicated products developed and manufactured in strategic partnerships with a number of its customers.

In the past decade alone, STMicroelectronics has significantly broadened and upgraded its range of products and technologies, while strengthening its manufacturing and distribution capabilities in Europe, the Asia-Pacific region, and the United States. The company is also in the phase of building new eight-inch-submicron plants around the world to augment the current eight-inch-wafer-manufacturing facilities.

STMicroelectronics is considered a world leader in both discrete and integrated power semiconductors that address such applications as computer printers and automotive and storage applications. In fact, STMicroelectronics is on the forefront of developing system-level integrated chips to operate handheld computers, game consoles, Internet phones, and other network appliances. This new technology will replace the more numerous and expensive chips currently used in these applications.

The company's superintergrated "system-on-a-chip" allows a complete system with full functionality to be built with substantial savings. These system chips can also be readily tailored to offer even greater cost benefits to specific high-volume applications.

"Potential customers are already creating prototype systems to use this chip as well as other integrated silicon," says Richard Pieranunzi, president and CEO of the Americas region. "As we break down existing cost barriers, we're enabling the creation of entirely new, high-volume markets. It's good for our business, good for our customers, and good for the consumer."

Excellence Pays Off

The company's success over the years can be traced in part to its commitment to creating an integrated presence wherever it goes, taking into account local needs and cultures in each marketplace. Additionally, STMicroelectronics is known for its long-term commitment to total quality management (TQM) principles in one of the most competitive high-tech areas of today's business world. Boasting ISO 9001 certification, the organization has been recognized by *Industry Week* and *Upside* magazines as one of the world's best companies. And in 1997, STMicroelectronics received the prestigious European Quality Award for innovation, customer service, employee involvement, market share, profitability, and impact on society.

For STMicroelectronics, productivity begins with people. From inception, the

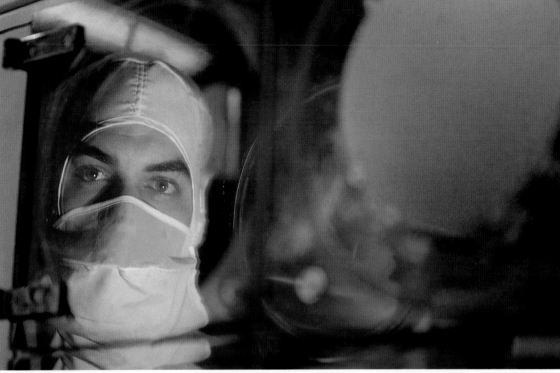

company recognized the tremendous asset represented by its employees, and made the commitment to place them squarely at the center of the enterprise. Putting the maximum emphasis on its human resources, STMicroelectronics invests in training and education to empower its people and unlock the enormous value embodied in their talent, creativity, and energy. As a result, the employees made the important transition from being actors to factors in the company's success. "One of the elements that sets us apart is our people," says Pieranunzi. "Our workforce

is cosmopolitan and diverse, a rich mix of talent."

The natural consequence of employee empowerment has been an increase in the productivity of the company's human resources, and of its operational and financial resources, as well. This has been aided by a TQM effort that permeates every aspect of the enterprise. The five key principles of this successful TQM effort are customer focus, employee empowerment, continuous improvement, fact-based decision making, and management commitment. But, above all, it is employee involvement and commitment, and not an abstract set of methodologies or processes, that make TQM work for STMicroelectronics and its customers.

Clockwise from top:
STMicroelectronics is known for its long-term commitment to total quality management principles in one of the most competitive high-tech areas of today's business world.

STMicroelectronics is considered a world leader in both discrete and integrated power semiconductors that address such applications as computer printers and automotive and storage applications.

Many semiconductor devices are manufactured on an eight-inch silicon wafer. These devices are tested, cut from the wafer, and typically packaged in multi-pin plastic packages.

EFDATA

EFData, now known as Adaptive Broadband Corporation, is one example of the fast-growth, high-technology businesses that are an integral part of the Valley of the Sun's economy. EFData's products provide critical communications connections from the farthest reaches of the Arctic Circle to the most remote earth stations in Antarctica, and everywhere in between. Today, EFData is the world's leading producer of digital satellite modems and radios, holding, on average, more than twice the market share

of its next-largest competitor. The company operates globally and its equipment is installed in almost every country in the world.

Growing with the Valley of the Sun

Founded in 1984, EFData quickly developed a reputation in the satellite communications industry for designing and manufacturing high-quality, error-free products. Error Free Choice, the company slogan, is the core of the company's philosophy and the standard by which products are manufactured.

EFData manufactures point-to-multipoint broadcast access equipment that is used in satellite-based communications services to reach users on land, at sea, or in the air. By transmitting data via satellite, communications can be delivered to isolated and remote regions that are typically outside the reach of traditional landline telephone service. Earthbound networks traditionally use wire connections, fiber optics, or microwave linking, while satellite networks—not limited by challenging terrain—can provide a practical, effective

communications solution. Equipment can be set up in a day, in contrast to the months and years necessary to build a landline network. Today, many remote communities are linked with the outside world, thanks to innovative contributions from EFData's research and development team. In addition to point-to-multipoint broadcast access solutions, Adaptive Broadband Corporation offers solutions for digital TV, satellite IP infrastructure, and on-line transaction processing (OLTP).

The Arizona company is leveraging its product leadership in the satellite sector to expand its capabilities and presence in the explosively growing broadband data networking market, which is hungry for high-speed Internet access. Time Division Multiple Access (TDMA) technology, combined with EFData's network management systems, is allowing the company to rapidly penetrate the market for broadband data bandwidth-on-demand solutions for private networks and service providers.

EFData's Integrated Services Digital Network (ISDN) solution, driven by the explosive growth of the Internet, has been

a first step in providing broadband data capability for business customers. Satellite ISDN-on-demand has many applications, including videoconferencing, distance learning, telemedicine, file transfers, and circuit restoration.

EFData has experienced tremendous growth in the past decade, and the company continually works hard to ensure that its customers and employees remain the focus of the business. EFData places a high level of importance upon developing collaborative relationships with its customers. Cross-functional teams are developed to work with members from the customer's organization to ascertain their current and future communications needs. This allows the company to develop products that address customers' complex and diverse communications requirements.

"EFData's reputation and continued growth are built around meeting and exceeding our customers' expectations," says Bob Treasure, vice president of sales and marketing. "We're in an exciting, rapidly changing business, and we work to form true partnerships with our cus-

EFData equipment is used in satellite-based communications.

tomers to ensure that they get the communications solutions that serve their unique applications."

From the beginning, EFData's commitment to its customers has been to provide quality products at an affordable price with unequaled field reliability. From receiving to shipping, each employee is committed to promoting quality. The company's total commitment to quality is evident throughout the design and development stages, in its advanced manufacturing processes, and in its distinguished customer service program.

Though EFData is serious about its business, it also endeavors to maintain a relaxed environment that promotes creativity and innovation. The company sponsors many events for the employees, including company picnics, product rollout celebrations, holiday parties, and appreciation lunches.

This attitude has resulted in many creative, yet functional, solutions. One example of such solutions addressed the problem of the physical distance between the engineering staff and the lab technicians. The engineering staff is located on the second floor of the facility; however, the test lab is located directly below on the first floor. When tests are being run on equipment, it is important for an engineer to respond quickly to a test technician's call. Because of this need for rapid response, a fire pole that leads from the Engineering Department directly to the lab was installed. Now, engineers can respond to important test issues within seconds. Customers also enjoy taking a ride down the pole when they visit the facility. Those who are brave enough to do so are awarded with a fireman's hat and a T-shirt that touts their brave feat.

Growing with the Company

EFData is very proud of its employees' contributions to the company. Many of the company's employees have been with the firm from the onset, and have grown both personally and professionally as the company has grown.

Frederick Castillo has been employed with EFData for more than eight years. He is the group leader for the RF/Microwave Product Chassis Group, and is responsible for ensuring that the products flow smoothly through the factory and that the product that ships to the customer is configured correctly.

Castillo has worked his way up in the organization. He started with EFData in a nontechnical position in the maintenance department. As he gained experience, Castillo was promoted to positions in other departments. He has held positions in the Shipping, Mechanical, and Prep departments, and appreciates the on-the-job training opportunities he has gained at EFData. Castillo enjoys the company of the people he works with and feels that they are like a family. He looks forward to the opportunities that are ahead of him at EFData.

Connecting with Family

One EFData employee, David Hoang, recently was afforded an opportunity to travel to his homeland, Vietnam, for a business trip for EFData. Hoang was a pilot

Employees get involved at the company-sponsored events (left).

Val Rhodes, an EFData engineer, takes a shortcut to the lab.

for his country in the Vietnam War; however, when the war ended, he fled the country to the United States. Due to his hurried escape from Vietnam, he was not able to let his family know his plans. After many years of waiting for his return from the war, the family lost hope and accepted that Hoang was another casualty.

Hoang used the opportunity of the business trip with EFData to search for his family. He made many inquiries to find the whereabouts of his family, and was eventually informed that they lived in Hanoi, about 80 miles from their original home. Hoang was able to locate his mother, brothers, sister, and their families—in all, 14 family members. Upon their first introduction, the family reached out to touch Hoang to make sure he was not just an illusion. All of these years, the family had relentlessly searched for his downed plane to no avail. Now, 21 years later, he stood before them.

Clockwise from top right:
Frederick Castillo and Bao Tran benefit from on-the-job training.

David Hoang is seen here with his manager, Gary Langguth.

Robert Martinez, Harold McGuire, Danny Garcia, and Carlos Ceballos make sure shipments get out the door.

Generations of Growth

As the main company receptionist for EFData for many years, Yoli Martinez was a friendly and welcoming voice to all of the firm's customers. In her eight years as the company receptionist, Martinez always made sure that customers received exceptional attention. Though everyone agreed that Martinez did an outstanding job as the company receptionist, she was also interested in developing a career with the company. In 1997, Martinez was promoted to a position in Human Resources. Since then, she has taken on additional responsibilities, and has returned to school to get her business degree with the help of EFData's tuition assistance program.

But Martinez is just one of the generations of families employed with EFData. Her daughter, Maritza, has been employed with the organization part-time for two years while she works toward her degree in marketing at Arizona State University. Maritza has also grown with EFData. She started out filling in for departments as they needed clerical support, and has since moved on to the Marketing Department, where she is gaining extensive experience in her field of interest.

Growing through Community Involvement

Although EFData is a global organization, it has close ties to the community. Because the company is one of the 10 largest employers in the Valley, it has a vested interest in supporting community events and charitable organizations.

Each year, EFData participates in the Muscular Dystrophy Association's MS Bike Ride for the local chapter. In addition to the funds that are raised through pledges to the riders, EFData also sponsors a bike team made up primarily of EFData employees. As some of the firm's employees have personal experiences with the crippling effects of this disease, this important cause receives considerable support.

The company also participates in monthly blood drives. Over the years, the firm has donated many pints of blood to area blood banks. This is one more way EFData gives back to the community.

Looking to the Future

Changing technologies offer EFData major opportunities to participate in projects in the telecommunications industry for both commercial and government applications. With unparalleled research and development facilities, EFData continues to supply the industry with the best per-

forming satellite communications equipment available in the marketplace today. The increasing convergence of satellite and terrestrial wireless systems means more growth and exceptional business opportunities for the Tempe-based manufacturer. By building on its established

processes of continuous improvement, commitment to quality, and a tradition of customer satisfaction, EFData is prepared to continue in its role as the leader in developing and supplying the industry's best-performing satellite communications equipment to the world.

Clockwise from top left:
Marie Handrahan of the accounting department participates in the yearly MS Bike Ride.

Employees gather to sign EFData's Commitment to Quality poster.

Yoli and Maritza Martinez represent two generations of employees that are growing with the company.

FORT McDOWELL CASINO

hen the 25,000-acre Fort McDowell Indian Reservation was created on September 15, 1903 to provide a home to the Yavapai, Mohave-Apache, and Apache tribes, there were no slot machines or neon lights. Even the most die-hard poker players could not have foreseen anything close to the spectacular, 150,000-square-foot Fort McDowell Casino that now attracts around 10,000 visitors every day. Known as The Fort, the facility offers 475 slot

machines, live keno, high-stakes bingo, pari-mutuel wagering, and one of Arizona's finest card rooms. More than 950 employees are dedicated to seeing that casino customers enjoy themselves seven days a week, 24 hours a day. Numbers swell to more than 30,000 during the Fourth of July and other special events when headline entertainers perform, and fireworks light up the evening sky above the Sonoran Desert.

Sovereignty Day

Following passage of the Indian Gaming Regulatory Act of 1988, the Fort McDowell Indian Community opened the first casino in the state, offering keno and video bingo in a 17,000-square-foot building. Initially led by a private management group, the tribe bought out the group's interest in 1991.

Though the casino simply provides an entertaining diversion for the public, it creates an economic development tool for 852 tribal members. Therefore, when federal agents seized 349 gaming machines on May 12, 1992, by order of a governor opposed to Native American gaming, tribal members banded together. Witnesses issued a community call to action, and every available car, truck, and piece of heavy machinery blockaded the casino access road, trapping the federal moving

vans in a three-week, nonviolent standoff. As a result, the governor signed a compact with the tribe, paving the way for Native American gaming in Arizona. May 12 is now an official tribal holiday known as Sovereignty Day.

Entertainment, Excitement, and Fun

The Fort meets casino customers' wants and needs by providing entertainment, excitement, and fun in a clean, secure environment. First-time players receive a fun kit with special incentive coupons to encourage them to try different gaming choices.

If poker is the customer's favorite game, he or she can stop by the Card Room and discover the widest variety of favorites, including seven-card stud, hold'em, and Omaha. Customers will

always find prompt, chair-side food and beverage service.

The state-of-the-art Bingo Hall is a bingo player's paradise, featuring more than 1,400 seats with an enclosed non-smoking area, free beverages, and free service at the bingo tables. Bingo action is definitely at The Fort.

There are 475 machines located in a beautiful and spacious setting. The Fort has a wide variety of slots, video keno, and video poker. If keno is the customer's favorite game, then he or she can take advantage of the live keno lounge where players have the chance to win up to $50,000. In the Turf Club, customers can watch the Thoroughbreds and greyhounds break out of the gates on one of the 18 big-screen TVs. While they enjoy the sport of kings, they can eat dinner in the Rotisserie.

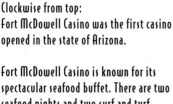

Clockwise from top:
Fort McDowell Casino was the first casino opened in the state of Arizona.

Fort McDowell Casino is known for its spectacular seafood buffet. There are two seafood nights and two surf and turf nights that bring in thousands of people on a weekly basis.

The Fort meets casino customers' wants and needs by providing entertainment, excitement, and fun in a clean, secure environment.

▲ MICHAEL WANAT

If the customer is looking for a special place to dine, Fort McDowell Casino has one of the finest buffets in the Valley of the Sun. The Red Rock Café features a delicious seafood buffet two nights a week with peel-and-eat shrimp and unlimited crab legs. If seafood is not the customer's favorite, there are always Mexican, Chinese, or surf and turf nights.

Supporting the Community

The Verde River runs through the reservation, and its banks are home to an assortment of wildlife and plants, notably the majestic saguaro cactus. Revenues from the casino build houses on this land, and improve the community infrastructure of streets and utilities. The casino also pays for a police department, a library, health care, and social services. A multimillion-

dollar fund was authorized in 1995 to provide low-interest loans for new and expanding businesses both on and off the reservation.

Income from the casino also furthers education in the community, building

MICHAEL WANAT

schools and providing scholarships for students wanting to continue their studies. Outside of Fort McDowell, the tribe has supported education with contributions of more than $1 million in scholarship funds to Arizona's three state universities. These scholarships create lifelong learning experiences for tribal members while maintaining cultural heritage and traditions.

Plans for the next century begin with a park for recreational vehicles, a destination resort, a golf course, and a live entertainment venue along the Beeline Highway in the shadow of the dominating Four Peaks. As Fort McDowell moves forward with its economic goals, it also ensures an optimistic outlook for its people while contributing to the local and state economy.

Clockwise from top:
The majestic Harris hawk is just one variety of wildlife in abundance at Fort McDowell.

Native American dancers such as the eagle dancer are among the many entertainers at Fort McDowell Casino's special events.

The Sonoran Desert provides a home to the 25,000-acre Fort McDowell Indian Reservation, which was created in 1903.

FORT MCDOWELL CASINO

Linthicum Constructors, Inc.

Building one-of-a-kind public and commercial structures—as well as exquisite custom homes—is the business of Linthicum Constructors, Inc., a full-service general contracting firm servin the Southwest since 1984. ❦ The building roots of the Linthicum family run deep. From th three Welsh carpenters who landed on the shores of Maryland in 1654 to the accomplishe contractor responsible for many of Arizona's notable modern-day landmarks, the Linthicum

name represents the essence of the truly professional builder.

The company has made its mark in several Valley markets and has carved a niche in the health care construction industry. Within the Linthicum management team alone, there are more than 50 years of health care construction experience. Over the years, Linthicum has built hospitals, family medicine clinics, women's centers, CT scan rooms, and respiratory therapy rooms. In addition, it has remodeled emergency rooms, open-heart surgical rooms, and a neurological center.

"We understand and respect the delicate environment within a medical facility, and we know how important it is for a construction crew to work in harmony with that environment and not as an intruder," explains Gary Linthicum, founder and president of Linthicum Constructors.

Building Lasting Partnerships

In starting a new project, Linthicum Constructors works hard to be involved in the schematic design. "What sets us apart is a genuine interest in being a true partner with the owners," says Linthicum. "This has provided us with many repeat business opportunities.

"We specialize in building on land that is unique to this area, such as in and around boulders and on mountainside properties," say Linthicum. "We pay particular attention to how a structure will ultimately rest on a property. And we are always looking for new solutions and new ideas."

This search for new solutions and new ideas is evident in the company's

The corporate headquarters for Linthicum Constructors, Inc. demonstrates a unique palette of materials and craftsmanship, all compatible with the desert environment it graces.

headquarters located in the Perimeter Center in North Scottsdale. A spectacular concrete entry wall welcomes visitors, clearly demonstrating the company's appreciation and use of natural materials. "This building is who we are," Linthicum says. Inside, polished concrete floors, stained and buffed to a bright patina resembling fine

leather, complement a custom-designed table with a rebar base in the conference room. Interesting curved walls and irregular spaces continue throughout the building.

The Linthicum headquarters represent the essence of the firm's philosophy of providing clients with projects that enhance their business, serve their communities,

Building the prestigious Troon North Country Club meant building around boulders, giant saguaros, and other native vegetation.

"We believe in each case the owner has the dream, the architect has the vision, and the builder must have the skill and talent to make that dream materialize. It's the most personal thing clients will ever go through with someone outside their family," Linthicum says, "so we try to make construction as enjoyable a process as possible."

To complete many of these truly unique homes, Linthicum partners with a variety of artisans for creative doors, cabinetry, and furnishings. Together, they create exquisite, one-of-a-kind homes in such distinguished communities as the Boulders, Biltmore, Paradise Valley, Desert Mountain, and Desert Highlands.

As Linthicum Constructors looks ahead to the future, the firm remains committed to following its well-defined business plan. "It's tempting to take on as much as possible, but our focus is not merely on growth," say Linthicum. "Meeting and exceeding the unique needs of each client remains our ultimate mission."

nd respect the delicate environment within and surrounding their structure.

While it may take extra time and care to protect a stately saguaro or a small, fragile prickly pear cactus on a desert site during construction, Linthicum considers it a priority. As recognition for these efforts, the Valley Forward Association awarded the company its coveted Crescordia Award for environmental excellence. Linthicum is proud of this honor that recognizes sensitivity to growth as well as professional accomplishment.

Stake in the Community

The company's craftsmanship—and its uncompromising dedication to quality and integrity—can also be seen in public gathering places throughout the Valley of the Sun, from the copper-roofed Troon North Country Club set in the pristine Sonoran Desert to the Third Street Bridge and Symphony Hall Deck in downtown Phoenix. The Scottsdale Baseball Stadium and a major expansion of the Scottsdale Civic Center Library also bear the Linthicum quality signature.

The company's dedication to sharing construction expertise with the community is evident in the Linthicum-built Desert House, an energy-efficient demonstration/experimental residence where a family lives on the grounds of the Desert Botanical Garden; and the Chrysalis Shelter for battered women in Scottsdale, for which the company donated time and materials.

Imaginative Residential Expertise

Ten years after the founding of Linthicum Constructors, a residential division was added after the direct urging of several Valley design professionals. These professionals wanted the quality in residential construction that Linthicum consistently demonstrated in its commercial projects. Linthicum consistently offered the skills,

know-how, and resources to bring imaginative—sometimes difficult—plans to life. For instance, one project involved two giant granite boulders forming a passage between the kitchen and the living room of a home, with the extra challenge of glass meeting the rock to form a window.

MARK BOISCLAIR

From top:
Scottsdale Stadium, located in the heart of downtown Scottsdale, has been referred to as a masterpiece by former Giants President Al Rosen.

Linthicum was recognized for its outstanding construction of the Scottsdale Civic Center Library expansion.

A beautiful single-story, contemporary, southwestern-style home is threaded among a natural desert setting and massive boulders.

Rowland Companies

A constant reminder of the timeless engineering feats and the exemplary craftsmanship achieved by ancient Egyptian builders, the pyramid logo of the Rowland Companies symbolizes the firm's goal of achieving excellence on each and every project. Rowland Companies is a full-service construction management and general contracting firm based in Greater Phoenix that serves clients throughout the West. It began as a commercial builder, specializing in health care facilities and religious campuses,

but the company has become known for its award-winning residential construction as well.

"Everything we do, our style, and our personality are reflected in our philosophy of achieving common goals with an uncommon commitment," says President Bill Rowland, who brings a lifetime of construction experience to the company.

Leading a Team Effort

Rowland Companies' services often begin by helping a client select the proper parcel of land and following through to completion of the entire project. "We are relationship based, and begin with that first handshake to develop a fair and trusting association with each client," Rowland says. Repeat business and referrals from satisfied clients account for most of the $50 million of construction business the firm does annually with its staff of 54 employees, including two generations of the Rowland family.

As development managers, the firm handles site development, infrastructure projects, and other real estate development activities. The company works with both owners and investors, offering total project management, cost estimation, scheduling, and environmental services. Rowland Companies has expertise in analyzing a site to determine whether it is appropriate for a particular project, and in looking at budget figures to make sensible, cost-effective recommendations.

Rowland Companies also offers construction management services for site development, infrastructure, and building projects. By coordinating work closely with design professionals, the firm routinely creates ways to deliver higher-quality projects at lower costs.

As general contractors, the firm leads the team effort when the assistance of qualified subcontractors is required to bring projects to completion on schedule and on budget. "We extend our philosophy of fairness and trust to the subcontractors we work with and to our suppliers," Rowland says, "and this tends to attract dedicated people who want to work with us."

Areas of Expertise

The company has an exceptional reputation for experience in creating religious campuses, which often require expertise in navigating community approval processes, as well as in planning and constructing the site. Rowland is building a fellowship family center for a 117-acre church campus in San Diego, and the firm is playing an integral part in the long-term development of the 150-acre Community Church of Joy master plan in Glendale, Arizona, the fastest-growing Lutheran Church in the nation. The firm serves the Lutheran congregation as construction manager for an ambitious, ongoing campus building plan scheduled for completion in 2015.

Rowland Companies has built specialty surgical hospitals, retirement housing,

In 1998, Rowland Companies' Apache Cottages project—a creative community of luxurious town homes in the Desert Mountain master-planned community—won the Best in the West Gold Nugget Award for attached homes of more than 1,800 square feet, competing with builders throughout the western United States and the Pacific Rim.

Rowland Companies began as a commercial builder, specializing in health care facilities and religious campuses, but the company has become known for its award-winning residential construction as well.

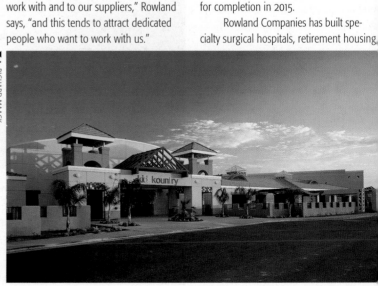

RICHARD MAACK

Rowland Custom Homes involves the future home owner in every decision affecting his or her new home, from site selection to the smallest finishing detail, and can offer experienced advice on building codes and planned community restrictions to assure compliance.

dementia units, skilled nursing facilities, and assisted-living units for a number of health care clients. The firm specializes in smaller facilities, often with about 20 patients to a unit. "We emphasize color and natural light for these projects," Rowland says. "This is where our business becomes interesting. We're always finding new ways to do things that help people thrive."

Rowland also has built schools, where the company tries to scale everything down to a child's size for an inviting learning atmosphere; corporate apartments to accommodate short-term business tenants; office and hotel properties; and other commercial and industrial facilities throughout the West. The firm looks for projects that encourage long-term working relationships and repeat business.

Rowland Custom Homes Inc. brings the company's reputation for honesty, integrity, and trust to the residential market. Rowland has managed the construction of custom homes in northeast Phoenix, Scottsdale, and Paradise Valley, ranging from $850,000 to $4 million in price. Rowland Custom Homes involves the future home owner in every decision affecting his or her new home, from site selection to the smallest finishing detail, and can offer experienced advice on building codes and planned community restrictions to assure compliance.

In 1998, Rowland's Apache Cottages project—a creative community of luxurious town homes in the Desert Mountain master-planned community—won the Best in the West Gold Nugget Award for attached homes of more than 1,800 square feet, competing with builders throughout the western United States and the Pacific Rim.

For clients who need their specialized expertise, Rowland also can provide litigation support, forensic investigations, and

RICHARD MAACK

expert testimony to property owners, surety companies, and attorneys concerning all phases of construction.

Giving Back to the Community

Contributing to the community is ingrained in the Rowland Companies' culture, and each year the firm selects opportunities to make a difference. "We believe that part of the heart of the community is in the arts," says Rowland. "The theater, the symphony, the art museum—they're an integral part of retaining the wholesomeness of our community." The company aided Horses Help, an organization that takes autistic and at-risk children horseback riding, as well as Christmas in April, which looks to the construction industry for volunteer labor and building expertise.

Rowland was selected as one of the inaugural builders in a competition creating custom playhouses to be auctioned to raise funds to help HomeAid Arizona renovate and build shelters for the transitionally homeless in the state.

Recently the company was presented with three awards for its Peter Pan's Pirate

Paradise playhouse. Rowland also participates in a special Christmas project that provides almost 500 gifts during the holidays for children in Nogales, Mexico.

"The good feeling of helping someone else helps bring us together internally as a company," Rowland says. "We encourage that."

RANDALL BOHL

SOUTHWEST GAS CORPORATION

outhwest Gas Corporation is the fastest-growing gas distribution company in the nation. It impressive numbers—1.2 million customers, more than 20,000 miles of pipeline—are a reflection o many factors. The desert Southwest is enjoying population growth and a healthy economy. Natural ga is clean energy. It's delivered through a safe and environmentally benign system. And Southwest Gas i a strong company of hardworking people who believe that service is the key to success—for themselves

the stockholders, and the communities in which they live.

It's this spirit that has enabled the company to become one of the many made-in-America success stories. Southwest Gas opened officially in 1931—not the most promising time to begin a business. But company founders were determined to follow through on the idea of distributing an energy source that could improve the lifestyle of home owners and help businesses thrive.

The first company employees sold bottled gas door-to-door in the dusty railroad town of Barstow. The company grew slowly and steadily over the next 20 years, switching to safer and more economical natural gas when the transcontinental pipeline was completed in the early 1950s.

About the same time, Southwest extended natural gas to industrial plants in Henderson, Nevada, and the fledgling Las Vegas gaming oasis. The company also entered the Arizona market in the 1950s with the purchase of a utility serving the cotton and copper region of central Arizona.

In 1979, acquisition of the gas system serving Tucson doubled the company's size overnight. Five years later, Southwest doubled its size again, purchasing natural gas properties in metropolitan Phoenix and surrounding communities.

"We bought the Phoenix system from a combination utility that emphasized electric energy," says Jim Lowman, senior vice president of the company's central Arizona division. "We started with a small market share and steadily built our business. Now,

85 percent of new homes in Greater Phoenix have the option of gas as a standard feature."

Part of the reason for Southwest's success is its focus on satisfying the customer. While many utility companies today are announcing that they have become customer driven, Southwest Gas long ago developed a customer-oriented culture. According to independent surveys, 95 percent of Southwest Gas customers are either satisfied or very satisfied with the service they received in 1997. In addition, a study on customer service by the University of Southern California rated Southwest Gas service as world class.

An investment in new technology is also helping enhance customer service. For example, the company has eliminated most paperwork in assigning orders to its nearly 90 service technicians. Each night around midnight, as many as 900 orders are sorted and routed with a computer keystroke. The next day, technicians at four locations around the Valley download the orders into handheld computer terminals.

Even customers themselves are taking advantage of technology by using the company's Web site on the Internet— www.swgas.com—to connect and disconnect service, or to make name changes to their accounts.

Clockwise from top:
Southwest Gas Corporation is proud of its customer service record. Instead of an automated, press-a-number answering system, friendly representatives answer all customer calls directly.

Company employees contribute thousands of volunteer hours to projects that improve the quality of life in Phoenix.

Natural gas fireplaces create the ambience of real wood, but require minimal care and are inexpensive, easy to use, and pollution free.

OPULENCE STUDIOS

Made in America

Another Southwest Gas priority is delivering gas safely and economically. And natural gas, with its underground pipeline network, has the most environmentally benign delivery system of the major energy supplies—no trucks, no trains, no tankers, and no overhead lines. Just an abundant, domestic product delivered to homes and businesses through a well-maintained network of underground pipelines. "It's safe, reliable, readily available, and made in America," says Lowman. "And because natural gas is also clean burning, it is well positioned to meet the challenges of today's marketplace."

Choosing Natural Gas

Because natural gas is clean energy, it is the perfect complement to today's lifestyle and business needs. For example, the natural gas that heats millions of homes and businesses, cooks our food, and generates electricity also powers more than 2,500 fleet vehicles throughout the Valley. Compared to gasoline or diesel, natural gas vehicles are cleaner, safer, and more economical. Southwest Gas has been a prime mover in this environmentally conscious shift, even opening a company fueling area to the public.

The versatility of natural gas is another reason it has been so popular in the marketplace, says Lowman. Precise temperature control for cooking and fast recovery time for water heaters are testaments to their efficiency. Now, though, natural gas appliances are also trend setting.

In fireplaces, for example, gas logs create the ambience of real wood with the advantages of minimal care, quick lighting,

and virtually no pollution. When the Maricopa Association of Governments adopted an ordinance requiring fireplaces in the county's new-home construction to be clean burning, natural gas logs easily met the test; also, the logs can be used on mandatory no-burn days.

Serving the Community

Technology, customer service, safety, and a strong product have contributed to the company's record-setting growth. But the foundation of Southwest Gas' success is its people. Individually, company employees serve on school boards and chambers of commerce, and contribute thousands of volunteer hours to improving the quality of life in their community. Working together through a volunteer team, they have renovated more than 40 houses, refurbished a homeless shelter's day care center, cleared neighborhood gardens, built a greenhouse at a senior center, adopted low-income families during the holidays, and worked with

the March of Dimes, United Way, Special Olympics, and Big Brothers /Big Sisters.

Clearly, the Southwest Gas focus is close to home—on the community and on customers. That emphasis will not change, even as the business adapts to issues such as utility deregulation and growth in the Southwest. "We are adding as many new customers each year as some gas companies in the East have in their entire service area," notes Lowman. "Managing under such circumstances is a challenge, but Southwest Gas anticipated the growth trend of the 1990s more than a dozen years ago. The company systematically planned and organized its workforce and infrastructure to ensure success. We're doing the same thing to meet the opportunities of deregulation."

Armed with its long-term plan of action and optimism about the future, Southwest Gas is well prepared to meet the needs of its customers now and for many years to come.

Clockwise from top:
Because natural gas is clean energy, it is becoming more and more popular as a vehicle fuel. Compressed natural gas currently powers more than 2,500 Phoenix-area fleet vehicles.

Since Southwest Gas entered the Phoenix market in 1984, the number of builders offering natural gas has soared.

The natural gas underground pipeline network is environmentally benign—no trucks, no trains, no tankers, and no overhead lines.

PARADISE VALLEY COMMUNITY COLLEGE

Paradise Valley Community College (PVCC), founded in August 1985, is dedicated to providing lifelong learning opportunities for its 6,500 students. One of the 10 Maricopa Community Colleges, PVCC provides a vital North Valley link in the largest multicollege district in the nation. ❦ PVCC offers flexible class schedules that provide instruction during the day, evening, and weekends to accommodate working students, who make up the majority of the student body. Academic information, including a class schedule, is available over the Internet at www.pvc.maricopa.edu, and students can register electronically.

Working with Business Partners

Class selections at PVCC are evaluated and improved continuously to meet the needs of students, businesses, and the community. Says PVCC President Raúl Cárdenas, "Ongoing partnerships with business and industry leaders assure that students in certificate and two-year degree programs are prepared for employment opportunities when they have completed their studies."

PVCC has teamed up with Microsoft, for instance, to become an official training center, offering certificate programs in computer information systems, networking, and maintenance that can lead to positions as network administrators and systems analysts.

The college's Center for International Studies offers associate degrees in international business and import/export trade, and has been designated a Regional Center for Asian Studies by the East-West Center in Hawaii. A full range of programs provides opportunities for student exchanges and international study for faculty and staff.

A growing demand for employees who are qualified to store, maintain, and dispose of hazardous materials prompted the college to create certificate and degree programs teaching practical technology as well as government compliance regulations. Similarly, a national trend toward the study of alternative or holistic health care encouraged the college to establish a certificate program in Asian Complementary Health Care Studies for doctors, nurses, and other interested health care professionals.

Postgraduate Opportunities

University transfer courses, including honors classes, lead to degrees in education, nursing, and engineering, all fully accredited by the Commission on Schools and Colleges of the North Central Association. Career work experience and cooperative education allow students to earn college credit through internships and other career-related positions in local companies.

Continuing education programs offer a wide selection of fine arts and special interest classes ranging from oil painting to the PVCC flute choir, to money management and estate planning, to ISO 9000 and ISO 14000 Quality System training.

Students are encouraged to become involved in campus activities through student government or one of the many organizations available to encourage special interests. A growing athletic program begun in 1994-1995 includes men's and women's track and cross-country, men's and women's tennis, and men's golf. Sanctioned by the Arizona Community College Athletic Conference and the National Junior College Athletic Association, the program has already produced two national women's cross-country champion teams.

Paradise Valley Community College continually strives to meet the needs of its students, area businesses, and the community, and is proud of its role as a valuable resource for the Greater Phoenix area.

Clockwise from top:
Paradise Valley Community College's (PVCC) remodeled and expanded Student Services Center won a design award from the Arizona chapter of the American Institute of Architects.

The unique sculpture—representing the educational process—which is located in the center of the campus, is a focal point of the college's spacious and beautiful grounds.

PVCC offers student activities that include a theater program that has brought to the stage productions such as the musical *Working*.

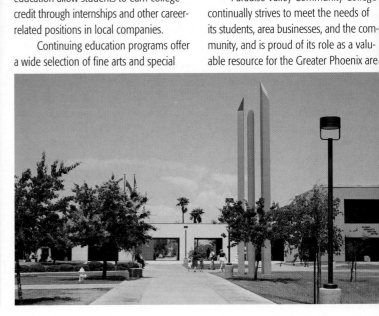

ith 199,790 members, PacifiCare of Arizona, Inc. is one of the largest health maintenance organizations (HMOs) in Arizona and the state's leading Medicare HMO for seniors. Secure Horizons, the seniors component, serves 88,521 of these members. The health care provider began operations in Arizona as FHP Health Care in October 1985, and was acquired by and became known as PacifiCare in 1997, creating a strong operation with a solid

leadership position in the western United States.

PacifiCare of Arizona's principal goal parallels that of its parent company, PacifiCare Health Systems: to be the best health maintenance organization in America. "By 'best,' we mean the most caring and unique in how we deliver health care, a company that both members and doctors view with confidence and trust," says Rick Badger, president and CEO of PacifiCare. The company is contracted with more than 1,000 primary care physicians and more than 2,000 specialists, who are provided with information from case studies and treatment results, as well as with timesaving systems to reduce duplication of effort and facilitate quick approval of referrals or additional tests.

Solid Leadership

PacifiCare endeavors to learn what the firm's members want and need, and then finds ways to offer it to them. "We believe that quality health care should be both responsive and responsible," Badger says.

Others recognize that PacifiCare is meeting members' expectations, as well. The company was ranked fourth in *Fortune*'s 1997 health care list of America's Most Admired Companies. Independent quality assessments, such as those done by the Healthcare Employer Data Information Set (HEDIS) and National Committee for Quality Assurance (NCQA), rate PacifiCare services well above state and national averages. And the Sachs Group, an independent health care information firm, ranks PacifiCare number one in three of its five Honor Roll categories, including access, convenience, and quality.

PacifiCare's members agree with these findings. Surveyed PacifiCare members say they like the personal service they receive, and more than 93 percent appreciate the lack of paperwork involved in receiving care. Nearly 90 percent like the range of services

and ready availability of information, and four of five rate the program highly when it comes to choosing a personal physician from the extensive network of available doctors.

Supporting the communities that PacifiCare serves is an ongoing part of its caring philosophy. Programs are funded to immunize children, and the Fit Kids Club promotes children's health and fitness. Senior fitness is encouraged through the National Senior Sports Classic, workouts with fitness guru Richard Simmons, and fellowship and companionship programs such as PALS (Partnering Animals with Loving Seniors) and OASIS (Older Adult Service and Information System).

Continually focusing on member needs and on delivering health services in the most caring, responsible manner possible, PacifiCare is sure to experience continued success and growth as it strives to be the best health maintenance organization in America.

With 199,790 members, PacifiCare of Arizona, Inc. is one of the largest health maintenance organizations (HMOs) in Arizona and the state's leading Medicare HMO for seniors.

MURRO CONSULTING INC.

urro Consulting Inc.'s motto—Building Performance Excellence—sums up the firm's results oriented approach to consulting. Under the direction of Ingrid Murro Botero, the compan helps businesses—ranging from large corporations to small, entrepreneurial companies—t improve their bottom line. 🌵 Botero founded Murro Consulting in 1986, with a visio of bringing together experienced people from many industries to provide first-rate servic

to her clients. Prior to starting the company, Botero was a vice president for Hay Career Consultants, where she opened Hay's Phoenix office and was instrumental in introducing the Phoenix business community to the concept of offering career continuation services for released employees. Much of the success of the company can be traced to her 20-plus years of domestic and international experience in consulting and human resources management. Another key to the company's

success has been Botero's generous giving of her time and energy to the community through various agencies, including the Valley of the Sun United Way and Greater Phoenix Leadership.

Murro Consulting's leadership development program assists companies with strategic planning, business planning, executive coaching, and team building. In addition, these programs help companies link their leadership development methods directly to their strategic business

needs. The company also assists businesses with changing their organizational culture, designs effective compensation programs, and helps employees take control of their careers. This is accomplished by using a strategic planning process to effectively link human resources practices and systems to a client's business strategies and goals.

Murro Consulting also conducts assessments to provide a baseline of information about its clients. Assessment tools include employee opinion surveys, leadership effectiveness evaluations, customer satisfaction surveys, and executive assessments. The firm uses a performance evaluation system to help clients both assess and develop employee performance. In addition, Murro Consulting helps clients identify the characteristics that are considered important to success, develop performance goals and measures, and resolve internal conflicts.

For companies that are undergoing changes, Murro offers a variety of outplacement programs—for key executives, groups, and individuals—to help companies and employees make this difficult transition. The firm also offers redeployment programs for firms that are reorganizing their workforce, and assists spouses in securing appropriate positions.

Murro Consulting is paving the way for future success in business by aligning with other consulting companies, in order to increase the firm's overall capabilities to meet the needs of its growing list of clients. The staffs in both the Phoenix and the Tucson offices now include senior professionals with extensive backgrounds in all facets of business. In fact, the firm's senior advisers bring more than 300 years of combined experience to clients in the banking, high-tech, service, manufacturing, distribution, utility, and health care industries.

"We're not just consultants; we're coaches," says Botero. "We have the expertise, tools, and resources needed to help businesses improve performance and increase profits. Our senior consultants work in partnership with clients, teaching them how to build performance excellence and raise their organization's level of performance to new heights."

The Murro Consulting Inc. management team includes (from left) Pat Kriegsfeld, Jack Milligan, Ken Helman, Ingrid Murro Botero, Marilyn Bechtold, Debbie Frank, and Gavin Robertson.

President Ingrid Murro Botero and Senior Consultant Gavin Robertson discuss a client's needs.

E ducation at the Humanities and Sciences Institute stems from a rigorous, accelerated academic program based on the teaching methods of Aristotle and Plato, which are intensely personal and usually involve small groups or one-on-one interaction. Whatever the method, teaching is always focused on what is most beneficial to the student. The goal is to prepare mature high school students in humanities and sciences for social responsibility, employability, and lifelong learning to enrich their lives. 🌵 Motivated students

thrive in this educational environment of self-paced learning. Studies include international languages, language arts, literature, social studies, mathematics, and natural sciences.

Students at this unique high school meet and exceed the state's requirements for graduation and have exposure to other types of learning environments such as field experiences. "Students can participate in activities that might include a working cattle ranch, the Intercultural Center for the Study of Deserts and Oceans in Mexico, or perhaps, research at the Grand Canyon," says Principal Curtis L. Ritland.

Students Make Community Contributions

Many projects allow students to meet educational goals and contribute to the community at the same time. For example, a group is helping the U.S. Fish and Wildlife Service and the YMCA restore the Agua Fria Riparian Forest Preserve while using this natural outdoor classroom to learn about riparian and basic ecology, botany, bird watching, hydrological cycles, forest communities, and Arizona's natural history.

All instruction integrates the Arizona Academic Standards and is based on the College Board's Advanced Placement curriculum, as well as the *Great Books of the Western World*.

Each student is encouraged to take an interest in athletic activities as a participant, not as a spectator, with interests

ranging from bowling to golf to martial arts to sailing. Students also attend theater productions, museum exhibitions, and legislative sessions as part of their educational growth.

Exceptional, Diverse Faculty

Each faculty member is qualified to teach at least two academic disciplines, and they have undergraduate degrees in diverse areas—including geography, anthropology, political science, humanities, and oceanography. All have outstanding academic credentials from prestigious colleges and universities throughout the country. Each speaks a language other than English, adding to the richness of the diversity they share.

Enrollment is limited to 320 students, who come from all over Maricopa County,

and the campus is open on a 12-month schedule. New classes begin weekly and instruction is available during extended hours six days a week. Some students attend in the daytime and others, who have jobs or other responsibilities, choose to attend in the evening. "Because we have open enrollment, students can graduate whenever they have completed requirements," Ritland says. Qualified students also may enroll concurrently in community college or university courses, and tuition is paid by the Institute.

The first graduates have fared well, earning scholarships and honors as they make their way to the next level of lifelong learning. Ritland looks forward to replicating the Central Phoenix facility in the East Valley, and, eventually, throughout the state.

"Students can participate in activities that might include a working cattle ranch, the Intercultural Center for the Study of Deserts and Oceans in Mexico, or perhaps, research at the Grand Canyon," says Curtis L. Ritland, principal of the Humanities and Sciences Institute .

Education at the Humanities and Sciences Institute stems from a rigorous, accelerated academic program based on the teaching methods of Aristotle and Plato, which are intensely personal and usually involve small groups or one-on-one interaction.

SPERR AND ASSOCIATES/ ARCHITECTURE

Founded in 1986, Sperr and Associates/Architecture has grown from a firm working on primarily design-oriented projects to a full-service architectural practice focused on providing expanded services to large corporate retail clients. 🌵 Over the past 13 years, Sperr and Associates has completed hundreds of projects, located primarily in Arizona, Nevada, and California. Clients have ranged from automobile dealerships to restaurants to drugstores to home and garden centers. Among the clients the firm has

served are CSK Auto, Chevron/McDonald's, Ernst Home and Garden Centers, and Houston's Restaurants. Currently, Sperr is managing major expansion projects for Rite Aid drugstores and PetsMart.

Headquartered in a gracious, historic, 70-year-old adobe home located at the northeast corner of Seventh Street and Northern Avenue, Sperr and Associates personifies the time-honored tradition of hand-holding service for its clients in combination with a technology-driven approach to project management and architecture.

"A primary key to our success and our clients' satisfaction is direct and solid communication," Douglas Sperr points out. Whether the client is across town or in another state, changes can be discussed and decisions made quickly using the technologically advanced tools available to the Sperr project teams. With the development of an interactive Web site, the entire team can exchange information, including digital photographs, CAD drawings, project schedules, or simple message posting. This type of automation, utilizing the Internet, provides Sperr

and Associates the opportunity to be on the leading edge of the architectural profession.

Neither niche marketing nor high technology can replace personal interaction, however, and Sperr and his staff of 12 professionals and technicians work hard to build and maintain ongoing relationships.

Michael Lorenz, a principal and the director of architecture, joined Sperr in 1994. Lorenz supervises the client lead managers and each of the production teams. His talent for team building

Douglas Sperr (left) and Michael Lorenz, the principals of Sperr and Associates/ Architecture, possess extensive and diverse experience in project design, management, and implementation.

brings the best synergies together for each project and promotes cooperation among clients, contractors, and the design team. "Our focus is on developing a strong, cohesive team of professionals who take a proactive approach to project management," says Lorenz. "That team includes the owner, the general contractor, land developers, and the architect in an interactive group, dependent on each other's success and avoiding the more common pitfalls of adversarial relationships. Our success in this approach has placed us in the position of creating national and regional development standards, and in problem-solving scenarios for other architectural firms."

Keeping Track of Progress

Meticulous records and technology-based systems keep projects profitable and the firm's clients continually informed

of increased costs and changing time lines. Sperr has spent more than two years developing a software system that he calls Profit Tracking, which analyzes and audits project-based financial information. Corporate retail projects require challenging design solutions to keep up with today's emerging technology. These design changes are many times retroactive to projects currently under construction. "Accurate tracking of these additional services is one of the keys to our financial success and our mastery of taking projects to completion on schedule and within budget," Sperr says.

This method of project management has become so effective that Sperr started a second business, US Global Network Communications, Inc., to offer Internet-based management applications to outside commercial and professional companies.

A Good Fit

Sperr encourages his employees to maintain a balance between professional and personal activities. This keeps ideas fresh and enthusiasm high. Staff members are encouraged to pursue advancement within the professional community and enjoy leisure time activities. In his spare time, Sperr can be found flying aerobatic sailplanes in the desert north of Phoenix, or creating platinum and gold jewelry, by hand, in his studio in the basement of the office.

Sperr is confident that his company's can-do philosophy works and will continue to provide success. "If we have a good management team, stay technically advanced, pay attention to our clients' needs, and create close relationships, our formula for success will provide a very positive future," Sperr concludes.

The Chevron/McDonald's Oil Alliance Program paired a McDonald's restaurant with a Chevron gas canopy and food mart. Sperr and Associates completed 17 of these projects in Arizona and Nevada.

The variety of Sperr and Associates' experience is reflected in the range of projects it has done. For example, this design for a Sheraton Hotel—proposed for the Phoenix Sky Harbor Airport—was created by the firm.

SuperShuttle International, Inc.

Each day, at 18 airports around the country, more than 800 familiar looking, blue-and-yellow vans transport almost 20,000 passengers door-to-door from their homes or hotels, and back again. Providing uncompromising quality, superb service, cleanliness, responsiveness, reliability, and safety is the standard upon which SuperShuttle® International, Inc. was built. ✵ As the national leader in the shared-ride ground transportation industry, the company's goal is to take better care of its guests than its local

competitors. The idea behind its winning service is simple—be on time, every time, and make no more than three stops. "Our philosophy sets the standard for the industry and travelers know they can depend on that same, consistent service no matter where they find the familiar blue-and-yellow vans," says Brian Wier, president and chief executive officer of SuperShuttle. Independent research supports his claim: 92 percent of all SuperShuttle customers rate its service as good or excellent.

RezCentral®, SuperShuttle's 24-hour, central reservation center located at its Phoenix headquarters, is the hub of the company's operations. With more than 8,000 calls daily, the center provides reliable service and accurate verification and reservation tracking capability.

Each city's operating center is equipped with a sophisticated operating system that supports RezCentral. SuperShuttle's digital dispatching system is revolutionizing ground transportation with real-time information and communication on van pickups and drop-offs; locations and revenue; and passenger information. The system uses global positioning system (GPS) technology to manage van movement and passenger routing. Dispatchers can determine the exact location of any van in

service and reroute it, if necessary, for even quicker response. Curbside coordinators use wireless, handheld data terminals to send reservation information to dispatch, and at the same time receive the status of the van's actual location, and RezCentral's ability to initiate an automated message telling guests the van's estimated arrival

time is a feature appreciated by passengers everywhere.

Serving Sky Harbor

SuperShuttle began in 1983 with 10 blue-and-yellow vans driven by trained employees—rather than independent contractors—who provided reliable, safe transportation to and from LAX Airport, and SuperShuttle soon became legendary for value, courtesy, and dependability. With excellent service and ever increasing customer demand for the convenience of SuperShuttle, operations began expanding. In 1985, SuperShuttle opened an operation in San Francisco. As residents of Arizona experienced SuperShuttle in California, demand for SuperShuttle service in Phoenix was ignited. In response to its customers, SuperShuttle began operations at Sky Harbor Airport in Phoenix/Scottsdale in 1986, and in 1994 moved its corporate headquarters there.

The next phase of expansion took SuperShuttle southeast to Dallas/Fort Worth and then to Miami. As word spread across the United States about this new transportation alternative, Philadelphia, Baltimore, and Washington, D.C., were added to the system. As expansion continued, Denver and Sacramento were added in the mid 1990s, and in June 1998,

SuperShuttle vans equipped with digital dispatch units allow drivers and dispatchers to serve the needs of more customers with greater accuracy (top).

In response to its customers, SuperShuttle began operations at Sky Harbor Airport in Phoenix/Scottsdale in 1986, and in 1994 moved its corporate headquarters there (bottom).

Technology like the global positioning system (GPS) is driving SuperShuttle's expansion.

SuperShuttle began serving New York City with operations to LaGuardia, JFK International, and Newark airports. The East Coast expansion continued into July 1998 with the opening of the Long Island SuperShuttle serving McArthur Airport and the other New York City airports.

SuperShuttle's fleet travels more than 60 million miles annually—equal to 270 trips to the moon and back. As an environmentally conscious company, SuperShuttle has always been a leader in using alternative fuels. Nationally, more than 50 percent of its fleet are alternative fuel vehicles.

Leader of the Pack

Shuttle transportation is often safer when compared with solitary walks to a car in a parking garage. Shared-ride is also an environmentally sound alternative to driving a car to the airport and back. "This is a service business, and we want to serve everyone," Wier says. "You can't be a leader in an industry if you aren't willing to go the extra mile to let customers know there is a reliable, convenient, and customer friendly service available to them when traveling."

While SuperShuttle takes guests to and from the airport, another division, ExecuCar®, appeals more to senior business executives for prompt, private, reliable sedan service to and from locations. ExecuCar began operating in Phoenix in 1989, when guests wanted a private, upscale alternative to shared-ride and taxis. Now ExecuCar serves most of Arizona's premier resorts, as well as local residences, and has expanded to Los Angeles and Dallas.

Private service contracts are another growing segment of SuperShuttle's business, shuttling employees from plant to plant for major corporations or as part of entertainment packages for theme parks or cruise ship lines and conventions. Because tour wholesalers in New York, Los Angeles, and Miami often include a SuperShuttle transfer in their voucher packages, the first person many international travelers meet is a friendly SuperShuttle driver.

One day, SuperShuttle plans to be the ground transportation of choice at more than 90 airports in the United States and abroad. Always keeping the customer in mind, the company also plans to make access to shuttle service as easy as going on-line, where guests can make reservations at www.supershuttle.com. This is just another way that SuperShuttle demonstrates its commitment to its customers.

The blue-and-yellow vans are the trademark of SuperShuttle's nationally recognized door-to-door airport ground transportation service.

The philosophy of the Mayo Clinic—the integration of clinical practice, research, and medical education, which is represented by the three shields in Mayo's logo—distinguishes this world-class clinic from other internationally known medical facilities. When Mayo Clinic Scottsdale opened the doors of its five-story outpatient facility in 1987, the fundamental, 100-year-old Mayo tradition of teamwork to heal the sick and to advance science was firmly ingrained in the clinic's culture.

Today, more than 250 physicians and 2,000 support staff tend to the medical needs of a growing patient population at this academic medical center. The clinic contains 240 exam rooms; an outpatient surgery center equipped for general anesthesia; a full-service laboratory, pharmacy, patient education library, and endoscopy suite; and a 188-seat auditorium for patient and physician education programs. About half of the patients are residents of the Phoenix metropolitan area, with the remainder coming from all over the United States and some 80 countries worldwide. Employees who know languages other than English are available to translate for patients, and more than 30 languages are represented.

Beginning in Minnesota

William Worrall Mayo, a frontier doctor who settled in Rochester, Minnesota, began his practice in 1863, which became a family tradition when his sons, Charles and William, joined him almost 20 years later. As the family's reputation and its practice grew, the Mayos invited other doctors to join them, initiating an innovative idea in American medicine—the multispecialty group practice. This encouraged doctors to take the time to thoroughly investigate patient problems, then quickly and easily get help from other specialists.

In 1919, the Mayo brothers dissolved their partnership and turned over the clinic's name and assets, including most of their life savings, to a private, not-for-profit charitable foundation. The brothers specified that any earnings from the practice, beyond operating expenses and funds needed to perpetuate the practice, be used for medical education and research. All Mayo staff members, including doctors, are paid a salary, and there is no profit sharing. Annual philanthropic support from more than 40,000 donors helps the clinic carry on its mission.

Although the Mayo brothers both died in 1939, their principles and ideals continue in the Mayo facilities in Rochester; Scottsdale; and Jacksonville, Florida. Patients come for diagnosis and treatment of difficult medical problems, the reassurance of a second opinion, surgery, or, perhaps, one of those famous Mayo checkups.

All in One Place

At Mayo Clinic Scottsdale, specialists are all in one location, and lab testing and analysis are done on-site, with results usually available within 24 hours. If necessary, satellite communications allow physicians in Scottsdale to collaborate with specialists at Mayo Clinic Rochester or Mayo Clinic Jacksonville to view data and discuss patient problems.

"We can tap the knowledge and experience of more than 1,000 highly trained Mayo medical experts," says Dr. Michael B. O'Sullivan, chairman of the board of governors, Mayo Clinic Scottsdale. "Because we continually review outcomes, we know which procedures are most promising and appropriate." Mayo's extensive involvement in medical research and education provides physicians and their patients with access to the latest technologies and treatment options as they emerge.

Referral is not necessary, and 90 percent of the clinic's patients make their own appointments. Following diagnosis, some patients obtain treatment at the clinic, while others return to their primary physicians. In either case, each patient's test results and history are maintained in a comprehensive patient file kept on record for perpetuity, always available to patients or their physicians for reference.

Mayo Clinic Hospital

A new, 440,000-square-foot hospital, the first planned, designed, and built by Mayo Clinic, is a key ingredient in the integration of the Arizona practice. All medical and surgical specialty programs, including the bone marrow transplant program at the clinic, are supported at the hospital, located at 56th Street and Mayo Boulevard just south of the future Pima Freeway. The

BILL TIMMERMAN

Mayo Clinic Scottsdale is a not-for-profit, multispecialty outpatient clinic with more than 250 physicians and a medical support staff of more than 1,800.

addition of a kidney and liver transplantation program is scheduled for implementation in the near future.

"We are able to provide medical services in a rapidly growing area that would be underserved if the hospital had not been built," says O'Sullivan, "and we were able to design it from the ground up with new, up-to-the-minute technology. This enhances the integration of our practice, which we believe serves the best interests of our patients."

Balconies on each floor of the hospital overlook the five-story atrium, which rises from the main lobby and is landscaped with live greenery. Each of the 178 patient rooms, brightened with natural light, is private and spacious. Mayo's never ending concern for patient care is evident in its arrangement of 12-room pods with a nursing station in the center, assuring that a nurse is within 20 steps of any room.

Technological innovations such as an electronic medical records system give physicians keystroke access to historical as well as up-to-the-minute information on test results, treatment plans, and patient progress. Filmless X-ray pictures can be viewed on a computer screen almost immediately, and physicians in multiple locations can see the images simultaneously, enlarging or enhancing them for better interpretation. The entire hospital is wired for telemetry so heart and other vital signs can be monitored from any patient room, and an integrated nurse call system uses advanced infrared technology to locate staff and patients.

Fourteen operating rooms in the three-quarters-of-an-acre surgical suite are built around a sterile core providing quick, convenient access to sterile instruments and supplies. Surgical specialties include general, cardiovascular and thoracic, colon and rectal, foot and ankle, gastrointestinal, gynecologic, hand, laparoscopic, neurologic, ophthalmologic, otolaryngological, orthopedic, plastic and reconstructive, urologic, and vascular surgeries.

Practicing in the Community
Mayo Thunderbird Primary Care Center, opened in 1994 as the first Mayo off-site primary care facility, was followed by others in Glendale, Fountain Hills, Scottsdale, and Phoenix. The Mayo Center for Women's Health opened in June 1997, and offers women's internal medicine and obstetrics/gynecology, and a full range of reproductive services including fertility treatments.

"We believe it's important to locate family and internal medicine in areas where our patients live," O'Sullivan says. "Our primary care facilities throughout the

Valley are key components in integrating services to provide effective and efficient patient care."

Research Improves Patient Care
The Samuel C. Johnson Medical Research Building, which opened in 1993, houses pioneering gene and complex molecular research through eight basic science programs, each led by a principal investigator. Scientists and physicians work closely together to learn new methods of diagnosing, treating, and even preventing major

illnesses. Ongoing collaboration with more than 1,000 physicians and scientists in Rochester and Jacksonville encourages new research ideas, communicates research findings, and speeds the application of discoveries to patient care.

"By studying the genes and complex molecules associated with birth defects, lung diseases, cystic fibrosis, arthritis, and cancer, our scientists hope to learn more about who is at risk for these diseases," O'Sullivan says. "They are looking for ways to help diagnose at an earlier stage when

The Doctors Mayo are shown together in a rare portrait: the father, Dr. William Worrall Mayo (seated), and his sons, Dr. Charles H. Mayo (left) and Dr. William J. Mayo. Active in Minnesota medical associations, the elder Mayo stimulated his sons, who subsequently played leading roles in the development of organized medicine in America.

Dr. William Worrall Mayo—pictured here in 1904—opened his medical practice in Rochester, Minnesota, in 1863.

treatment is more effective, and perhaps avoid these diseases altogether."

In addition to the basic research, more than 600 ongoing clinical research studies are under way, with enrollment averaging 600 new patients each year. These studies include hematology-oncology, gastroenterology, cardiology, neurology, endocrinology, and urology.

In research, as in the clinical practice, tradition is long-standing and productive. Mayo scientists first developed a method of analyzing surgical tissue for quick diagnosis and a system for grading the severity of cancers in the early 1900s. They developed the first accurate test for measuring anemia, set up the nation's first blood bank, and created the first oxygen mask and pressurized suit for pilots. Slipped disk surgery, heart catheterization, pulmonary function testing, and CT scanning were all pioneered at Mayo. Perhaps Mayo's best-known accomplishment is the discovery of cortisone, which was recognized with a Nobel Prize in 1950, culminating 36 years of dedicated research.

Sharing Medical Expertise

Mayo takes its mission to share medical expertise and promote continuing education seriously. In the last decade, more than 12,000 medical colleagues from throughout the world have studied and trained at the Scottsdale campus. Medical education includes physician training programs, continuing medical education courses, and visiting lecture programs.

Thirteen specialties are offered in the Scottsdale-based residency and fellowship programs, including internal medicine, family medicine, general surgery, and anesthesiology. Residency candidates from programs at Mayo Clinic Rochester, as well as from non-Mayo residency programs throughout the Phoenix metropolitan area, also receive training.

Intensive seminars and workshops, covering a wide range of topics, are dedicated to the ongoing training of practicing professionals. Through the Visiting Clinician Programs, Mayo offers individually tailored education experiences not available through conventional continuing education courses or formal graduate medical programs. Since 1992, visiting clinicians have traveled from other parts of the United States, Russia, China, Mexico, Spain, Italy, Saudi Arabia, Turkey, Bolivia, Chile, and Canada to learn on the Mayo Clinic Scottsdale campus.

Encouraging Patient Education

Mayo also encourages patients to be proactive in their health care. In 1998, a Patient and Health Education Center opened at

◄ BILL TIMMERMAN

Mayo combines a heritage of medical expertise with careful attention to each individual patient. This combination results in the clinic's thorough yet personal approach to medical diagnosis and treatment.

Satellite telecommunication impacts care by providing patients access to all of Mayo Clinic's medical expertise, no matter which location the patient visits.

Mayo Clinic Scottsdale housing a library with medical reference books, brochures, pamphlets, and magazines. The center also provides computers with CD-ROMs, including *Mayo Clinic Family Health Book, Mayo Clinic: The Total Heart,* and *Mayo Clinic Health Encyclopedia,* among others. It is open to the public during regular clinic hours.

For Your Health, a series of complimentary community education seminars taught throughout the Valley by teams of Mayo specialists, addresses important contemporary health issues. More than 14,000 people have had the opportunity to learn more about medical concerns and gain insight into preserving their health. Classes in the ongoing series are structured around specific diseases, behavior modification, and healthy lifestyle changes, and have included such issues as asthma education, glaucoma and macular degeneration, smoking cessation, staying healthy in the desert, and sleeping disorders.

Supporting the Community

Mayo's long-standing tradition of giving back to the community in which its staff lives and works has strong support in Arizona. The staff donates time to more than 100 professional, community, civic, and cultural organizations. For instance, the clinic has adopted Palomino Elementary School and its surrounding neighborhood,

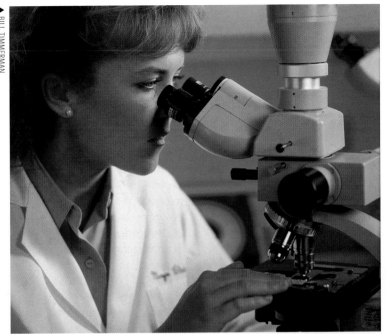

providing free health screenings and immunization clinics several times a year. During the holidays, food and toy drives benefit families in the neighborhood.

Scholarships, internships, and invitations to the clinic encourage students to learn about careers in medicine and science and to continue their education. Fourth-year medical students are offered the opportunity to gain clinical experience under the supervision of Mayo staff physicians; students from Mayo Medical School, the University

of Arizona, and other national and international medical schools have participated.

As Mayo looks at the future of health care, quality and access are major concerns. Creating new practices, sending Mayo specialists into the community, and exploring the use of communications technology to meet the needs of employees are some of the ways Mayo will meet the challenges of the next century. One thought remains clear at Mayo, however: the needs of the patient always will come first.

Mayo supports medical research as the promise of the future of medicine. The clinic's research keeps it at the forefront of discovery and extends the most current knowledge to its patients.

Mayo's multispecialty team approach to medicine gives its patients the opportunity to consult with specialists from virtually every medical field. Mayo has used the team approach successfully for more than a century.

GREATER PHOENIX ECONOMIC COUNCIL

The Greater Phoenix Economic Council (GPEC) is an economic development partnership composed of county and city governments, private businesses, and educational institutions. GPEC's core business is to leverage public and private resources to attract new and expanding employers to the metropolitan area to create jobs for the 2.8 million people who call Greater Phoenix home. Led by President and CEO Rick Weddle, GPEC is recognized as a national model for public/private partnerships. In 1995,

Site Selection magazine named GPEC one of the top 10 economic development organizations in the country. In its 1997-1998 fiscal year, GPEC helped 28 companies locate or expand in Greater Phoenix, creating more than 5,400 new jobs. These businesses will create total annual payrolls of more than $167 million, and represent almost $203 million in capital investment.

GPEC targets those companies that fall within the 10 industry clusters outlined by the Governor's Strategic Partnership for Economic Development: bioindustry; business services; environmental technology; food, fiber, and natural products; high technology; mining and minerals; optics; software; tourism; and transportation. In recent years, Greater Phoenix has attracted a high number of companies in the high-technology and business services clusters. In fact, high technology has led Arizona's growth throughout the 1990s and supports, either directly or indirectly, one of every five jobs in the state.

"We have been able to attract high-paying, desirable jobs that any community would welcome," Weddle says. "At the same time, we have kept a regional perspective and an eye to quality industrial development. We want to ensure that Greater Phoenix retains the unique qualities that encouraged this prosperity in the first place."

Attracting New Businesses

GPEC works with member communities Avondale, Buckeye, Chandler, El Mirage,

Gilbert, Glendale, Goodyear, Mesa, Peoria, Phoenix, Scottsdale, Surprise, Tempe, and Maricopa County, as well as more than 150 private-sector investors to improve the region's business image, build a stronger business climate, and diversify the economic base by attracting desirable new and expanding business and industry.

By serving as a first point of contact for a business considering a move to Greater Phoenix, GPEC brings together the talent and resources needed to evaluate the region at no cost to the inquiring company. Comprehensive, confidential services include custom tours, meetings with community leaders, introductions to necessary business contacts, and advocacy with government agencies when a relocating company has special needs.

GPEC works with each prospective company to determine the amount and type of space it needs, the infrastructure required to support the business, any necessary distribution channels, and workforce requirements. GPEC then sends the request to its member communities, which,

The Greater Phoenix Economic Council, led by President and CEO Rick Weddle, unites the public and private sectors to create an environment where business can thrive.

GPEC touts the region's strong, qualified labor pool to companies looking to expand or locate in Greater Phoenix.

GPEC markets Greater Phoenix as an ideal business location and an excellent place to live.

in turn, evaluate the data to determine whether the business fits their resources. After a business has made the decision to move to Greater Phoenix, GPEC helps the firm successfully integrate into the local business community.

GPEC utilizes advertising, targeted direct mail, editorial marketing campaigns, and high-profile events to attract key decision makers to Greater Phoenix. In addition, members of GPEC's corporate locations staff make prospect trips to numerous cities to nurture personal relationships with executives of targeted companies and their site location consultants.

Combined Community Strength

GPEC was formed after a 1988 economic summit was held to address a negative

article on Greater Phoenix printed in *Barron's*. The region's economy was failing, and efforts to attract businesses weren't working. It was determined that a regional approach, in which a single, collaborative group would represent the entire region, was needed. The Greater Phoenix Economic Council was formed, and has continued to hold an economic summit every year since. The most recent summit meeting focused on the critical success factors that will determine the region's ability to prosper into the 21st century.

Greater Phoenix offers a positive business climate; reliable distribution channels; steady population growth, which brings an educated, ready workforce; affordable housing; and a superior quality of life. The region's well-respected

educational institutions include Arizona State University, the internationally acclaimed American Graduate School of International Management (Thunderbird), and the second-largest community college district in the nation, Maricopa Community Colleges.

"Our diverse economic base and positive business climate allow Greater Phoenix to compete both nationally and internationally," Weddle says. "GPEC's challenge is to continue to unite the resources available in the community to ensure long-term success."

SADDLEBACK HANDCRAFTED HOMES

addleback Handcrafted Homes gives a whole new meaning to the word shelter. In the gated community being built by the company on the side of Troon Mountain, each of the 113 semi-custom homes is a feast for the eyes, inspired by the timeless beauty of California mission and Tuscan architecture, with flexible designs, detailed craftsmanship, and an efficient use of space. The new homes share the private enclave with the spectacular natural surroundings of massive boulder fields, soaring mountain cliffs, and majestic saguaros.

"We selected the finest piece of high Sonoran Desert property that we could find, and we are building homes that truly are for the next millennium," says Chairman Larry Kush, who, with his wife, Sandra, is personally involved in the building of each property. "Our goal is to create great architecture that is harmonious with its surroundings, subtle yet stately, grand yet unimposing, with timeless designs to complement the beauty of nature."

Saddleback provides clients a foundation of eight creative floor plans, which they then use as a base to customize—which helps to remove the guesswork from building a truly special home. Some of the best architectural, land planning, and contracting talent available has been selected by Saddleback, to ensure that the finished products meet everyone's expectations. Home designs ranging from 2,860 to 6,970 square feet are built on one-third- to one-and-one-half-acre lots. Depending on the site selected and the home and landscaping options, prices range from $415,000 to $815,000.

Livable Elegance

People from all walks of life find the natural desert setting and Saddleback's uncompromising sensitivity to the environment appealing. "These are not predictable, cookie-cutter homes," Kush says. "We want to build each one so the mountain looks better with our homes on it than it did without them."

The company's classic designs are inward looking, with private courtyards, rounded turrets, and tall, narrow windows that control light, in direct contrast to the open floor plans and walls of glass in many new homes today. They meet futurist Faith Popcorn's description of "cocooning," where people can retreat to the warmth and security of their homes, and focus on family and private time. In a high-pressure world where everything is rushed, these homes are planned as places for people to unwind and recharge.

Saddleback homes tend toward defined rooms that can be individually personalized by each home owner, and which are designed for multiple uses as families and lifestyles change. Home offices and gyms are included, along with well-equipped, user-friendly kitchens with

Saddleback Handcrafted Homes and its team of seasoned consultants design the homes to be built into the varying heights of the mountainous landscape, reducing the need for lot grading and ensuring that the great boulder gardens dotting the land remain untouched.

By punching a few buttons on a cell phone, a home owner can turn on the lights, set mood music, light the fireplace, and draw a warm bath—all on the way home from work.

every imaginable option available for customization. Kush calls his comprehensive plans "four-sided" architecture, "where the backs and sides look just as good as the fronts."

This vision of livable elegance is complemented by the latest in construction technology. Cutting-edge air-cleaning and indoor weather systems—20 to 40 times more efficient than regular furnace filters—remove 95 percent of aggravating pollen, dirt, dust, grease, tobacco, and cooking smoke. An extra-quiet heating and cooling system allows each home to be divided into as many as eight different zones to increase efficiency.

The homes are wired for Internet access, satellite television, home security systems, home office electronics, and home LAN systems. An advanced home management system from SmartOne can control virtually every electronic and mechanical system in the house. By punching a few buttons on a cell phone, a home owner can turn on the lights, set mood music, light the fireplace, and draw a warm bath—all on the way home from work. It's also possible to see who is knocking on the front door—or check out what just splashed in the pool—from any television in the house.

Preserving the Environment

Saddleback and its team of seasoned consultants design the homes to be built into the varying heights of the mountainous landscape, reducing the need for lot grading and ensuring that the great boulder gardens dotting the land remain untouched.

"Never before has so much creative talent and cutting-edge technology been brought together to create a community of this magnitude," Larry Kush says of the exceptional architecture and complementary home management technology that ensure the new homes will be in harmony with their environment for years to come.

Larry and Sandra Kush launched Saddleback Homes, Ltd., in 1989 with just 20 homes. From the beginning, they had an ability to incorporate unique architectural design and quality custom features with the desert landscape. Their success has been recognized with numerous awards, including highly prized national and international Gold Nuggets for home-building excellence.

Larry Kush is a life director of the Home Builders Association of Central Arizona and was board chairman in 1993. He is a national director, and also serves on the association's building materials task force. Having built more than 3,000 homes, he is a respected leader in the industry, and is called upon frequently to provide expert commentary on home building and related issues.

As cofounder and president of Saddleback Handcrafted Homes, Sandra Kush has established an in-house design company to provide the highest-quality design services and products available for clients who custom design their homes. She recently became one of four building professionals in Arizona to receive the Certified Marketing Professional designation by the National Association of Home Builders, and she is a nationally known speaker on home-building and design topics.

Together, the Kushes have built a lasting legacy of gracious, custom-built homes, designed to more than meet the needs of today's home owners, while respecting the natural beauty of the region's mountains and deserts.

Saddleback provides clients a foundation of eight creative floor plans, which they then use as a base to customize—which helps to remove the guesswork from building a truly special home.

MILNE SCALI & COMPANY

ilne Scali & Company offers a full range of insurance services to clients in Phoenix and the Southwest. These services include commercial insurance, bonds, employee benefits, personal insurance, claims management, and risk control. When Richard W. Milne Jr. and Terrence M. Scali founded the company, their goal was to provide all clients with exceptional service. They knew from experience that this goal would best be achieved as independent brokers. In this

capacity, they are the link between the client and the insurance company. They are in a position to negotiate terms to reduce insurance costs, manage claims, and simplify the often confusing process for the client. By pooling a wealth of experience and training, and by forging strong relationships with numerous and varied insurance companies, Milne and Scali have built an agency possessing all the tools needed to provide each client the best program available—one that is tailor-made for the client's situation.

With a sales volume of close to $100 million in annual premiums, Milne Scali is one of the largest privately owned insurance brokerages in Phoenix. "We have put together a team of hardworking professionals with an understanding and knowledge of the business that is unsurpassed in the industry," says Milne, "and we encourage people to continue to learn and grow to their potential." This management philosophy has resulted in an environment where "everyone feels they are in a partnership; here, we are working with our coworkers, not for someone," according to Bob Shcolnik, vice president of sales and marketing. "Communication flows freely and decisions are made quickly, resulting in the best insurance products to serve the

Clockwise from top:
Milne Scali is one of the largest privately owned insurance brokerages in Phoenix. Pictured here are founding partners Richard W. Milne Jr. and Terrence M. Scali.

Milne Scali offers a full range of insurance services.

The 20,000-square-foot stone and copper Milne Scali building on Glendale near the Squaw Peak Freeway was designed and built for the company in 1995.

client's special needs," according to Scali. "Because we are high-volume producers, insurers give our clients VIP attention in many ways, one of which is by giving us better premium pricing which we pass on to our clients. We also have more clout in solving problems and tailoring coverage. Clients appreciate our entrepreneurial advantages."

As a further service to its clients, Milne Scali has a risk control safety engineer on staff, unique for an independent agency. The engineer studies a client's work environment from a safety standpoint and recommends ways in which the client can reduce risk and, consequently, lower premiums. Milne Scali's efficient claims

department is equipped with sophisticated automated tools that track the claims history of a company. With this record, the claims department can identify trends in the type and frequency of a client's claims. Once a problem is identified, procedures can be implemented to eliminate or reduce it. This is especially effective for national accounts with offices in multiple cities or states. Clients receive timely claims reports and their employees receive training seminars where the latest safety procedures are discussed.

Milne Scali's client base ranges from sole proprietorships with growing needs to large, self-insured, national corporations in fields as diverse as construction, real estate development, manufacturing, retail sales, service, and health care. The com-

pany also works with business associations such as the Western Petroleum Marketers Association, Arizona Concrete Contractors, and Arizona Association of Industries. Milne Scali designs insurance programs to meet these special industry needs. Most of the firm's clients are in the middle business market, but it is always on the alert for niches that are not being adequately served by the insurance industry. A group of enterprising employees recently identified a growing market that was not being properly served by the insurance industry. The company now provides workers' compensation and other products to fairs and carnivals across the country. Clients in this group range from large traveling companies with hundreds of employees to small family operations that provide entertainment at birthday parties.

Milne Scali & Company has a staff of more than 100 professionals working in three locations in the Valley. Two of the buildings are company owned. The stone and copper Milne Scali building on Glendale Avenue near the Squaw Peak Freeway was designed and built for the company in 1995. This 20,000-square-foot building was designed to support a flat management structure and the team approach. Low-walled workstations encourage the sharing of information and provide a feeling of space. Another building on Central Avenue near Camelback Road was acquired in 1997. The third location is an office in the East Valley. "We

want to continue to focus on growing here; owning our buildings signifies a long-term commitment to this community," says Milne. Scali says, "We are competitive with the largest national firms and are intent on becoming one of the largest independently owned insurance brokers in the Southwest. We can achieve that goal by continuing to develop unique solutions that bring value to our clients and build lasting relationships along the way."

Clockwise from top:
Milne Scali & Company has a staff of more than 100 professionals working in three locations in the Valley.

Milne Scali & Company has a risk control safety engineer on staff, unique for an independent agency.

At Milne Scali, the sales and service staff is the company's greatest asset.

Hermosa Inn

Hand built in the 1930s by artist Lon Megargee as his home and studio, the historic Hermosa Inn is nestled comfortably on six and a half acres of land in a secluded residential area of Paradise Valley. Situated among gracious olive and mesquite trees, towering palms, and blooming flowers, the inn's 35 unique casitas and charming main lodge exist in harmony with their desert surroundings. Megargee was known for his paintings of the Old West, and his projects ranged from large murals for the Arizona

State Capitol Building to the famous design of the cowboy and his horse that appears inside all Stetson hats. His paintings first appeared in *Arizona Highways* magazine in 1939, and in the 1940s, he was commissioned to do four paintings for the A-1 Brewing Company, two of which were to become his most famous: *Black Bart* and *A Cowboy's Dream*. Still admired today, Megargee's murals for the state capitol building—now a museum—are being restored for the museum's centennial anniversary.

Megargee built his home to reflect the culture and traditional architecture of the Southwest. As Megargee's vision took shape and his home grew, the artist decided to run it as a guest ranch and named it Casa Hermosa, or "handsome house." Today, no two of the tile-roofed residential accommodations are alike; guests can choose from cozy adobe rooms to generous villas, each distinctly decorated to maintain the charming ranch ambience that invites guests to stay a night or a month. High-profile corporate travelers and vacationers looking for an intimate desert hideaway are attracted by the inn's seclusion and personalized, responsive service; companies will sometimes book the entire hotel for their exclusive use.

"Our customer is our priority," says General Manager Richard Behr. "We're here to make each stay a special and memorable experience." Behr plans to fulfill this goal by transforming the bed-and-breakfast atmosphere into one of a boutique hotel—24-hour, full-service staff assistance—while enhancing the inn's reputation for southwestern hospitality.

A Gracious Blend of Old and New

All 35 spacious guest casitas have vaulted ceilings, handpainted Mexican tile, and private patios, plus modern necessities such as telephones with dataports and remote control color televisions. Hand-built adobe rooms called ranchos—many with beehive fireplaces—comfortably accommodate two guests, while casitas are larger, with living rooms or sitting areas. Haciendas have a large living room and French doors that open onto a guest patio or garden, and are set in a beautiful garden courtyard with access to a sunken spa. The large, luxurious villas offer two separate bedroom suites that easily accommodate four guests,

Clockwise from top:
Hand built in the 1930s by cowboy artist Lon Megargee, Casa Hermosa (handsome house) has been restored to embody a warm, southwestern spirit.

Thick adobe walls, original beams, beehive fireplaces, and handsome ironwork create a historic hacienda ambience at the Hermosa Inn's award-winning restaurant, LON's *at the hermosa*.

There are no standard rooms at the Hermosa Inn. Accommodations range from spacious villas to cozy adobe casitas, each uniquely decorated with a warm and charming southwestern ranch style.

Clockwise from top left:
Throughout the main lodge, the art of Lon Megargee is displayed as it was in the 1930s, when he built Casa Hermosa as his studio and guest ranch.

LON's *at the hermosa* offers contemporary American cuisine with a southwestern flavor.

Quiet elegance and comfortable seclusion are the hallmarks of the historic Hermosa Inn.

fully equipped kitchens, and spacious living rooms.

The inn has become a favorite gathering site for meetings, as it offers a degree of privacy unusual in a hotel setting. The charming locale has attracted high-technology, financial, and creative companies looking for a relaxing, gracious atmosphere for focused learning or creative brainstorming. The private Stetson Room, seating up to 70, can be used for meetings, receptions, and special functions; the Megargee Room is semiprivate and seats 14 people at a large harvest table. Receptions can also be held on the patio, and smaller lunches and dinners can be catered in the villas and haciendas.

Executive Chef Patrick Poblete's distinctive cuisine is served at Lon's *at the hermosa*, the Hermosa Inn's signature restaurant, which opened in 1994. In this critically acclaimed establishment, diners can enjoy either the warmth of historic photographs and the hacienda decor indoors, or the spectacular views of Camelback Mountain beneath star-studded skies on the front patio. A lifelong gardener, Poblete plans many evening specials around the harvest of the day from his 10,000-square-foot garden of fresh herbs, vegetables, and fruits. The restaurant, named one of the top four in Phoenix by *USA Today*, also has been singled out by the *New York Times, Travel & Leisure,* and *Gourmet Magazine*.

Part of the Community

A local, family-owned company, Spring Creek Development owns and manages the Hermosa Inn, and is dedicated to preserving the history of the community and the character that comes with the ruggedness of living with the desert. "We built this business with the community in mind," says Behr, "and the success of the Hermosa Inn has been because the community has supported us."

It was in 1992 that Paradise Valley residents Fred and Jennifer Unger, principals of Spring Creek Development, became intrigued with the resort and its history, bought the property, and began working to restore its original charm. Over the years, different owners had added a pool, tennis courts, and the outlying casitas and villas. One of the few remaining authentic Southwestern haciendas, the ranch had experienced a devastating fire that had severely damaged the main building—Megargee's old home—in 1987.

Working with builder and designer Dan MacBeth, also a Paradise Valley neighbor, the Ungers saved the adobe walls of the fire-damaged main building, restored the charred old beams, and cleaned up the original ironwork that graces the building both inside and out. The interior of the building, which houses an intimate cantina, the restaurant, and the inn's reception area, was furnished to encourage visitors to step back in time to the 1930s, when Megargee called Casa Hermosa home.

The Ungers, who also restored the historic Royal Palms Hotel at the southern base of Camelback Mountain, are now concentrating on the Canals of Scottsdale, a half mile along the canal running through the central core of that community's downtown. The Ungers plan to extend to their new project the same personal attention to detail and creative problem solving that made the Hermosa Inn a desirable destination and a reflection of the best Arizona has to offer.

SunAMERICA SECURITIES, INC.

ulfilling individual dreams of financial security is the ultimate goal of SunAmerica Securities, Inc., a financial services firm specializing in retirement planning and investment products. ❧ SunAmerica Securities, Inc. has sophisticated management and products, and a seasoned, entrepreneurial culture. The business is backed by its parent company, Los Angeles-based SunAmerica, Inc., which had $2.1 billion in revenue and assets of $42 billion in 1997. With retirement savings emerging as the fastest-growing sector of the

financial services market, SunAmerica Securities, Inc. has become a leader as a full-service firm offering a diverse menu of investment and retirement products with a powerful distribution network to sell them. SunAmerica, Inc. is ranked among the largest issuers of fixed and variable annuities in the country.

"We are supported by the financial strength and resources of our parent company, SunAmerica, Inc., which was an early visionary in stressing the importance of building individual net worth, particularly for retirement," says SunAmerica Securities, Inc. President Vince Asaro, "and we offer a broad cross section of approved investment and insurance products to build a solid, integrated financial program for every client."

Wide Array of Financial Products

SunAmerica Securities, Inc. is headquartered in Phoenix with 2,500 registered representatives throughout the continental United States, Hawaii, and Alaska. Representatives are individual practice managers, who are affiliates rather than employees of the nationally recognized firm. Through SunAmerica Securities, Inc., they can offer

their clients a wide array of products and services, and they have access to an impressive range of support services, including on-line links to client data, research, and pricing. In addition to leading-edge technology, SunAmerica Securities, Inc. provides strong educational and compliance support, keeping representatives up to date with the complex issues and regulations of the securities industry.

An early investment in technology and, more recently, a program known as Vision 2020 position the firm well with a sophisticated, fully integrated system to manage client information and transactions on-line, as well as interactive retirement planning software to create customized financial plans for clients. Technology has helped SunAmerica Securities, Inc. move toward a paperless back office that pro-

cesses critical documents in a fraction of the time typically required, helping maintain its high standard of customer service.

SunAmerica Securities, Inc. holds and oversees the use of licenses needed by its representatives, and because representatives are not tied to a specific family of funds or other financial products, they are free to provide unbiased financial advice to their clients.

Encouraging Overall Planning

Representatives encourage their clients toward overall financial and estate planning, which establishes goals toward a secure future and improved lifestyle. Investment options include annuities, money market funds, mutual funds, individual stocks, fixed-income investments, and a wide array of insurance products. Repre-

SunAmerica Securities, Inc. ranks among the top independent broker/dealers in the country (top).

SunAmerica Securities University is designed specifically to meet the needs of financial services professionals in both personal and professional development (bottom).

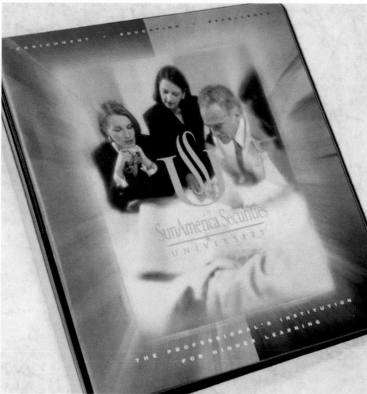

sentatives also provide advisory services such as money management, wrap fee accounts, fee-based investment advisory, and asset allocation.

The Trading and Operations departments in Phoenix process more than 1 million transactions every year. General Securities and client account orders are cleared through the largest clearing agent in the industry. As a member of the Securities Investor Protection Corporation (SIPC), securities are protected in each client's account up to $500,000, with additional coverage of up to $74 million available through commercial riders.

"We select new registered representatives carefully, adding quality people who are knowledgeable in many areas of financial services," Asaro says. "Continuing education is mandatory, and each one must follow established office procedures and record-keeping systems." Transactions are carefully monitored, and compliance requirements for industry rules and regulations are as stringent as any in the industry.

Educating Representatives

SunAmerica Securities University (SSU), established in 1996, provides a unique education and training opportunity to representatives for both professional and personal advancement. Through partnerships with the University of Phoenix and the College of Financial Planning in Denver, SunAmerica Securities, Inc. has established the strongest education track record in the industry through forums, academic workshops, and conferences. Many learning experiences also are available through an electronic Internet Campus at the University of Phoenix.

This forward-looking program not only provides a means for representatives to obtain continuing education credits, but also focuses on encouraging them to become certified financial planners. In addition, representatives can improve their knowledge of financial markets and industry trends through regional meetings and an annual National Education Conference.

The spirit of giving back to the community is encouraged throughout the SunAmerica organization. In lieu of awards, the firm recognizes outstanding representatives by contributing to a charity of each honoree's choice.

As SunAmerica Securities, Inc. looks ahead to retaining and expanding its position in the marketplace, the firm remains dedicated to developing innovative financial choices, educating its representatives, and ensuring a continuing philosophy stressing integrity and industry compliance.

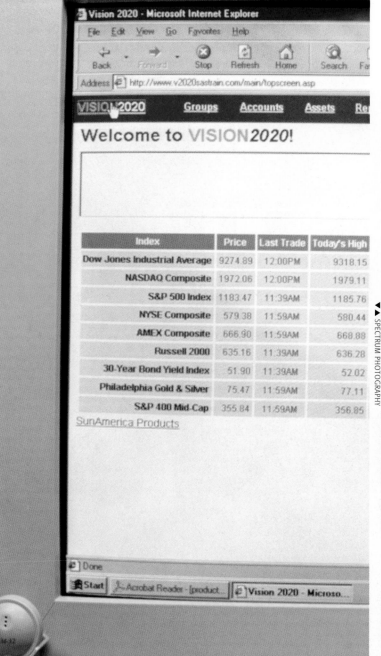

▶ SPECTRUM PHOTOGRAPHY

◀ ▶ SPECTRUM PHOTOGRAPHY

Clockwise from top:
SunAmerica Securities, Inc. is headquartered in Phoenix, Arizona.

Education, enrichment, and excellence are the focuses of the year-round programs offered throughout the country by SunAmerica Securities University.

A Web-based computer system provides broker direct on-line services for SunAmerica Securities, Inc.

American International Group, Inc. (AIG) has announced the merger of SunAmerica Securities, Inc. into AIG, effective as of January 1, 1999. AIG is the leading U.S.-based international insurance organization among the largest underwriters of commercial and industrial insurance in the United States.

EQUITY RESIDENTIAL PROPERTIES TRUST

Equity Residential Properties Trust (EQR), a real estate investment trust (REIT) with more than 680 properties across 35 states, is the nation's largest publicly traded owner and operator of apartment communities. Substantial holdings valued at around $9 billion include more than 70 properties in the local Phoenix and Tucson markets. ❧ Founded in 1969 by Sam Zell, chairman of the board of trustees, the company went public in 1993, trading on the New York Stock Exchange. With CEO Douglas Crocker II directing

company operations, EQR grew to more than six times its original size in its first five years as a public company, far surpassing projected goals. By the end of the decade, the trust is expected to include around 200,000 units with a market capitalization between $13 billion and $15 billion.

An understanding of public equity markets encouraged the company's leadership to create a program that courts institutional investment firms, and it has successfully attracted more institutional investment dollars than any other apartment REIT. In 1997, net income totaled $176.6 million, a 74 percent increase over the previous year, with dividends up 18 percent. Through special tax treatment as a REIT, EQR is not subject to corporate income tax as long as

it meets certain requirements, including distributing at least 95 percent of what the company earns among its shareholders.

Acquisitions Fuel Growth

Acquisitions have been and will continue to be the cornerstone of EQR's rapid growth rate. Generally, the company acquires garden-style apartment communities in parklike, suburban settings, concentrating on the broad middle tier of the industry. Properties have amenities such as swimming pools, tennis courts, spas, fitness centers, gas barbecues, and covered parking. New services such as health clubs and office service centers for home-based businesses give the communities competitive advantages.

In December 1997, EQR was adding properties on an average of 200 units a day with an acquisition team led by Executive Vice President Alan George. Heading a multidisciplinary, in-house group including accounting, legal, asset management, and finance professionals, George draws on the team's collective experience in operations, marketing, maintenance, and development. Their in-depth, preacquisition analyses of properties determine favorable return on investment in the locations they recommend for addition to the company's portfolio.

"While our growth is phenomenal, it certainly has not been by chance," Crocker says. "We are leading the transformation of the apartment industry by taking a

Ready, affordable financing and a determination to dominate the national residential apartment market will continue to drive Equity Residential Properties Trust (EQR) forward well into the next century.

EQR, a real estate investment trust (REIT) with more than 680 properties across 35 states, is the nation's largest publicly traded owner and operator of apartment communities (top and bottom).

corporate approach to real estate and applying professional management practices to a fragmented cottage industry."

Setting New Standards

Corporate culture at EQR emphasizes drive, competitiveness, and an eagerness to excel. Senior executives average 27 years of industry experience, bringing a unique blend of entrepreneurial initiative and market leadership to the company. Their knowledge, vision, and expertise—combined with EQR's size, reputation, competitive compensation, and incentive programs—attract the best people in the

industry to help guide the company's rapid growth.

"Our stock option programs encourage employees to think like owners and grow with the company," says Crocker. "We're all working as a team to set new standards for service in this industry." Long-term share option plans are available to on-site managers and maintenance supervisors, giving most employees a chance to share in the company's success.

Open, two-way communication and employee training and support are hallmarks of EQR's nationwide operations. Both formal and informal recognition programs

commend outstanding accomplishments and encourage personal growth. Operating manuals, which take the form of guidelines instead of strict procedures, encourage managers to think for themselves and take well-reasoned risks. The company's size also offers more opportunities for individuals to explore their potential, and several of those who have risen to the rank of vice president started out as on-site leasing or maintenance workers.

A network of 23 local offices is supported by seven regional centers directing day-to-day operations in the Atlantic, southeastern, midwestern, southwestern,

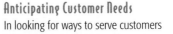

western, and Pacific northwestern states and Arizona. Local professionals in each market support individual properties with marketing, maintenance, leasing, and management, continually sharing insight into changing local needs and conditions with corporate headquarters in Chicago. Each self-sufficient regional operations center has a regional vice president as well as accounting, marketing, technical services, human resources, and training professionals. All levels of management understand the advantages of operating economies.

EQR has developed one of the most comprehensive training programs in the industry. Offered free to its staff of more than 6,000 people through Equity University, the training emphasizes the importance of knowledge of the real estate industry. Formal classroom training ranges from fair housing and employment law to financial management and customer service and

The Phoenix office of EQR has developed the Rent Direct marketing program, which offers detailed information about every EQR property in the area. Using the program, prospective residents can find the exact location, size, and features they are seeking with a single, toll-free telephone call.

hiring skills. Plans call for a formal accreditation system that will measure the progress of every employee and suggest areas for further career development.

Anticipating Customer Needs
In looking for ways to serve customers better, the company is seeking to improve

the services it already offers, as well as developing new, value-added incentives to keep residents happy. Its sophisticated Web site, www.eqr.com, features information on properties throughout the country. Prospective residents can preview amenities through photographs, download maps for directions, look at floor plans, and compare rental fees and terms.

EQR is dedicated to providing customers with a wide range of options. For example, some apartment communities cater to military personnel, offering furnished accommodations for temporary duty assignments, as well as longer lease arrangements. Others are intended for college students as an alternative to dormitory living. They respond to student needs with special considerations such as preleasing for the following term, campus shuttle buses, extra bookcases, and sports facilities that include basketball courts and table tennis.

In some locations, the unique Rent with Equity program gives residents the opportunity to apply rent credit toward the purchase of a new home. They can apply 25 percent of the total rent they pay each month, up to 6 percent of their total home purchase, to moving into a home of their own.

To help manage properties, EQR has created a new, computer-based system to

streamline the flow of information and allow managers to chart historical performance of each property and identify areas for improvement. The Phoenix office also has developed the Rent Direct marketing program, which offers detailed information about every EQR property in the area. Using the program, prospective residents can find the exact location, size, and features they are seeking with a single, toll-free telephone call.

To assist short-term business clients, a corporate housing program offers furnished one-, two-, and three-bedroom apartment homes in EQR communities. These apartment homes provide a less expensive, more comfortable alternative to hotel accommodations for corporate guests who are on assignment or are relocating from another area. Apartments in this program are fully equipped with housewares, and include local telephone service and basic cable television. The company tries to make its extended-stay corporate residents' time away from home enjoyable, and some properties even allow small pets.

All properties are conveniently located near dining, shopping, and entertainment facilities.

Communicating the Message

In an effort to communicate to potential renters throughout the country, EQR leverages its marketing dollars by modifying innovative advertising and promotions developed for one market to meet the demands of others. Cooperative partnerships with national and local vendors—from restaurants to telephone companies—bring added value to residents, helping to make the properties even more desirable places to live. When residents need to relocate, EQR can provide them with information about company properties in their new location.

As prices for existing properties rise to near replacement costs, the company, which has concentrated on acquiring properties, now sees new opportunities in development as well. A joint venture with Lincoln Property Company, a national multifamily residential developer, is slated to invest approximately $1 billion in new

properties in target markets over the next three years. To limit risk, EQR plans to take ownership of these properties only after they are built and partially leased. As the company continues to add attractive, affordable housing, this strategy will allow greater control over the quality of properties in its portfolio while increasing EQR's capability to add as many as 7,000 new units a year.

The company's Arizona interests increased substantially in 1997 when a $1 billion merger was completed with Evans Withycombe Residential, adding 55 properties totaling 15,948 units. As part of the merger agreement, a development oversight group joined EQR to monitor and expand the company's relationships with third-party developers, such as Lincoln, in markets that offer good prospects for growth.

Ready, affordable financing and a determination to dominate the national residential apartment market will continue to drive EQR forward well into the next century.

EQR is dedicated to providing customers with a wide range of options. For example, some apartment communities cater to military personnel, while others are intended for college students as an alternative to dormitory living.

TURNER CONSTRUCTION COMPANY

urner Construction Company has a broader geographic presence in the United States than any other firm in the industry and completed approximately $4 billion of construction in 1998. Its services include preconstruction consulting, general contracting, construction management, construction consulting, design-build, design-build/finance, program management, and building maintenance. Leadership in any industry is difficult to achieve and even harder to maintain, but Turner's

Scottsdale's Hyatt Gainey Ranch is one of the premier resort properties in the country and required the coordination of more than 300 different subcontractors to complete work in an extremely short time frame while meeting the stringent building specifications of the client. Turner Construction Company's depth of construction management skills and its solid relationships with quality subcontractors created one of the most attractive hospitality properties in Greater Phoenix.

Leadership in any industry is difficult to achieve and even harder to maintain, but Turner's growing range of services and aptitude for securing repeat business from a stellar client list—including Motorola and American Express—continually place the company at the top of annual industry rankings for major national contractors in almost every category.

growing range of services and aptitude for securing repeat business from a stellar client list continually place the company at the top of annual industry rankings for major national contractors in almost every category. Turner has worked toward innovative, ethical leadership in the industry since its founding in 1902. In its early years, the company made its mark in the construction industry by pioneering the use of reinforced concrete.

"Innovation and team relationships are the hallmarks of our accomplishments locally," says Marvin D. Doster, general manager, "and the basis for our success in exceeding our clients' expectations in terms of quality and on-time completion of projects." In Arizona, there are four different divisions of Turner Construction—commercial, education, health care, and industrial/technology. The industrial/technology division is known throughout the local high-technology business sector as Turner/On-Site.

In-Depth Experience and Resources
Through its extensive network of offices, Turner combines the accessibility and support of a local firm with the strength, stability, and resources of a national corporation. Its employees are active local citizens, building relationships in the surrounding communities and working closely with area customers, architects, subcontractors, labor, and municipal agencies to secure Turner Construction's reputation as a quality company and an excellent, ethical,

dependable builder. The Tempe office has the added support and resources of 3,400 Turner Corporation employees in 38 business units throughout the continental United States.

The commercial division's dedication to excellence in construction services is seen in high-profile structures that have been built throughout the Valley. Scottsdale's Hyatt Gainey Ranch, for example, is one of the premier resort properties in the country and required the coordination of more than 300 different subcontractors to complete work in an extremely short time frame while meeting the stringent building specifications of the client. Turner's depth of construction management skills and its solid relationships with quality subcontractors created one of the most attractive hospitality properties in Greater Phoenix.

Turner recently completed additional grandstand seating and luxury suites for International Speedway Corp. at Phoenix International Raceway's world-class, one-mile, paved oval, and is continuing with the expansion project. Concurrently, Turner is constructing improvements at several of International Speedway's other racing facilities in Florida, Missouri, and New York.

The owner of Sierra Vista Mall, serving Cochise County in the southern part of the state, is another national client with regional interests in Arizona who recognizes the broad, versatile expertise that Turner management brings to a project.

Excellence in Health Care Facilities
Ranked as the largest health care facilities builder in the United States by *Modern Healthcare* magazine for 12 years in a row,

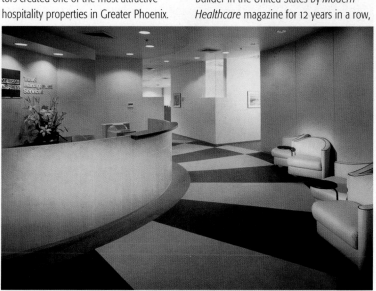

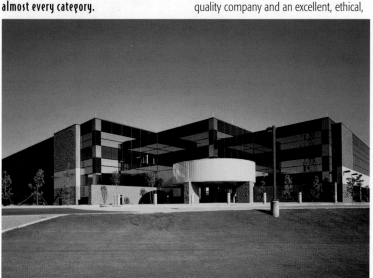

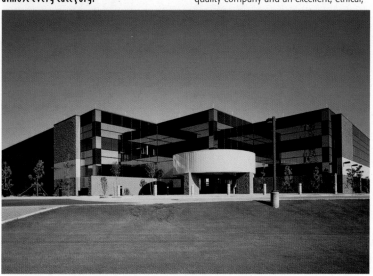

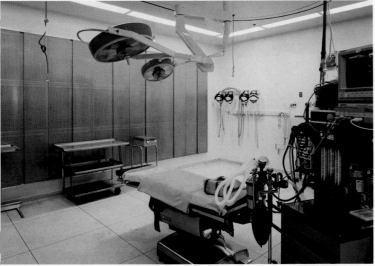

Turner has built a number of projects in the Valley, including the Palm Valley campus of Phoenix Memorial Hospital and the Gilbert Medical Office building. "We excel at projects with technical challenges such as those we encounter in the ever changing health care industry," Doster says.

Several years ago, Turner Corporation saw special opportunities in the high-technology side of the construction business and looked to On-Site Project Management as an established Arizona presence in the field. The two companies merged in 1994, melding the diversification and technical skills of each firm into what is now known as Turner/On-Site. Today, this Arizona division counts the major semiconductor industry players in the Valley among its clients.

"Our system accountability process begins at the start of each project and is continuously monitored through completion," says Doster. "We have found this results in a minimal punch list and meets our clients' schedules and financial goals

time and again." By providing early notice of important issues, they can be addressed as the project progresses instead of at the end of construction, when changes can be costly and time consuming.

This process worked flawlessly when early occupancy was the critical need for Building 99, Motorola's 161,000-square-foot, two-story structural steel, metal, and concrete curtain wall office/laboratory facility in Tempe. Turner/On-Site delivered the project on time and on budget in seven months. Its reputation for having a highly skilled, reliable staff encouraged Medtronic Micro-Rel to select Turner/On-Site to construct a 102,000-square-foot addition to its Tempe property, including a wafer fabrication facility that was both flexible and economical.

A New Concentration

Education construction is a new emphasis for Turner Construction in Arizona, but again, the company has a depth of experience to call on with a strong track record

in other markets. Turner is well versed in helping school districts in meeting the challenges education faces today to maximize value and stretch their construction dollars. "We can provide expertise up front so their bid process brings the most value in procuring services they need," says Doster.

To keep skilled employees coming into the Turner Construction pipeline and to encourage the construction industry's ability to provide employment into the next century, the company actively supports the Del E. Webb School of Construction at Arizona State University and hires interns to provide on-the-job experience.

The company's emphasis is on building relationships that last and on nurturing repeat business. "We have the desire and the expertise to provide quality products, and we want our clients to think of Turner Construction first," says Doster. "We know that begins with meeting and exceeding our commitments and their expectations each and every time."

Ranked as the largest health care facilities builder in the United States by *Modern Healthcare* magazine for 12 years in a row, Turner has built a number of projects in the Valley, including the Gilbert Medical Office building, ASM America's lithography clean room, and the Desert Samaritan Hospital operating room.

CABLE SYSTEMS INTERNATIONAL INC.

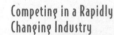

Ｗith annual sales of more than $400 million, Cable Systems International Inc. (CSI) is one of the largest privately held manufacturing companies in Arizona and a leading manufacturer of cable products for the telecommunications industry. Customer demand for leading-edge telecommunications products drives CSI's profitability. CSI's customers include regional Bell Operating Companies, Lucent Technologies, and original equipment manufacturers and distributors.

CSI was created as a subsidiary of the Phoenix-based Cable Systems Holding Company in 1995 when AT&T decided to spin off the copper cable products group. Today, the Cable Systems Holding Company is one of 85 major U.S. businesses in the Citicorp Venture Capital portfolio, and operates two subsidiaries—CSI and LoDan Electronics. LoDan Electronics, acquired in 1997, is a contract assembly service provider and a designer and manufacturer of specialized cable assemblies.

In 1998, CSI acquired a minority equity interest in IPC Information Systems. IPC, with annual revenues of $270 million, supports the financial trading industry through the design, manufacture, installation, and service of high-speed trading room workstations known as turret systems, and through the design, installation, and operations of a global wide area network supporting the financial services industry. Customers include global brokerage houses, banks, insurance companies, and financial services firms throughout the world.

Competing in a Rapidly Changing Industry

More change has occurred in the last five years in the fast-growing telecommunica-

tions industry than in the past 50 years. Eight-party telephone lines, for example, were once good enough for residential customers, but eventually one private line became the norm. Today, households with multiple telephones, computers with Internet connections, and fax machines demand two, three, and even four lines per dwelling. Through these years of growth and change, and even with the growth of wireless communications, cable and wire have continued to be the predominant medium for interconnecting customers. CSI's roots in the Bell System have been instrumental in bringing premier products to its customers. The company's reputation has always been built on a solid foundation of reliability, integrity, cutting-edge design, product quality, and customer service.

"You can't compete in the telecommunications business without listening to your customers and understanding their plans and goals," says Peter Woog, president and CEO of CSI, "because customer needs are changing almost daily, and you have to be able to change with them."

CSI leads the way in creating products that continually strive to connect its customers better, faster, and easier. For example, the product engineering team has developed VeloCSIty™, a revolutionary new Category 5 high-performance, plenum-rated local area network (LAN) cable using a unique foam skin insulation material coupled with proprietary jacketing materials. Even after accelerated aging to simulate long-term conditions in CSI's plenums, VeloCSIty™ cables meet the standards for burn compliance and electrical performance.

Another new company product is composite cables, which are copper twisted pairs jacketed together with fiber-optic, coaxial, or service distribution wire. These were developed to deliver the next generation of data and telephony services to residential and commercial subscribers. OptiCopper™ is ideal for networks, which require both fiber optics for broadband service and copper pairs to power the fiber-optic electronics or for complementary voice transmission. While some predict that fiber optics will eventually replace copper altogether as the premier transmission method in telecommunications

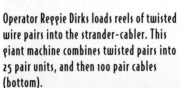

Under the leadership of President and CEO Peter A. Woog, Cable Systems International Inc. (CSI) earned its debut in Arthur Andersen's Arizona 100—the top privately held businesses in the state—ranking number seven in 1998 (top).

Operator Reggie Dirks loads reels of twisted wire pairs into the strander-cabler. This giant machine combines twisted pairs into 25 pair units, and then 100 pair cables (bottom).

Strand operator Danny Campos checks the position of twisted pairs as they move through the strand faceplate (top).

Where it all began: CSI's plastic insulated cables (PICs) have provided reliable, quality telephone service to cities across America for more than 30 years (bottom).

networks, it is today too expensive for everyday residential use, and a copper cable is still required to bring power to the fiber-optic electronics.

Whether customers need CSI's connectorized products to support standard service or the advanced technology of the future, they can count on CSI to produce them. Using CAD/CAM systems, the company can translate custom specifications into product designs quickly and cost efficiently, providing the customer with prototype samples at critical stages in the process. In its cable assembly manufacturing operations, CSI has more than 10,000 cable-plug variations to choose from and can terminate virtually every type of connector. As an ISO 9001-certified business, CSI manufactures assemblies to the highest standards in the world to support cellular telephony, digital transmission, multimedia and radio applications, the medical industry, aerospace, and various LAN applications.

The CSI Process

The manufacturing process at CSI uses the talents of 1,800 employees—enough people to run a small town, and with just as much diversity. CSI's team includes engineering, sales, marketing, production, maintenance, training, and administrative employees. Everything needed to run an

autonomous business, including food service and a medical clinic, is located on the premises.

Round-the-clock production turns 16,000-pound coils of five-sixteenth-inch copper rod into thin strands of wire that are insulated, twisted, and combined to eventually transmit voice and data in telecommunications systems. More than 200 pounds of insulated copper wiring run through the average American home, ensuring that light switches, televisions, appliances, and telecommunications equipment such as telephones and computers operate safely and efficiently. CSI's products address the outside plant infrastructure as well as the data and telecom wiring required inside homes and businesses.

CSI's 1.3 million-square-foot Phoenix plant—an area equal to 25 football fields—is located on 120 acres fronting 51st Avenue just south of I-10. The manufacturing process begins with copper rod and plastic, and continues until completed cable and wire products are shipped to customers. The plant was built in 1968 by Western Electric as the manufacturing arm of the Bell System. Then surrounded by sheep and cotton fields, the location was chosen for access to the southwestern market of the United States. The Bell System divestiture in 1984 transitioned it into an AT&T

facility until the Citicorp Venture Capital purchase in 1995 created CSI.

Building Relationships

By forming work teams, strategic partnerships, and joint ventures, CSI is expanding traditional boundaries and relationships. A 42,000-square-foot building has been built north of the plant for lease to Web Industries as part of a long-term supply

agreement for on-site slitting of raw materials needed in the manufacturing process. This partnership is expected to increase operating efficiencies and enhance CSI's financial development and performance. Long-term agreements also exist with Union Carbide for the supply of plastics and with Corella Electric Wire and Cable, a minority-owned business enterprise that insulates and supplies wire to CSI for pro-

cessing into finished cable. John Corella operates the business in a state-of-the-art manufacturing plant built by CSI just north of its main facility.

The company's special commitment to working with Minority and Women Business Enterprises (MWBEs) has been documented in a *Harvard Business Review* case study, and serves as a model for many other businesses. Corella received the Arizona Entrepreneurial Success Award from the Small Business Administration in 1996, and was named 1997 Outstanding Hispanic Executive by the Arizona Hispanic Chamber of Commerce for his successful business practices.

Fostering a New Corporate Culture

Strategic thinking has guided CSI's business development from the beginning. The firm started with an established product and a strong, well-defined client base, supported by long-term supply contracts already in place. A skilled workforce, technological know-how, and a committed senior management team provided a smooth transition from a former association with one of the largest corporations in the world to being new entrepreneurs. Continued success is dependent on more than the introduction of new products, increased market share, and acquisition growth. It involves a vision of a culture that fosters employee talent, promotes synergy between organizations and teams, and encourages employees to achieve their personal best.

Two strategic moves helped drive this shift toward a corporate culture that emphasized mutual earned respect and entrepreneurial spirit. First, an agreement was reached with the company's union, the Communications Workers of America, to develop labor partnerships that drive both employee and company growth. An innovative profit sharing program was developed, which rewards employees with profit sharing payouts that are linked to business performance. "We're asking for more employee involvement and accountability. This program allows us to reward employee involvement," says Woog.

Secondly, a continuous quality and process improvement program was introduced and implemented in all areas of the business—from order entry to manufacturing, delivery, and customer invoicing. This program instills pride in CSI's employees, lowers costs, streamlines processes, and continually improves products and service to the customer.

Establishing a Tradition of Community Support

Successfully supporting the community where its employees live and raise families

Poly-jacketing line assistant Stephen French monitors the measurement readings as a cable receives its protective exterior jacket (top).

Finished reels of PIC are transported via an overhead crane to the final test area for inspection (bottom).

...as been as important at CSI as its business success. That's why, in 1996, the firm developed and implemented CSI's Community Programs Initiatives—designed to lend the growing community a helping hand.

Community support activities are promoted through five distinct program initiatives: the CSI Foundation, CSI's Matching Funds for Volunteer Hours, the Company Store, CSI's Gifts in Kind program, and its ongoing United Way support. The programs support Valley citizens in the areas of education, health and human services, arts and culture, and community development.

Each year, the CSI Foundation receives a percentage of the company's profits to help provide community services. To make the decisions about foundation funding, a volunteer employee committee was formed from members of management and the union's executive board. Company employees also have the opportunity to earn recognition and additional financial aid for their favorite nonprofit organizations by volunteering personal time and earning matching funds for their volunteer hours. CSI has an on-site company store that offers employees a variety of gift items, and coordinates periodic employee specialty sales like the semiannual book fair. The profits generated from store sales help fund CSI's Matching Funds for Volunteer Hours program. The company's Gifts in Kind program also enables nonprofit and educational organizations to make

donation requests for both CSI products and obsolete resources. This program has helped fulfill school needs for networked classroom wiring to enable schools to promote new learning opportunity through the use of the Internet. And lastly, the annual event that helps to unify the company and bond it with the community is the Valley of the Sun United Way Campaign. This initiative serves the community by providing Valley citizens added support through a successful employee campaign and a generous foundation grant.

Planning for the Future
In positioning itself as a global telecommunications industry leader of the future,

CSI is expanding the company's product portfolio through new product offerings and looking for opportunities for additional growth partnerships with suppliers and vendors. Both its domestic and global reach will undoubtedly expand, as strategic acquisitions are identified to support expansion into new industries and new countries.

Cox Communications, Inc.

ox Communications, Inc. serves approximately 600,000 cable television customers throughout the Greater Phoenix area and is intent on becoming the preferred provider of residential and commercial digital television, digital telephone, and high-speed Internet access services. A superior, state-of-the-art, fiber-optic network provides Cox the competitive advantage of greater bandwidth that makes it possible to expand video programming options and offer additional telecommunication

services, including digital telephone and high-speed Internet access, in one convenient service package.

Cox Communications has been in the cable business since 1962, when the company purchased cable systems in Pennsylvania, followed by systems in California, Oregon, and Washington. The company's hybrid fiber-coaxial (HFC) distribution architecture replaces microwave and traditional coaxial cable technology to ensure increased channel capacity, improved reliability, and the best picture quality available for Cox's cable customers. This distribution system also positions Cox Communications at the forefront of telecommunications trends by combining digital television with digital telephone and high-speed data transmission services, and offers the customer the convenient, hassle-free, and economical advantage of using one telecommunications provider without having to add or maintain a second communications line. Once completed, the network upgrade will include 10,000 miles of infrastructure, making it the most extensive HFC network in the United States.

"We're rolling out this technology throughout the Valley in phases as techni-

cal upgrades are completed," says Gregg Holmes, vice president and general manager of Cox Communications in Phoenix. "This allows us to ensure continued high-quality customer service." About 60 percent of the 10,000 miles of network has been completely upgraded, and Cox estimates that almost every home throughout the Valley will have access to the upgraded network by the end of 2001.

Mind-Boggling Internet Speed

Cox@Home connects personal computers to the Internet via a cable modem at speeds in the 1.5 to 3 Mbps range, at least 100 times faster than telephone modem connections. This means, for example, that a data file that requires eight minutes to download using a standard 28.8 modem connection and two minutes to download on ISDN, requires only eight seconds with Cox@Home. Cox Communications' broadband network allows 24-hour-a-day, unlimited access and continued uninterrupted service. In other words, the service is always on, while the telephone lines in the customer's home remain free for voice use. Subscribers can enjoy real-time delivery of news and information, whether it's local,

national, or international. New services via the cable modem are developing daily.

"To ensure total customer satisfaction, we send a highly skilled Cox technician to the subscriber's home to install the PC connection for Cox@Home," says Holmes. "Our technician loads and configures all necessary software, tests for a successful connection, and provides the Cox@Home customer with a 20-minute training program. If a question arises any time afterward, we offer on-line customer service support as well as customer call center support, whichever the customer prefers."

Digital television will add channels to Cox's core cable selections and allow multiplexing, so the same premium pay services, such as HBO and Showtime, are available at variable times, and subscribers can enjoy the convenience of choosing when they watch a show instead of being tied to one specific programming schedule. A navigator channel sorts the options and customers select what is most convenient for them from an interactive program guide. As many as 12 digital channels are inserted into the space of one traditional analog channel, which greatly enhances

Cox Communications' multimillion-dollar Master Telecommunications Center in Chandler features a DMS 500 telephone switch to deliver phone service over Cox's hybrid fiber-coaxial network.

ay-per-view services and digital music
elections.

Cox Communications, a multiple
system operator (MSO), is publicly traded
(NYSE:COX) and based in Atlanta. Cox
expanded its operations into Arizona in
1995 with the acquisition of Dimension
Cable. A number of Dimension's staff
transitioned to Cox, adding continuity to
a high-powered and highly experienced
management team. Cox is an employer
of choice with more than 1,500 employees
dedicated to providing operational excellence and exceptional customer service. Ten
offices throughout the Valley are available
for customers served by 10,000 miles of
cable passing more than a million homes.

More then 35,000 homes and customers are added each year in Cox's local
service area, making Cox Communications
in Phoenix one of the largest and fastest
growing among the company's urban cable
systems. As the company has grown, quality customer service has continued as the
number one priority. The addition of new
services and products is making the subscriber acceptance rate even greater in
the rapidly growing Phoenix market.

Cox Communications is the first cable
operator ever to receive the J.D. Powers
customer service award. It also enjoys the
unprecedented recognition of being named
Cable Operator of the Year twice within a
five-year period by *Cablevision Magazine*.

"We want our customers to expect
the best," Holmes says, "and we have reor-
ganized operations and designed our new
services to exceed our customers' expectations." The company has revamped its
billing system and call center to respond
more efficiently as a full-service communications provider. Subscribers can also find
additional information on Arizona innovations on the company's Web page at
www.phx.cox.com.

Supporting the Community

Close ties with the community and good
corporate citizenship are important in Cox's
corporate culture. The company is commit-
ed to supporting community development,
youth, and education through many programs and charitable efforts. More than
$6 million in annual corporate donations,
in-kind donations, on-air public service
announcements, education and community
organization partnerships, and community
event sponsorships allows the company to
be an active participant. Cox Communications
leaders serve on economic development
committees, local chambers of commerce,
and boards of nonprofit organizations
such as Chicanos por la Causa, Urban
League, Make-a-Wish Foundation, Valley

Big Brothers/Big Sisters, and Arizona
Education Foundation.

Free cable service and courtesy
cable modem connectivity are also provided to schools in the Cox service area,
supported by teacher training, curriculum
materials, media literacy programs, distance
learning events, and 525 hours a month of
commercial-free educational programming.
Cox's annual Teacher of the Year and Excellence in Education and Technology
programs recognize and encourage outstanding educators and educational practices.
All combined, the company's generous
support of local nonprofit organizations
and education firmly positions Cox as an
anchor in the community.

Into the Future

Driven by increased demand for more
competitive residential and commercial

access to technology, the Telecommunications Reform Act was passed in 1996. This
legislation has dramatically changed the
ground rules for competition and regulation
throughout the communications industry.
The act's elimination of cross-market entry
barriers has created new opportunities such
as Cox@Home and Cox Digital Telephone,
and enables Cox to provide the added value
of convenient, one-stop, total communications service to its customers.

Future development includes
Cox@Work, where high-speed data will be
extended to businesses across the Valley.
Delivering high-quality customer service
and being on the forefront of technological
developments help to assure Cox's telecommunications capability as a full-service,
facilities-based communications provider
offering new services well into the next
century.

Cox Communications' new high-speed Internet access service, Cox@Home, offers
a lower-cost, higher-performance Internet
access service (top).

Summer campers participating in the third
annual Camp Cox get ready for a team-
building program. Camp Cox is one of the
many annual community service programs
sponsored by Cox Communications to
benefit local youth (bottom).

Business travelers who come to Scottsdale for stays of more than a few days find comfortable, inviting accommodations at Homestead Village, which is within walking distance of excellent restaurants, movie theaters, shopping areas, and walking paths. This home-away-from-home is one of five Homestead Village properties in Greater Phoenix meeting the needs of extended-stay visitors who want consistent, quality lodging at a moderate price. Other Homestead Village locations in the Valley

are in Tempe, Northwest Valley, Deer Valley, and Mesa.

A publicly traded company headquartered in Atlanta, Homestead Village is a nationally known developer, owner, and operator of more than 120 moderately priced, extended-stay lodging properties across the United States that are built especially for the business traveler. Guests are provided with all the essentials for a consistent, quality stay, whether it's for a few days, a week, a month, or longer. "Recent industry studies show that extended stay is the fastest-growing segment of the hospitality market," says Homestead Village Scottsdale General Manager James Tevault. "And less than one-quarter of that demand currently is being met."

There are 120 Homestead Village properties in 20 states with 20 more currently under construction. The Scottsdale property is jointly owned with locally based SCG Realty Company.

A Host of Amenities

To meet practical, everyday needs, the attractively furnished studios at Homestead Village feature a fully equipped kitchen, which includes a full-size refrigerator, a microwave oven, a coffeemaker, a toaster, and a double-burner cooktop. In addition, a 24-hour guest laundry is available on the premises, and daily housekeeping and towel services are provided.

All rooms include an easy chair or sofa, and an iron and ironing board. Free local telephone calls and complimentary incoming domestic faxes are a plus for business travelers, and each studio has telephones with data ports, personalized voice mail, and separate work areas. Copy service is available on the premises, and all messages, mail, overnight packages, and faxes are delivered to each guest's room at the end of each business day.

Guest services are provided by a personable staff that looks forward to making each visitor's stay a pleasant one. "We get to know our guests on a first-name basis," says Tevault. "We're a family here, and we want to do everything we can to exceed their expectations."

Convenient Locations

The Scottsdale property is within walking distance or a short drive of many of the attractions that draw thousands of visitors annually to the city, including Old Town Scottsdale. The Olive Garden, Z Tejas, P.F. Chang's China Bistro, Roy's, Ruth's Chris Steak House, Baby Kay's Cajun Kitchen, and Cafe Terra Cotta are just a sampling of the many globe-spanning restaurants that are convenient to Scottsdale's Homestead Village. Guests who are willing to drive a little farther can step back in time for a real western dining adventure at the world-famous Rawhide Steakhouse, which is

Business travelers who come to Scottsdale for stays of more than a few days find comfortable, inviting accommodations at Homestead Village, which is within walking distance of excellent restaurants, movie theaters, shopping areas, and walking paths (top).

To meet practical, everyday needs, the attractively furnished studios at Homestead Village feature a fully equipped kitchen, which includes a full-size refrigerator, a microwave oven, a coffeemaker, a toaster, and a double-burner cooktop (bottom).

This home-away-from-home is one of five Homestead Village properties in Greater Phoenix meeting the needs of extended-stay visitors who want consistent, quality lodging at a moderate price.

surrounded by a life-size replica of an 1880s western town complete with live country-western music, saloon girls, a crooked card dealer, and real cowboys.

Scottsdale is a utopia for sports enthusiasts with more than 100 world-class, traditional, and desert golf courses, plus the attraction of the San Francisco Giants' spring training in March at nearby Scottsdale Stadium. College and professional football games at Sun Devil Stadium are just a few minutes south of Homestead Village on the Arizona State University (ASU) campus. Shopping aficionados will be equally satisfied with a visit to Scottsdale Fashion Square, offering more than 175 renowned retailers. Extended hours every Thursday night encourage an evening Art Walk just a few blocks away with special exhibitions, demonstrations, entertain-

ment, and refreshments; and an ambitious schedule of music, dance, and theater performances are featured at the Scottsdale Center for the Arts in Civic Center Plaza.

Homestead Village in Tempe is convenient to the Phoenix Zoo, the Desert Botanical Garden, live productions at Grady Gammage Auditorium on the ASU campus, and the Arizona Mills Mall featuring shops, restaurants, and a 16-screen movie complex. Access to Interstate 17 places the Northwest Valley Homestead Village on West Dunlap in close proximity to downtown Phoenix with restaurants, shopping, and entertainment at the Arizona Center; professional basketball and hockey at America West Arena; and professional baseball at Bank One Ballpark.

The northernmost Homestead Village in Greater Phoenix at Deer Valley is a good

jumping off point for visits to Flagstaff, Sedona, and the Grand Canyon. It's also near Arrowhead Mall and Metro Center Mall, and convenient to a number of restaurants, including Outback Steakhouse, Native New Yorker, Garcia's, and Bill Johnson's Big Apple. Mesa's Homestead Village is near Fiesta Mall, as well as a number of popular local eateries.

As the national network of Homestead Village locations grows, the company conducts extensive consumer research to ensure that property designs meet the special needs of the growing extended-stay market. Responding to feedback from its guests, Homestead Village continues to improve its amenities to ensure that customers will return to the properties whenever they have a need for long-term accommodations.

PERNA LUXURY REAL ESTATE

The unique needs of a changing, upscale marketplace inspired Lou and Jane Perna to establish Perna Luxury Real Estate in Scottsdale, and their personal style and classic marketing strategies have proved successful far beyond their original projections. ❧ As a consultant in buying and selling residential property, acreage/ranches, and investment real estate, Perna Luxury Real Estate is uniquely qualified for any luxury real estate transaction. The company's experience extends to northeast Scottsdale golf

The unique needs of a changing, upscale marketplace inspired Lou and Jane Perna to establish Perna Luxury Real Estate in Scottsdale, and their personal style and classic marketing strategies have proved successful far beyond their original projections.

communities such as Desert Mountain, Terravita, Troon, North Troon, Estancia, Greyhawk, DC Ranch, and Legend Trail. Its ranch/acreage experience, like the John Wayne-Wingfield Ranch in Nogales, Arizona, and the De La Montana Development in Tubac, Arizona, assures clients that the company has a solid understanding of the luxury real estate market throughout Arizona.

Filling a Market Need

"If you're going to look for a million-dollar home in the northeast market, you need to see us," says CEO Lou Perna. "We have found our niche as a top-notch luxury real estate company staffed by high-quality professionals who know how to make buying a home a good experience."

Perna's typical buyer owns his or her own business, or is a high-level CEO with an annual income of $250,000-plus and net worth of $3 million or more. For many, it's a second, third, or fourth home, and a significant number are purchased for cash. While Perna sells many homes in the $400,000 to $500,000 range, sales also have pushed upward to $3 million, with the firm's average transaction being around $850,000. In the thriving market where they concentrate their efforts, the Pernas

find plenty of choices to offer clients; in 1998, the firm generated $42 million in sales revenue.

Personalized Approach for Surprising Results

The Pernas' commonsense approach begins with careful listening, and follows through with experienced consulting and the sharing of proven advice to help buyers realize their goals. An initial meeting allows the parties to get acquainted; the Pernas learn about the individuals involved—who they are, what they like and don't like, their hobbies and interests, their

objectives in buying a home, their expectations, the timetable, and any special concerns that might affect the purchase.

Once the Pernas have established a confident relationship, a search is made using their thorough knowledge of the luxury market and all available technological resources to identify the properties that meet each client's special requirements. In the time they take to identify close fits, the Pernas systematically sift through hundreds of possible properties, but the final selections are nearly always right on target—to the surprise and pleasure of their buyers.

Perna Luxury Real Estate boasts offices in north Scottsdale and Denver, as well as in Kitzbühel, Austria, and London, England, to handle prospective European clients.

Sellers look to Perna for maximum exposure for their properties through its extensive contacts in the Scottsdale market, as well as the firm's relationship with 24 strategically located luxury real estate brokerage firms around the country. International affiliations also increase sales opportunities.

"There are a lot of wealthy people in Europe who want to invest in the West, and they love Arizona for the warmth and the beauty and the desert," says Perna.

Perna's staff and agents use their knowledge of the luxury market and all available technological resources to identify the properties that meet each client's special requirements.

Perna Luxury Real Estate is uniquely qualified for any luxury real estate transaction, listing homes such as the 10-acre hacienda-style Goldfield Ranch with 360-degree views and the 7,100-square-foot Village of Eagle Feather with a rambling covered patio and a fountain courtyard.

"There are more than 123,000 visitors a year from Germany alone." They need to know whom they can trust, what the tax laws are, what is permissible under those laws—the same concerns a U.S. citizen would have when considering buying property in a foreign country.

When a European buyer dials Perna's office in Kitzbühel or London for information, a fellow European answers the phone and forms that reliable link from the beginning as someone who knows the customer's language and understands his or her culture. Perna also has aligned its business with a CPA firm that has an international representative who can discuss tax ramifications both in the United States and in the buyer's country. A law firm with an experienced international person on its staff is also available to explain the legal ramifications of a deal.

Relying on Experience

Perna's phenomenal success and growing reputation are not by accident, but the result of a disciplined, strategic plan influenced by Jane Perna's decade in commercial and residential real estate and Lou Perna's 27 years of experience as an executive with Procter & Gamble, and later in directing sales and marketing for Desert Mountain.

"We carefully select our advertising vehicles and we spend 10 times more of our revenues on advertising than any other real estate company," Lou Perna says. "From the beginning, we have worked to position the company, not a specific property." Building that reputation, both nationally and internationally, has taken time and

patience, but that up-front investment is paying off. Perna also gives credit to Wes Sparling at SC&M Services, and his award-winning advertising counsel.

Membership in organizations such as the International Real Estate Federation (FIABCI-USA) links the firm with 4,000 contacts in countries around the world, and the company's advertisements in hand-picked European publications are increasingly influencing European buyers to look to Perna for home buying expertise. As the business grows, word of mouth from a growing list of satisfied clients also helps Perna build on its reputation for

trustworthiness and exceptional service, both domestically and abroad.

"We want to be recognized universally as a quality company that walks the talk—the kind of company that follows through and really makes a difference," says Perna. For the future, the company looks toward growing its Scottsdale operations and to future expansion in Europe—but the Pernas' aspirations don't stop there. Casting an ambitious eye on establishing contacts throughout the Pacific Rim, the Pernas look forward to the day when the sun never sets on Perna Luxury Real Estate operations.

The earliest visitors to the Southwest were intrigued by the chili pepper—which represents the true symbol of warmth and hospitality—and they never forgot the first time they experienced it. That's why Sun Destinations Scottsdale attaches a chili pepper wreath to the front door to intrigue and welcome the company's visitors to its premier vacation rental properties. Sun Destinations manages privately owned, beautifully furnished, luxury and moderately priced vacation residences, providing visitors with all

the comforts of a home away from home plus the amenities of a top Scottsdale resort. The company has helped more than 2,000 people find homes, and a substantial number of its renters represent repeat business. The company's sites are so popular that wise visitors book for the year ahead as they are leaving to ensure that they will get the accommodations they want—often the same house or condominium each year.

The success of Sun Destinations has been determined not by one single action, but through its attention to the hundreds of little details that make each stay enjoyable. "We try to put ourselves in our clients shoes," says President Thomas D. Kuffler. "Our visitors are in a strange town, maybe a strange country, and there's a special satisfaction in helping them feel comfortable." More and more visitors are coming from Canada and Europe, where travelers accustomed to staying in villas find private homes an attractive option.

Sun Destinations, founded in 1996, is managed by Kuffler and his founding partners Grant Sardachuk and Paul Kuffler. Together, they offer more than 60 years of real estate experience. "'We're involved on a day-to-day basis with managing and marketing," Kuffler says, "and we continually work to provide the best service for our two client groups--the guests who rent the properties and the property owners."

Comforts of Home

All Sun Destinations homes are attractive properties in preferred areas, renting for between 40 to 60 percent less than a hotel or resort with peak season rates

Together, Thomas D. Kuffler, president of Sun Destinations, and partners Grant Sardachuk and Paul Kuffler have more than 60 years of real estate and business experience.

Sun Destinations' staff is comprised of highly trained, dedicated travel and real estate professionals.

Many of Sun Destinations' managed properties capture the very essence of the southwestern lifestyle.

(December 20 to April 18) ranging from $3,000 to $10,000 monthly. Arriving visitors find all the comforts of home--fresh linens; fully equipped kitchens with cookware, appliances, and table service; attractive furnishings; cable television; swimming pools; and free local telephone calls. Often, special arrangements can even be made for the family pet.

The company's exclusive Platinum Collection are world-class properties that include premier custom homes and patio homes that usually feature a private pool and tremendous views. The Gold Collection's luxury choices include some of the finest patio homes, condos, and townhomes throughout the Scottsdale area. Surprisingly affordable, the Silver Collection includes locations more comfortable and economical than most hotels with convenient locations to all the amenities the Valley has to offer.

In addition to private residences, Sun Destinations also manages Scottsdale Desert Casitas, 95 newly renovated, fully furnished one-bedroom suites near Scottsdale's fine shops, art museums, and parks. Desert Casitas offers the convenience of a hotel and the space and amenities of a comfortably furnished apartment complex, including a full staff and on-site check-in capability. The suites are rented predominantly to longer-term snowbirds and corporate relocations. Moderately priced, including utilities, the apartment-style units offer weekly maid service, fully equipped

kitchens, gas barbecues, laundry facilities, and some even have business stations.

Desert Casitas guests can enjoy beautifully landscaped grounds with a heated swimming pool, a spa, and two tennis courts, as well as complimentary membership to a nearby L.A. Fitness facility. Located on Miller Road just south of McDowell Road, Desert Casitas is adjacent to Scottsdale's famous greenbelt, known as Indian Bend Wash, which runs 25 miles from north Scottsdale all the way south to Tempe. Guests discover bike paths, lakes, in-line skating, or leisurely walks are just a few steps from each casita's door. Visitors who fly in and out of the city find the location convenient to Sky Harbor International Airport.

Business and Pleasure

Sun Destinations' guests for all of these properties are vacationing families, international tourists, traveling businesspeople, or any other business or leisure travelers needing a place to stay for as little as a week or as long as several months. Many Valley corporations, including Motorola, UPS, and American Express Travel, use Sun Destinations' services for temporary housing for new trainees and relocating employees or for luxury lodging for incoming executives and clients. Some renters simply need a home while they are searching for permanent housing or waiting for their home to be built.

With a state-of-the-art, computerized reservation system, Sun Destinations' reservationists are able to spend more time exploring every want and need of the company's guests.

Rental arrangements are completed by Sun Destinations' cordial, bilingual reservations staff, which handles all aspects of the rental process from helping visitors select just the right property to sending out confirmations and collecting rents. The staff's state-of-the-art computer system was especially designed to handle phone traffic, Internet inquiries, and reservations.

"Our biggest challenge is matching people with exactly what they are looking for, so they enjoy themselves and come back," says Noelle Fournier, director of reservations. "We have so many choices and locations to offer and we listen carefully to determine their individual wants and needs." Fournier notes that many out-of-state guests ask for a pool, which Sun Destinations considers standard in the Scottsdale area.

The reservations staff also can help visitors coordinate golf packages at one of more than two dozen championship golf courses within minutes of most residences—whether visitors are looking for lush fairways or a unique desert experience. Reservationists also are resources for advice in arranging tennis, hiking, boating, or fitness programs for more active visitors, as well as more relaxing activities such as shopping, dining, spa visits, and sight-seeing. Scottsdale is the destination for most leisure visitors, but Sun Destinations' homes also serve as a hub for trips to other parts of the state.

Trustworthy Service

Such exceptional residences often belong to second-home owners who want an agency they can trust to maintain and rent their property when they are not in town. Owners can use their homes six weeks of the year without sacrificing rental opportunities. In other instances, owners have

purchased the homes specifically to generate investment income. All homes must qualify to become a Sun Destinations property by passing a series of inspections and market analysis based on location, size, number of rooms, and amenities. "We look carefully at each unit to be certain it meets the expectations of our rental clients," says Kuffler, "and if necessary we make recommendations to the owner where we believe a change or improvement is needed."

Sun Destinations' maintenance department takes care of regular services like pest control and air-conditioning, as well as responding to emergency concerns on a 24-hour basis. For a flat fee, Sun Destinations also will safeguard and maintain a residence for home owners who do not want to rent out their property.

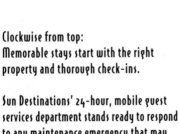

Clockwise from top:
Memorable stays start with the right property and thorough check-ins.

Sun Destinations' 24-hour, mobile guest services department stands ready to respond to any maintenance emergency that may arise.

Managed properties are well appointed with outstanding amenities and appealing surroundings.

MAY PHOTOGRAPHY

in Arizona for Canada's 7,000-member Royal LePage Realtor network. Sun Destinations is also a member of the Vacation Rental Managers Association, an industry association of similar management companies throughout the United States and Canada. And, on a broader scope, Sun Destinations has forged a unique partnership with Resort Condominiums International (RCI), the largest time share operator in the world. For a modest fee, owner clients of Sun Destinations can join RCI and vacation in any of its 3,000 resorts in 80 countries.

While corporate headquarters is in Scottsdale, where increasing the number of properties under management is a primary goal, Sun Destinations' management team also is exploring other resort areas for expansion. "We're looking at Summit County in Colorado, where we see potential opportunity in the Vail Valley, and the Palm Springs and the Palm Desert markets," Kuffler says. Sun Destinations' goal is to take the management successes experienced in Scottsdale to new locations, while retaining the company's regional uniqueness and local flavor wherever it goes.

Scottsdale Desert Casitas prides itself on exceptional guest services; offers excellent amenities and a warm, inviting atmosphere; and has been newly renovated, with both work and play in mind.

Property management is Sun Destinations' only business, which encourages property owners' confidence in the care and attention their homes receive.

Complete trust-fund accounting services provide detailed monthly reports, which show rental activities and expenses so owners can easily track the financial performance of their property.

High-Tech Connections

Sun Destinations' worldwide, comprehensive marketing program is carefully designed to differentiate it from other management services, and it reaches out to local, regional, national, and international publications through advertising as well as direct mail and sales promotions. The company's reputation for quality and professionalism extends to its Web site at www.sundestinations.com, which has been a focal point of its marketing program from the beginning.

Nearly 45 percent of Sun Destinations' business comes via the Internet, where the Rental Wizard guides potential visitors from anywhere in the world to each property's photograph and description. Most clients come from the Midwest and western Canada, and about 50 percent of Sun Destinations' guests come with families.

Locally, the company is affiliated with the Scottsdale Chamber of Commerce,

the Tempe Chamber of Commerce, the Greater Phoenix Convention & Visitors Bureau, and the Scottsdale Association of Realtors, and is the exclusive provider of luxury vacation home rentals to the Barrett-Jackson Classic Car Auction, which annually attracts 10,000 visitors to the Valley of the Sun.

More than 7,000 registered travel agents and 3,000 Realtors are affiliated with Sun Destinations through the Travel Partners Network, and Sun Destinations has been designated the Snowbird Connection

POWERTRUSION 2000 INTERNATIONAL, INC.

S o often today, we hear more about environmental disasters and problems than we do about environmental solutions. Global warming, pollution, and deforestation are critical issues that citizens of the world must address, but finding solutions to these problems is an overwhelming and seemingly impossible task. Fortunately, an innovative Scottsdale business has found a way to play a significant role in lessening our impact on the planet while helping improve the standard of living worldwide. 🌵 Founded in 1997

by entrepreneur Dr. Daryl V. Turner, Powertrusion 2000 International, Inc. is committed to helping the United States and developing countries meet their growth needs without destroying the environment. As the population continues to expand in the United States and even more rapidly in the developing world, new roads will be built, power will be generated, and goods will be transported. Powertrusion 2000 is a company that can help supply communities around the world with innovative products made from re-

cycled or recyclable materials, helping them achieve their infrastructure development goals in a sustainable manner. Powertrusion 2000 has positioned itself to become the leader in environmentally sound alternative materials to be used in infrastructure products traditionally made from scarce resources like wood, metals, or petrochemicals.

Over the past few years, Powertrusion 2000 has accomplished more than most businesses achieve in 10 years. In fact, the time between when a product is con-

ceived and when it enters the market has been reduced to just one year, a fraction of the time it takes other companies at the same level of development in similar industries.

The first Powertrusion 2000 product, a composite polymer utility pole, hit the market in 1998, and has received significant attention from the press and the firm's customers due to its revolutionary concept. The PT 2000 pole aims to provide an environmentally responsible alternative to the 5 million-plus trees that are cut down each year in the United States for utility poles. PT 2000 poles are unique because they do not need the preservatives or chemicals—such as creosote and copper arsenic—required to impregnate wooden poles, emit no emissions to adjacent waterways, and leave nothing behind for marine life to eat and later expel into the environment. There are no emissions into the air and no hazardous wastes to dispose of at the end of the pole's useful life, and the poles will not rot, rust, or corrode. The poles are relatively maintenance free for their up-to-80-year lifetime, and afterward are 100 percent recyclable.

In partnership with American Forest's Global Re-Leaf 2000 Program, the company not only saves a tree, but plants a tree at the company's cost for every power pole it sells. "Just imagine, for every million poles we sell a year, we save a million trees, and then we plant another million trees throughout the world," says Turner. "In America alone, 5 million trees are cut down each year to supply the need for power poles and every year it compounds, so you can see what a powerful statement this is." The second product that the company was contracted to develop and manufacture is a container top designed to be used with intermodal shipping containers. These container tops will be made from recycled plastics, and will be replacing their steel and fiberglass predecessors. With the millions of containers used for cargo shipped around the world, Powertrusion 2000's container tops will create a signifi-

Powertrusion 2000 International, Inc. and its founder, Dr. Daryl V. Turner, plan to make the company's composite utility poles the benchmark for the power distribution industry.

RICK MUELLER PHOTOGRAPHY

cant new market for recycled plastics. In addition, they are energy saving and easier to use and handle.

The technology invented by Powertrusion 2000 is also being applied to other products currently under development, such as highway guardrails, low-cost telephone poles, cable trays, bridges, support beams, shipping pallets, marine pilings, and automotive and aerospace parts.

Many of Powertrusion 2000's relationships are global, and the company plans to manufacture its products directly in the markets where they are needed. This relationship with the host country helps contribute to the local economy, protects the country's hard currency reserves, and increases the level of development through the transfer of technology. The company's first international joint venture was established in 1998 in Mexico, and other joint venture plants are planned for developing countries such as the Philippines, United Arab Emirates, China, Greece, India, South Africa, and Chile.

Powertrusion 2000's multitalented, internationally savvy management team readily meets the special challenges presented by the global nature of their business. The company has attracted staff members who speak two or more languages fluently, and most have experience working with other international businesses. A close association with Thunderbird, the American Graduate School of International Manage-

ment, and Arizona State University ensures that the company is always up to date on the latest information on international business, environmental solutions, and engineering.

Powertrusion 2000's strong commitment to sustainable international development and environmental innovation will lead the company to the forefront of the battle to find solutions to the world's most pressing environmental concerns. By providing high-quality, economical materials that can be used in the place of scarce natural resources, Powertrusion 2000 International, Inc. is ensuring that governments around the world have the alternatives they need to make wise environmental decisions.

Powertrusion 2000's management team believes that innovative, high-tech materials and products are the key to the company's success.

AVNET, INC.

s a middleman in the electronics and computer distribution business, Avnet, Inc. isn't exactly a household name. Many consumers may not recognize the company's name, but this multinational corporation boasts more than 8,800 employees and affects almost everyone's life through the products it distributes for the manufacture of everything from computers and cameras to cellular phones and airplanes. ❦ The company traces its roots back to 1921, when Charles Avnet began as a broker of radio parts for

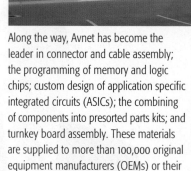

ship radio operators and ham radio enthusiasts who had homemade equipment. It evolved into a franchise distribution business in the mid-1920s, supplying parts to radio dealers and manufacturers when factory-made radios became available to consumers. This small, family business went public in 1956, and by the end of the 1970s, had exceeded $1 billion in sales.

The now-$6 billion business—which relocated to the Valley in 1998 from its home base of Great Neck, New York—markets, inventories, and improves the products of some of the world's most prestigious electronic component and computer-equipment manufacturers. Avnet is a leading distributor of computer products, semiconductors, and interconnect, passive, and electromechanical components. Avnet has sales in 58 countries, with an emphasis on industrial customers in the United States, Canada, Mexico, Europe, Asia, Australia, New Zealand, and South Africa.

The company today focuses on the marketing of electronics and computers, and is franchised by more than 250 of the industry's best-known suppliers, including Motorola, Intel, Hewlett-Packard, Texas Instruments, Compaq, and IBM, for a host of industry customers, among them AlliedSignal, Boeing, and Honeywell.

Along the way, Avnet has become the leader in connector and cable assembly; the programming of memory and logic chips; custom design of application specific integrated circuits (ASICs); the combining of components into presorted parts kits; and turnkey board assembly. These materials are supplied to more than 100,000 original equipment manufacturers (OEMs) or their contract manufacturers.

Supplying a Wide Range of Products

Avnet's Computer Marketing organization is composed of two principal businesses, as well as smaller niche companies such as Avnetdirect.com, which sells mid-range servers directly to smaller companies over the Internet.

The first principal business within Avnet's Computer Marketing organization is Avnet Computer, which sells directly to a management information systems (MIS) customer base within the Fortune 1,000. Avnet Computer supplies these customers with an array of benefits such as consulting

and services integration, which provides troubleshooting and problem-solving assistance.

The division's second principal business within the Computer Marketing organization is Hall-Mark Computer Products, which deals with value-added resellers (VARs) and supports them in their interaction with their account base. Hall-Mark

Clockwise from top:
Avnet, Inc.'s global headquarters is located in Phoenix.

Roy Vallee is chairman and CEO of Avnet.

Avnet employees are always ready to respond to customers' needs.

Avnet's headquarters was relocated from Great Neck, New York, to the Valley in 1998.

Avnet's Computer Marketing organization sells to both consumers and value-added resellers alike.

also provides credit services, marketing, lead generation programs, and leasing. In addition, this division is now in line for significant global growth through a series of acquisitions and start-up operations in Europe and Asia, providing these new clients with the same high level of quality that Hall-Mark delivers to its North American customers.

Avnet Electronics Marketing was formed as a result of an extensive, four-month evaluation based on interviews with approximately 1,200 customers, 15 suppliers, and 1,000 Avnet employees. The company also conducted benchmark surveys on successful companies both within and beyond the electronics-distribution industry. What this research showed was that customers wanted access to Avnet's entire supplier line card—a list of the various suppliers and their product offerings—and value-added services through one account manager. They also wanted account managers who focus on customers with similar business and technical needs, as well as sales representatives who are product experts working in close geographic proximity to their customers.

By combining the services of the former Hamilton Hallmark, Time Electronics, and Penstock divisions, Avnet Electronics Marketing now offers full customer access for all Avnet products, services, and brands through a single account manager. Customers have the ability to move between Avnet's namesake products and other brands simultaneously, and without the hassle of dealing with numerous account managers.

Connecting to Its Customers

To better serve its OEM customers who outsource all or most of their materials from multiple Avnet divisions, the company

The Avnet Data Center in Chandler handles calls from all around the world.

formed an innovative Electronics Marketing Group (EMG) unit, Avnet Integrated Material Services (IMS), centralizing customer access to all needed materials, technical support, and value-added services regardless of the originating Avnet division. A Hewlett-Packard server in Chandler allows the company and its customers to communicate 24 hours a day anywhere in the world they need to be connected.

Customers can electronically send their orders to Avnet's computer system, which then reserves parts from its inventory to be shipped as needed or pipelined directly to IMS customers from Avnet's various suppliers. This delivery flexibility has created a dramatic shift in distribution for suppliers who formerly sold most of their volume directly to customers. By joining forces with Avnet IMS, suppliers find that their customers can quickly counteract upside and downside changes in demand that have plagued them and the industry from time to time in the past. With more than $1 billion worth of electronic components in inventory worldwide, Avnet can act as an industry shock absorber for materials management, and agreements with supplying manufacturers allow Avnet

to be credited for components that become obsolete or have been reduced in price.

Outsourcing materials management to Avnet allows customers to reduce their materials and logistics costs significantly, and assures them that production components or subassemblies will be delivered to their factory floor or contract manufacturer's assembly stations on a just-in-time basis.

Pictured here is the Avnet Programming Center in Chandler.

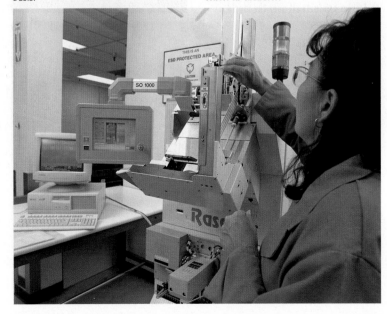

Avnet keeps these products either in its own warehouse or in on-site stores with Avnet IMS employees in charge. Components are released by the customer's electronic signal to Avnet IMS through an assortment of proprietary auto-replenishment systems. This shortens design cycles and time-to-market for products, allowing customers to build their products to correspond with incoming orders without incurring shortages or having to stockpile components or finished products.

At Home in Greater Phoenix

Avnet's move to the Valley from Great Neck was a strategic decision led by the need to select a single corporate location to bring the holding company's myriad entities under one geographic roof, which results in better—not to mention faster—business decisions.

Avnet first considered California for its new home; the company's Electronics Marketing Group was already headquartered there, as was a major distribution center in Culver City with an inventory

base of about $100 million. The Coalinga earthquake of 1983, however, made it obvious that, in the event of another quake, the company might not be able to supply its customers for days, weeks, even months. Avnet also looked at Dallas, home of Hall-Mark Electronics, which had been the third-largest electronics distributor in North America before it was acquired by Avnet in 1993. New York, center of Avnet's legal and financial departments, also was considered before the company opted for Phoenix.

"The move was a good business and personal fit," says Roy Vallee, Avnet chairman and CEO. "We wanted a western location because of our concentration of customers, and the Valley appealed to us, with weather and a time zone that allow us to get every shipment out every day. Also, we realized that whenever we recruited people to come here, they liked it and stayed." Vallee finds the business-friendly government policies, the strong educational infrastructure, and the availability of a highly skilled workforce attractive, as well.

The company now has 2,200 employees and close to a million square feet of local facilities, making it the largest public company headquartered in Greater Phoenix.

Avnet already had a presence in the Valley with a components warehouse in Chandler, built 12 years ago and recently increased to more than 400,000 square feet at a capital cost of more than $20 million. At the firm's computer distribution facility, also in Chandler, 800 employees work from 6 a.m. to midnight, processing millions of sales orders and inventory requests coming in daily from around the world. Avnet has other facilities internationally that supplement these two major warehouses.

Avnet is committed to the use of technology in best serving its customers. The company's electronic data interchange network—which is linked to major customers and suppliers—provides customers with on-line pricing and availability information, direct-order entry, inventory analysis, shipment scheduling, and electronic shipping advice and invoicing. Any order taken by

Avnet's Programming Center can customize the company's products to customers' specifications.

Avnet's highly trained employees utilize the company's state-of-the-art facilities to deliver products all over the world.

6 p.m. is shipped that same night. Avnet stocks more than 1 million different components in its warehouses, and about a third of those shipped are customized to individual client specifications.

A Worldwide Industry Leader

Acknowledged today as the industry leader in the use of integrated materials management techniques, value-added services, and advanced logistics and information technologies, Avnet shows no sign of losing that position. With its strong financial base and dedication to quality service, the company will continue to build on its ability to supply its worldwide customers with top product lines, broad inventories, extensive value-added capabilities, the highest level of technical support, and cost-effective materials management services.

"Our customers are going global and so are we," Vallee says. "They need a distributor who can service their needs the same way in Ireland as in Singapore and Bombay. Avnet's customers tend to deal with a few technically advanced, financially sound, global distributors who possess the top products. Domestic customers who outsource materials management to Avnet often want the capability world-

wide." Avnet acquired its first overseas companies in the United Kingdom, France, and Scandinavia in 1991.

The company's pan-European, wide-area computer network—the leading transaction-processing multilingual, multicurrency system among European distributors—offers an example of how Avnet is staying ahead of the international competitive curve. The system eliminates problems with different computer systems, languages, and currencies, and allows the productivity advantages and economies of scale achieved by centralized logistics. Using this centralized, automated system, the company sold $5.9 billion worth of components in fiscal 1998.

More than 20 acquisitions in the past six years have bolstered Avnet's universal expansion. The company made its way into the Asian market in January 1995, followed by five more acquisitions there, which produced $300 million of business. The company has opened facilities in three cities in mainland China and is looking for similar long-term strategic opportunities throughout the region.

While much of the company's growth is predicted to come from the Asian market, especially mainland China, Avnet is looking at Latin America and Eastern Europe as expanding sources of opportunity as well.

"Right now, we see three key areas of opportunity," Vallee explains. "Integrated materials services, both domestically and internationally; business development in Asia; and the computer products business. We will go anywhere in the world that electronic equipment is being built and computers are being bought."

Phoenix's talented workforce is one of Avnet's greatest assets.

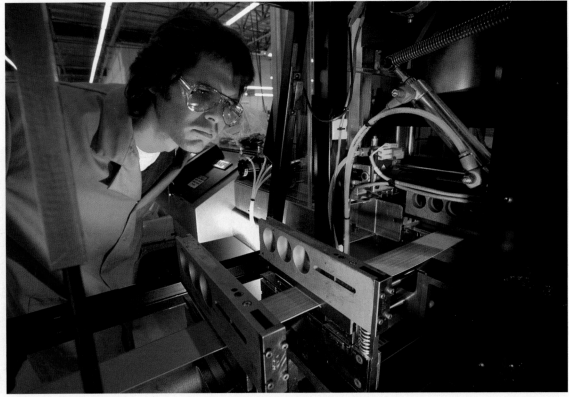

GRAND BAY HOTELS & RESORTS

Grand Bay Hotels & Resorts was created to become one of the world's finest collections of highly distinctive destination resorts and urban hotels. Each offers travelers a magnificent experience, graced by every imaginable pleasure and convenience in an atmosphere of comfort, splendor, and ease. ❦ What separates the collection from other luxury hotels and resorts is an emphasis on choices that provide a more stress-free, relaxing experience for vacation travelers and a more

productive, efficient experience for business travelers.

Grand Bay Hotels & Resorts was created in 1998 when Patriot American Hospitality, one of the world's largest hotel companies, formed a new Luxury Division by merging two luxury hotel and resort companies. One was Grand Bay Hotels and the other was Carefree Resorts, which had its roots in the Valley of the Sun. Carefree Resorts got its start as a division of Westcor, known for developing such shopping malls as Metrocenter, Scottsdale Fashion Square, and Paradise Valley Mall, along with local hotels and resorts including The Buttes and The Boulders.

The Grand Bay Hotels & Resorts collection features destination resorts including (clockwise from top right) The Boulders in the high Sonoran Desert foothills north of Scottsdale, Las Casitas Village at Puerto Rico's El Conquistador Resort & Country Club, and The Peaks Resort & Spa in Telluride.

Headquartered in Phoenix, Grand Bay Hotels & Resorts offers tempting choices for healthy, relaxing, productive travel, as shown by its acquisition of Golden Door, North America's premier destination spa. Golden Door has been ranked as America's number one spa every year since the Zagat U.S. Survey began awarding the honor in 1988. Grand Bay Hotels & Resorts is creating a Golden Door Spa at each of its resorts and a Golden Door CitySpa at each hotel.

That's just the beginning of the appealing differences that characterize Grand Bay Hotels & Resorts. Guest room amenities, for example, reinforce the concept of healthy choices. Among the pleasures are Golden Door skin care products, fresh workout clothes daily, exercise equipment, and lavishly stocked refreshment centers with healthy snacks as well as traditional treats.

Another distinctive element is service. Guests' needs and requests are not only anticipated, but remembered. When a guest visits again—or even visits a sister hotel or resort—those same personal preferences are carefully observed. The company's attitude toward service is reflected in its motto: "Seek opportunities to create memories."

The Grand Bay Hotels & Resorts collection features destination resorts including The Boulders in Carefree; Carmel Valley Ranch on California's Monterey Peninsula; Grand Bay Hotel Puerto de la Navidad in Manzanillo, Mexico; Las Casitas Village at Puerto Rico's El Conquistador Resort & Country Club; The Lodge at Ventana

Canyon in Tucson; and The Peaks Resort & Spa at Telluride. Also featured are luxury hotels including Grand Bay Hotel Coconut Grove in Miami and Grand Bay Hotel Toronto in the fashionable Yorkville district. And coming soon are Grand Bay Hotel Chicago, Grand Bay Hotel Philadelphia, Grand Bay Key Biscayne, and Grand Bay Laguna Niguel.

Grand Bay Hotels & Resorts continues to look for premier hotels and resorts to enhance its collection, in order to emphasize the pleasure of travel by offering truly exceptional amenities, delightfully superior facilities, and the highest levels of service in the world.

TOWERY PUBLISHING, INC.

Beginning as a small publisher of local newspapers in the 1930s, Towery Publishing, Inc. today produces a wide range of community-oriented materials, including books (Urban Tapestry Series), business directories, magazines, and Internet sites. Building on its long heritage of excellence, the company has become global in scope, with cities from San Diego to Sydney represented by Towery products. In all its endeavors, this Memphis-based company strives to be synonymous with service, utility, and quality.

A Diversity of Community-Based Products

Over the years, Towery has become the largest producer of published materials for North American chambers of commerce. From membership directories that enhance business-to-business communication to visitor and relocation guides tailored to reflect the unique qualities of the communities they cover, the company's chamber-oriented materials offer comprehensive information on dozens of topics, including housing, education, leisure activities, health care, and local government.

In 1998, the company acquired Cincinnati-based Target Marketing, an established provider of detailed city street maps to more than 300 chambers of commerce throughout the United States and Canada. Now a division of Towery, Target offers full-color maps that include local landmarks and points of interest, such as parks, shopping centers, golf courses, schools, industrial parks, city and county limits, subdivision names, public buildings, and even block numbers on most streets.

In 1990, Towery launched the Urban Tapestry Series, an award-winning collection of oversized, hardbound photojournals detailing the people, history, culture, environment, and commerce of various metropolitan areas. These coffee-table books highlight a community through three basic elements: an introductory essay by a noted local individual; an exquisite collection of four-color photographs; and profiles of the companies and organizations that animate the area's business life.

To date, more than 80 Urban Tapestry Series editions have been published in cities around the world, from New York to Vancouver to Sydney. Authors of the books' introductory essays include former President Gerald Ford (Grand Rapids), former Alberta Premier Peter Lougheed (Calgary), CBS anchor Dan Rather (Austin), ABC anchor Hugh Downs (Phoenix), bestselling mystery author Robert B. Parker (Boston), American Movie Classics host Nick Clooney (Cincinnati), Senator Richard Lugar (Indianapolis), and Challenger Center founder Dr. June Scobee Rodgers (Chattanooga).

To maintain hands-on quality in all of its periodicals and books, Towery has long used the latest production methods available. The company was the first in the country to combine a desktop workstation environment with advanced graphic systems to provide color separations, image scanning, and finished film delivery under one roof. Today, Towery relies on state-of-the-art digital prepress services to produce more than 8,000 pages each year, containing well over 30,000 high-quality color images.

An Internet Pioneer

By combining its long-standing expertise in community-oriented published materials with advanced production capabilities, a global sales force, and extensive data management expertise, Towery has emerged as a significant Internet provider. In keeping with its overall focus on community-based resources, the company's Internet sites represent a natural step in the evolution of the business. There are two main product lines within the Internet division: introCity® and the American Community Network (ACN).

Towery's introCity sites introduce newcomers, visitors, and longtime residents to every facet of a particular community, while also placing the local chamber of commerce at the forefront of the city's Internet activity. The sites include newcomer information, calendars, photos, citywide business listings with everything from nightlife to shopping to family fun, and on-line maps pinpointing the exact location of businesses, schools, attractions, and much more.

Towery Publishing President and CEO J. Robert Towery has expanded the business his parents started in the 1930s to include a growing array of traditional and electronic published materials, as well as Internet and multimedia services, that are marketed locally, nationally, and internationally.

STEVE DAVIS

decades earlier. Soon thereafter, he expanded the scope of the company's published materials to include *Memphis* magazine and other successful regional and national publications. In 1985, after selling its locally focused assets, Towery began the trajectory on which it continues today, creating community-oriented materials that are often produced in conjunction with chambers of commerce and other business organizations.

Despite the decades of change, Towery himself follows a long-standing family philosophy of unmatched service and unflinching quality. That approach extends throughout the entire organization to include more than 130 employees at the Memphis headquarters, another 60 located in Northern Kentucky outside Cincinnati, and more than 50 sales, marketing, and editorial staff traveling to and working in a growing list of client cities. All of its products, and more information about the company, are featured on the Internet at www.towery.com.

In summing up his company's steady growth, Towery restates the essential formula that has driven the business since its first pages were published: "The creative energies of our staff drive us toward innovation and invention. Our people make the highest possible demands on themselves, so I know that our future is secure if the ingredients for success remain a focus on service and quality."

Towery Publishing was the first in the country to combine a digital desktop environment with advanced graphic systems to provide color separations, image scanning, and finished film delivery under one roof. Today, the company's state-of-the-art network of Macintosh and Windows workstations allows it to produce more than 8,000 pages each year, containing well over 30,000 high-quality color images.

ACN, Towery's other Internet product, is the only searchable on-line database of statistical information for all of the country's 3,141 counties and 315 metropolitan statistical areas. Each community's statistical profile includes vital information on such topics as population, workforce, transportation, education, taxes, and incentives. ACN serves as a national gateway to chambers of commerce, private companies, and other organizations and communities on the Web, making it an ideal resource for finding and comparing data on communities suitable for a plant or office location.

Decades of Publishing Expertise

In 1972, current President and CEO J. Robert Towery succeeded his parents in managing the printing and publishing business they had founded nearly four

The Towery family's publishing roots can be traced to 1935, when R.W. Towery began producing a series of community histories in Tennessee, Mississippi, and Texas. Throughout the company's history, the founding family has consistently exhibited a commitment to clarity, precision, innovation, and vision.

ALAN BENOIT received a bachelor of fine arts degree from Arizona State University. His photographs have appeared in numerous publications, including *Travel & Leisure*, *Condé Nast Traveler*, *USA Today*, *Arizona Highways*, and *National Geographic Traveler*. Benoit is a four-time winner of the Nikon/Outdoor Writers of America's *Great American Outdoors* exhibition.

DAN COOGAN, an Eagle Scout and a certified scuba diver, fulfilled his lifelong dream by becoming a photographer. His images have been published in *Aviation Week & Space Technology*, *Inc.*, *Air & Space/ Smithsonian*, and *PC Week*, and his clients include Motorola, Phelps Dodge, Intel, and Caterpillar. Coogan was raised in Kent, Ohio, and—after 23 years of snow—sought the hot and sunny state of Arizona.

JIM CORWIN earned a bachelor's degree from the University of Washington and a degree in photography from Everett Community College. He spent 12 years working for photo labs in the Seattle area before opening his own business in 1990. A native of Portland, Oregon, Corwin specializes in travel, nature, people, and sports photography, and he has worked for such clients as the Boeing Company, Safeway, US West Communications, GTE, and Microsoft. His work has been published in *National Geographic Traveler*, *Audubon*, *Mother Earth News*, and *Business Week*, in addition to Towery Publishing's *Seattle: Pacific Gem* and *San Diego: World-Class City*.

MICHAEL DERR, a native of Wisconsin, earned a bachelor of arts degree in journalism from the University of Wisconsin at Madison. Formerly the executive news editor of the *Mesa Tribune* and managing editor of *Phoenix Magazine*, he has been editor of award-winning *America West Airlines Magazine* for the past 12 years. Derr is also a publishing consultant, a freelance book editor, and a photographer who specializes in landscapes.

DICK DIETRICH first seriously began making photographs when he was 11 and has continued in the commercial photography business for more than 30 years. Now, his time is devoted to traveling across the country producing work for national and international advertisers and publishers. A native of Maine, Dietrich, along with his family, now calls Arizona home.

LINDA ENGER, owner of Linda Enger Photography, specializes in images of locations and people. Winner of the 1997 Prisma Award, Enger has worked with *Phoenix Home & Garden*; Zila, Inc.; and the Phoenix Arts Commission.

LEE FOSTER is a veteran travel writer and photographer who lives in Berkeley. His work has been published in a number of major travel magazines and newspapers, and he maintains a stock photo library that features more than 250 worldwide destinations. Foster's full travel-publishing efforts can be viewed on his Web site at www.fostertravel.com. His work can also be seen in Towery Publishing's *Salt Lake City: Welcoming the World*.

PAT GORRAIZ is currently studying art at Arizona State University and is employed by Image Craft Ltd. He was born and raised in Phoenix.

DARIN IPEMA, originally from Chicago, received a bachelor of fine arts degree in communication from the University of Memphis. He specializes in cinematography, and has shot two independent feature films, as well as several music videos. This is the first time Ipema's photographs have appeared in print.

JERRY D. JACKA has illustrated a total of 14 books and collaborated with his wife on five books about Native American art. Jacka also produced a video that received a 1989 Rocky Mountain Emmy Award.

KERRICK JAMES, specializing in destination and adventure travel photography, has been published in *Arizona Highways*, *America West Airlines Magazine*, *Travel Holiday*, and *Alaska Airlines Magazine*. In his spare time he enjoys kayaking, river rafting, and literature.

CHRISTINE KEITH is a staff photographer for the *Arizona Republic*. She received a bachelor of arts degree from Prescott College and a master of arts degree from Ohio University. Keith's images have appeared in a variety of national magazines, including *Smithsonian*, *Better Homes & Gardens*, and *Natural History Magazine*. She has won a Leica Medal of Excellence and a Paul Schutzer Memorial Award.

JAMES LEMASS studied art in his native Ireland before moving to Cambridge, Massachusetts, in 1987. His areas of specialty include people and travel photography, and his work can be seen in publications by Aer Lingus, British Airways, and USAir, as well as the Nynex Yellow Pages. Lemass has also worked for the Massachusetts Office of Travel and Tourism, and his photographs have appeared in several other Towery publications, including *New York: Metropolis of the American Dream*; *Treasures on Tampa Bay: Tampa, St. Petersburg, Clearwater*; *Washington: City on a Hill*; *Orlando: The City Beautiful*; and *San Diego: World-Class City*.

CHUCK LAWSON, originally from Columbus, Ohio, moved to Glendale, Arizona, in 1971. His areas of photography include architecture, human interest, recreation, and studio. Lawson has had a lifetime fascination with trains, leading to a project for *Arizona Highways* that highlights the Grand Canyon Railway.

AIMEE MADSEN earned a degree in photojournalism from Laramie County Community College. Through her studio, Aimee Madsen Photography, she specializes in editorial, landscape, and wildlife images. Madsen's photographs have been published in *Arizona Highways*, *Worth Magazine*, and *Phoenix Magazine*, and she is represented by Gamma-Liaison World Press Agency.

LES MANEVITZ, originally from Massachusetts, attended the Brooks Institute of Photography. He specializes in images of nature and archaeology.

DEBS METZONG served in the U.S. Army, where he did some military photography while stationed in Japan. He was employed by Mountain Bell/US West for 32 years, including 10 years as a photographer, until his retirement. Metzong now freelances regularly.

J. PETER MORTIMER is a contributing editor and former picture editor of *Arizona Highways*. As an award-winning photographer, Mortimer has worked with a client list that ranges from Eastman Kodak to *National Geographic*, and is affiliated with Gamma-Liaison World Press Agency in New York and Paris. Mortimer has a bachelor's degree in journalism and telecommunications, and has supervised and taught the photojournalism curriculum at Arizona State University.

MIKE PADIAN originally studied and worked in sign and mural painting, but found a niche for his love of the outdoors in action and outdoor adventure photography. Now a veteran professional photographer, Padian has contributed photography to *Bike*; *Powder, the Skier's Magazine*; *Vertical*; *SWEAT* (South West Exercise and Training); and *Mountain Bike*.

PHOTOPHILE, established in San Diego in 1967, is owned and operated by Nancy Likins-Mastern. An internationally known stock photography agency, the company houses more than 1 million color images, culled from more than 90 contributing local and international photographers. Subjects range from extensive coverage

of the West Coast, business and industry, people and lifestyles, health, medicine, travel, scenics, wildlife, and adventure sports, plus 200 additional categories.

BRETT SHOAF, a resident of San Diego since 1958, studied photography, telecommunications, and film production at San Diego City College and Grossmont College, where he earned an associate arts degree. Shoaf is self-employed at Artistic Visuals, and his work includes stock, commercial, and instructional/tutorial photography, as well as ad design. His clients include IVID Communications, Vortex Interactive, Shelter Island Inc., Bartell Hotels, and the San Diego Visitor Information Center. His stock photography has been published in the *San Diegan* and *San Diego Official Visitors Planning Guide*, as well as in Towery Publishing's *San Diego: World-Class City*. With a special interest in nature photography, Shoaf has photographed the natural beauty of such places as Kauai, Switzerland, and Utah.

GEORGE STOCKING, owner of Phoenix-based Coyote Howls Photography, specializes in landscape and travel photography. His work has appeared on numerous calendars and in books and magazines.

RICHARD D. STRANGE, originally from Indianapolis, moved to Phoenix in 1972. His images have appeared in *Arizona Highways*, *Sierra*, and *Life*, and have been used in the Annual Grand Canyon Calendar.

BOB TREHEARNE is a freelance photographer specializing in the outdoors, specifically western scenes such as horse drives, rodeos, and powwows. His work has been published in *National Geographic Traveler* and *Arizona Highways*, as well as in two books about the West. Trehearne maintains stock photography files and sells limited edition prints.

NIK WHEELER, a native of Hitchin, England, began his photographic career in Bangkok, where he copublished a travel supplement and guidebook on Thailand. In 1967, he worked in Vietnam as a combat photographer. Since that time, Wheeler has covered the 1968 Tet Offensive, the Jordan Civil War, the fall of Saigon, the Montreal Olympics, and the coronation of the king of Nepal. His clients include *Time*, *National Geographic*, *Newsweek*, *Geo*, *Travel & Leisure*, and *International Wildlife*. Wheeler has pub-

lished four books; has copublished and photographed for the *Insider's Guide* series, including Japan, Hawaii, California, and Spain; and has appeared on *The Merv Griffin Show* and Regis Philbin's *Morning Show*.

GREGORY WILLIAMS, a lifelong resident of Savannah, graduated from the Savannah Technical Institute and has studied under renowned nature photographer John Earl. In his freelance career, Williams specializes in landscape, unique architecture, and abstract photography, and many of his images are used in chamber of commerce guides across the nation. He has won several regional Sierra Club photo contests and, in 1996, mounted an exhibit titled *Savannah and the Georgia Coast*. His images have also appeared in Towery Publishing's *Seattle: Pacific Gem* and *Jacksonville: Reflections of Excellence*.

BOB WILLIS, a former television travel host, is a self-taught photographer. A member of the Society of American Travel Writers, he is a travel guidebook writer for Fodor's, Access Guides, and Globe Pequot Press. Willis is a two-time top winner of the Chesapeake Bay Photo Contest, and his images have been used by Teldon Calendars and on a U.S. Commerce Department poster.

MARK ZEMNICK has been taking photographs for more than 20 years. Owner of Zemnick Photography, he specializes in photographing people on location.

FRANK ZULLO earned a bachelor of science degree in visual communications design from Arizona State University. His photographs have been published in a wide variety of print media, including *Life*, *Time*, *National Geographic World*, and *Astronomy*. Zullo's clients also include Grolier, Prentice Hall, and Random House.

Other photographers and organizations that contributed to *Greater Phoenix: The Desert in Bloom* include AllSport, Ed Mell, and Phoenix International Raceway.

LIBRARY OF CONGRESS CATATLOGING-IN-PUBLICATION INFORMATION

Downs, Hugh.
Greater Phoenix : the desert in bloom / by Hugh Downs.
   p. cm. – (Urban tapestry series)
Includes index.
ISBN 1-881096-69-6 (alk. paper)
1. Phoenix Region (Ariz.)–Civilization. 2. Phoenix Region (Ariz.)–Pictorial works. 3. Business enterprises–Arizona–Phoenix Region. 4. Phoenix Region (Ariz.)–Economic conditions. I. Title. II. Series.
F819.P57D69   1999
979.1'73'00222–dc21   98-21337

Printed in Canada
Copyright © 1999 by Towery Publishing, Inc.

TOWERY PUBLISHING, INC.
THE TOWERY BUILDING
1835 UNION AVENUE
MEMPHIS, TN 38104

PUBLISHER: J. Robert Towery
EXECUTIVE PUBLISHER: Jenny McDowell
ASSOCIATE PUBLISHER: Michael C. James
NATIONAL SALES MANAGER: Stephen Hung
MARKETING DIRECTOR: Carol Culpepper
PROJECT DIRECTORS: Dean Daly, Linda Frank, Linda Heintz, Karen Riva

EXECUTIVE EDITOR: David B. Dawson
MANAGING EDITOR: Lynn Conlee
SENIOR EDITOR: Carlisle Hacker
EDITOR/PROFILE MANAGER: Brian Johnston
EDITORS: Mary Jane Adams, Jana Files, John Floyd, Heather Ramsey
ASSISTANT EDITOR: Rebecca Green
EDITORIAL ASSISTANT: Sunni Thompson
PROFILE WRITER: Sandy Doubleday
CAPTION WRITER: Linnea Maxwell

PHOTOGRAPHY EDITOR: Jonathan Postal
PHOTOGRAPHY COORDINATOR: Robin McGehee
PROFILE DESIGNERS: Laurie Beck, Kelley Pratt, Ann Ward
PRODUCTION ASSISTANTS: Loretta Drew, Melissa Ellis
PRODUCTION RESOURCES MANAGER: Dave Dunlap Jr.
PRODUCTION COORDINATOR: Brenda Pattat
DIGITAL COLOR SUPERVISOR: Darin Ipema
DIGITAL COLOR TECHNICIANS: Amanda Bozeman, Eric Friedl, Deidre Kesler, Brent Salazar
PRINT COORDINATOR: Tonda Thomas

FILM, CAMERAS
SUNGLASSES
AVAILABLE AT
SALOON

RETURN GOLD PANS
HERE
THE GOLD-SILVER NUGGETS ARE
IN ROCK TROUGHS AND STREAM BED.